I0729696

CONTEMPORARY FLOWERS IN MIXED MEDIA

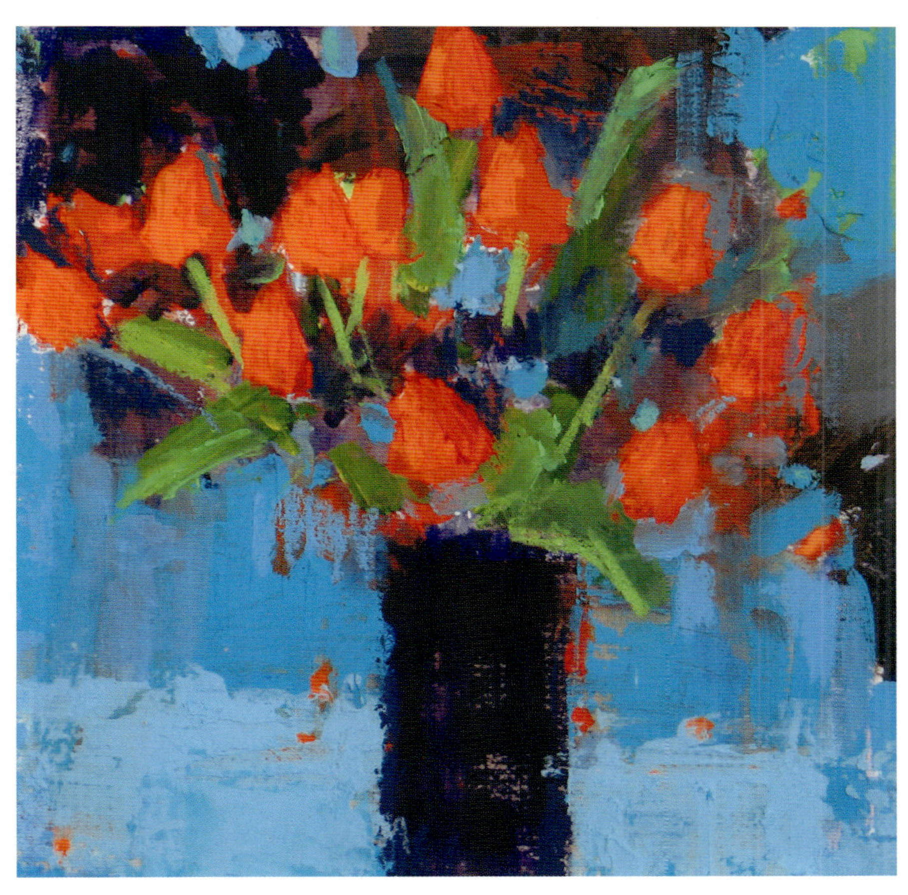

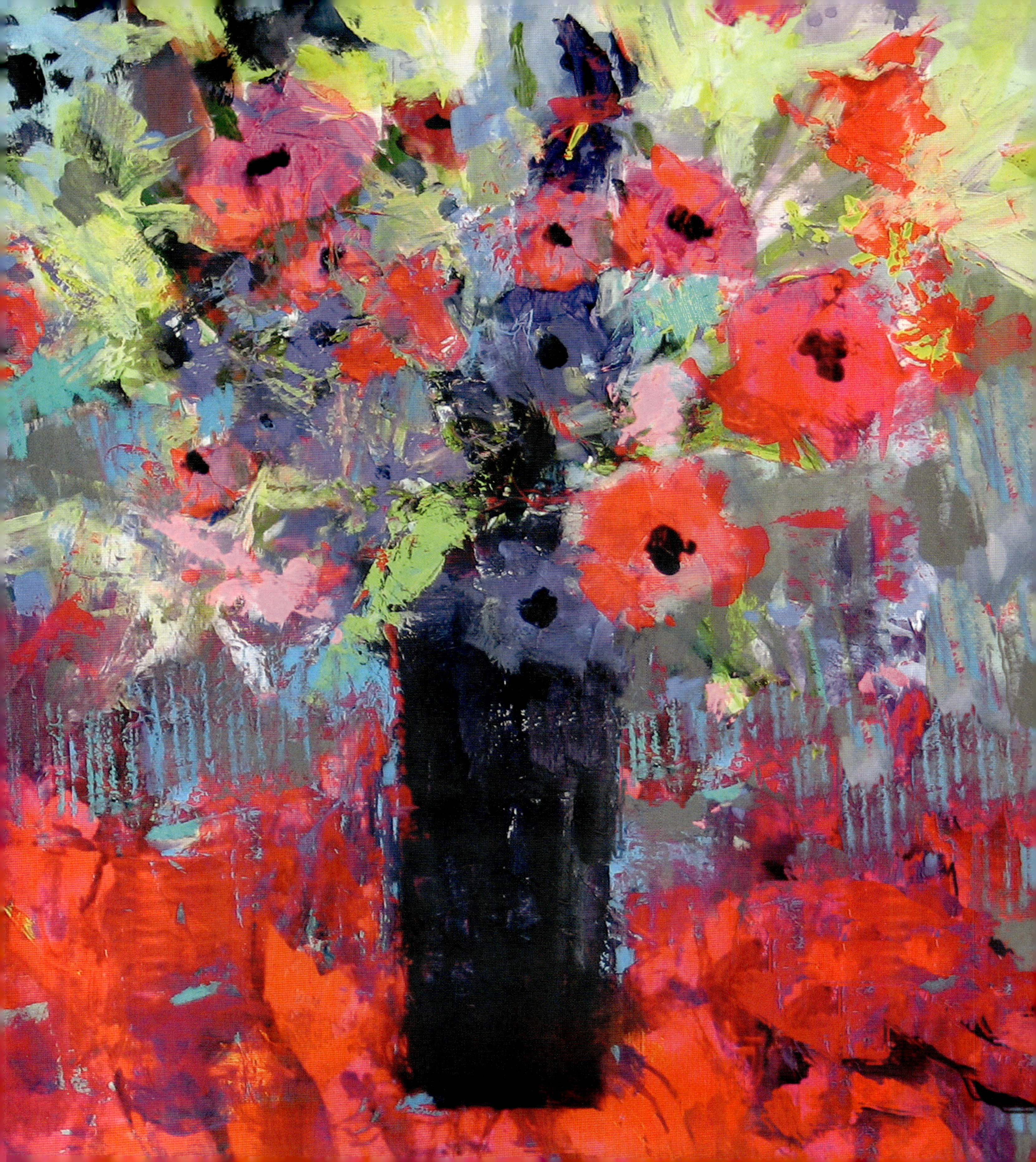

CONTEMPORARY FLOWERS IN MIXED MEDIA

SORAYA FRENCH

BATSFORD

To my beloved trio, Tim, Yasmin and Saasha,
whose mixture of gentle encouragement and
brutally honest criticism motivates me to try harder.
Without their help and support none of this would
be possible. xxx

First published in the United Kingdom in 2021 by
Batsford
43 Great Ormond Street
London
WC1N 3HZ

ISBN 978-1-84994-614-8

A CIP catalogue record for this book is available from the
British Library.

10 9 8 7 6 5 4 3 2 1

Reproduction by Rival Colour Ltd, UK
Printed and bound by Toppan Leefung, China

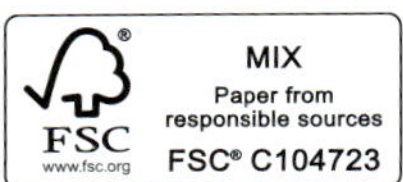

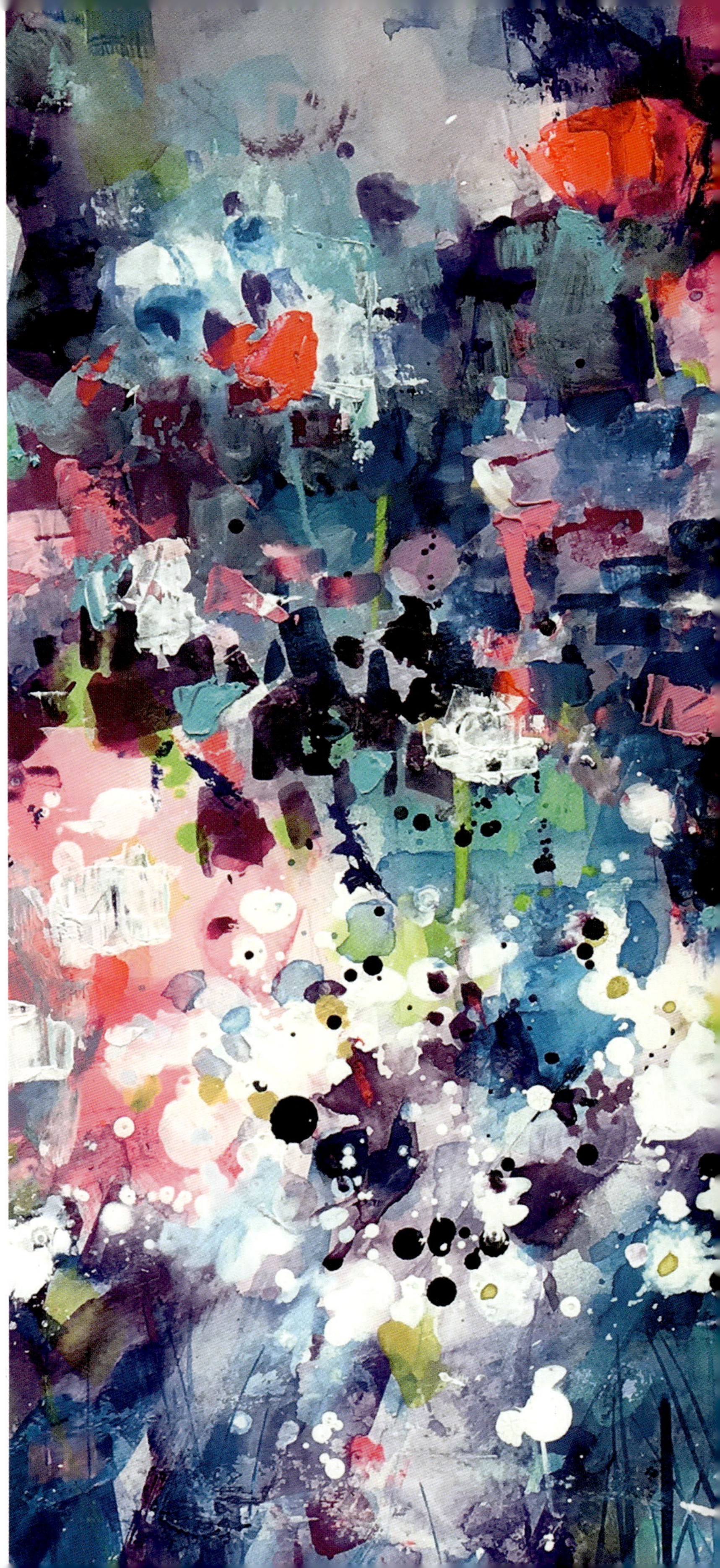

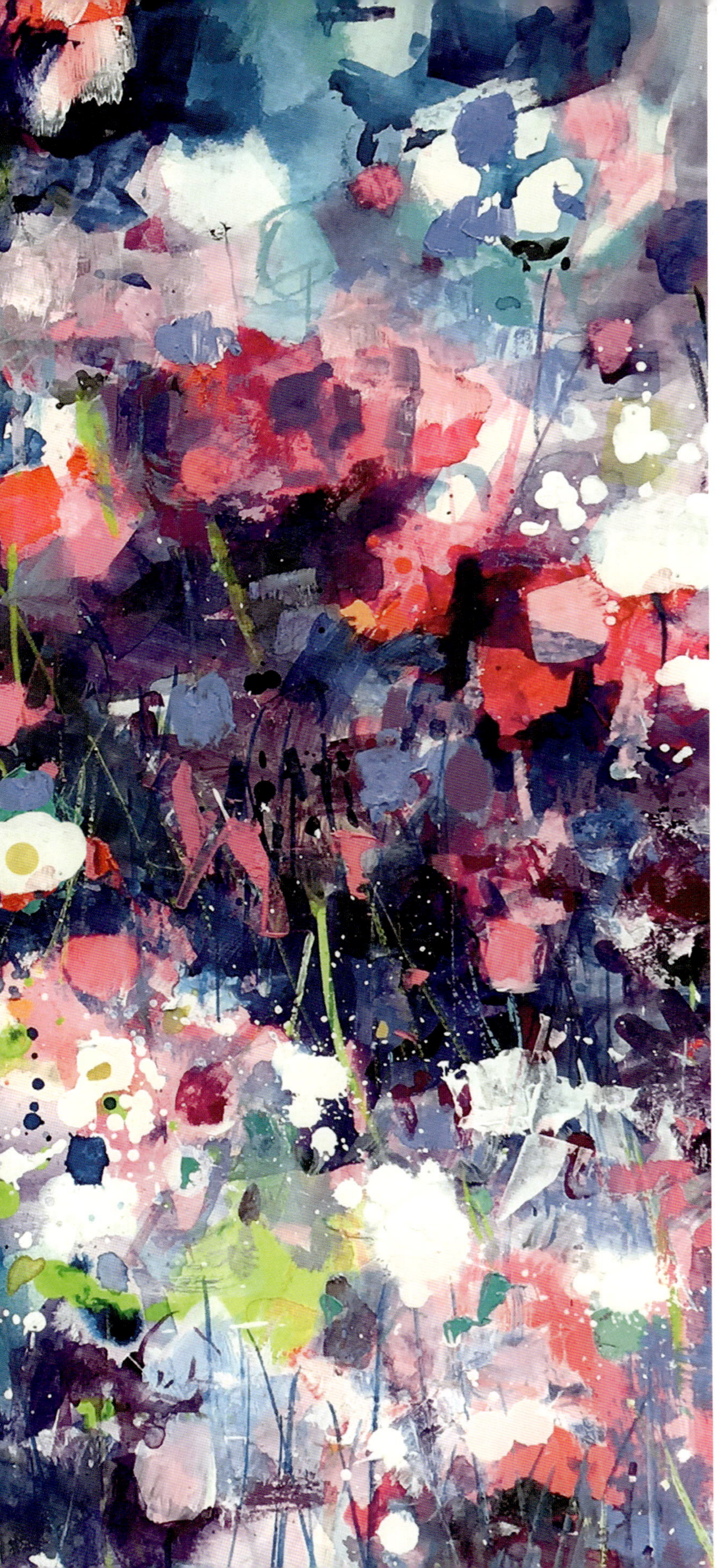

CONTENTS

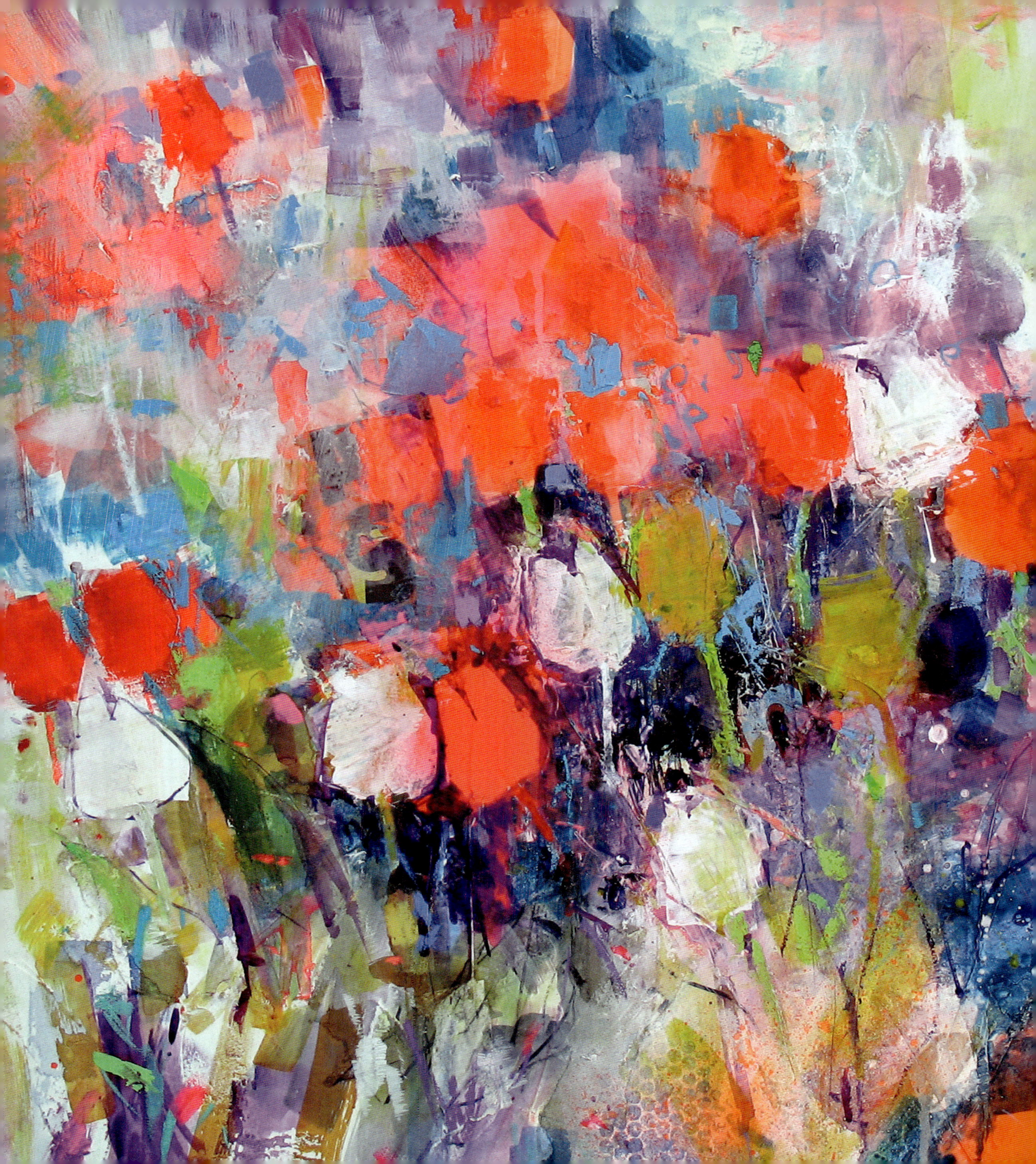

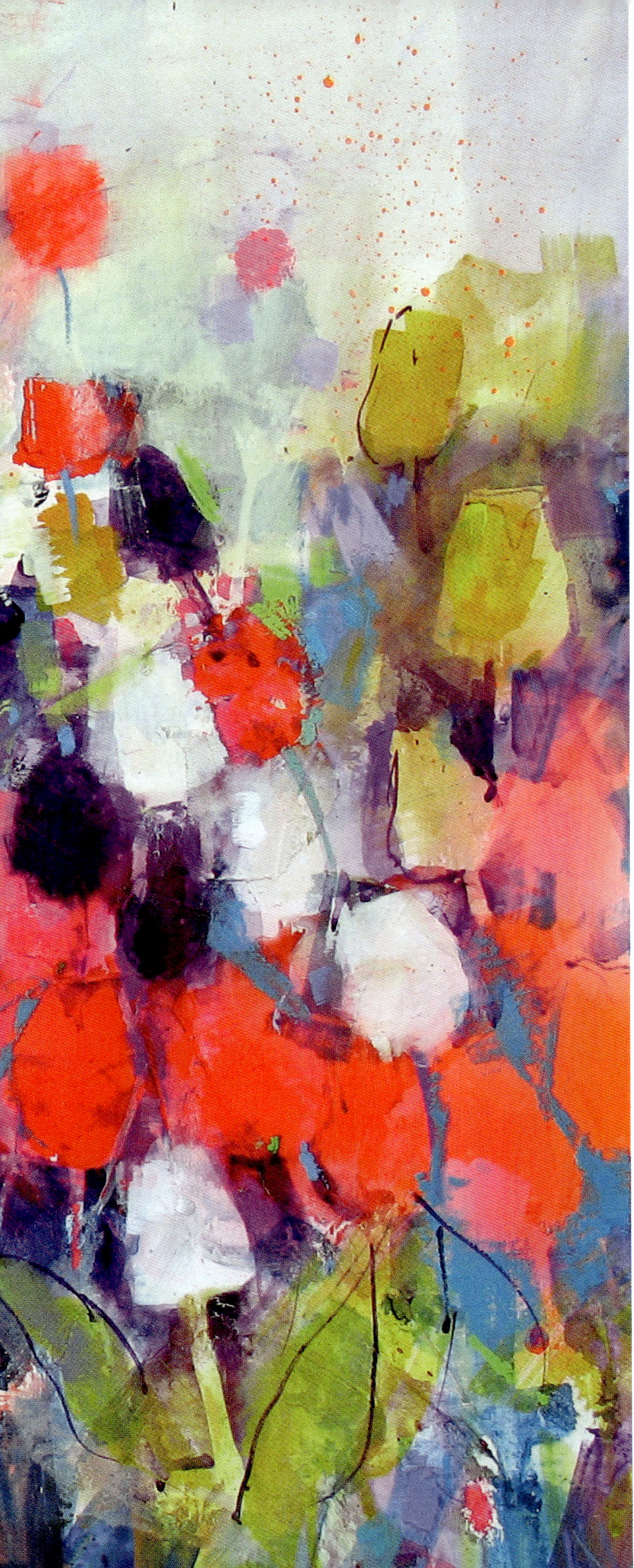

WELCOME

Painting flowers in mixed media presents the artist with the opportunity to combine exquisite transparent washes of inks and watercolours with the vivid colours of opaque wet and dry media to interpret the stunning colours of nature. Spontaneity, versatility and unpredictability are at the core of painting contemporary semi-abstract flowers in mixed media, but it is the degree of control that is the most appealing feature of working in this expressive and exciting way – decisions can be made and remade numerous times to allow a painting to evolve and find its natural flow and rhythm in a more unrestrained manner than can result from a laborious and tentative process.

Tulip Fusion

76 × 56 cm (30 × 22 in)

Mixed media on watercolour paper

ABOUT THIS BOOK

If you are reading this book then I hope you are ready to take a leap of faith and step into the complex but fascinating world of painting semi-abstract flowers in mixed media. There is no competing with mother nature, the greatest artist of all, so this book is my attempt to encourage you not to recreate, but to interpret the incredible amount of inspiring visual information flowers offer as a subject, in the most unique and individual way to you.

This versatile and transformative form of expression encompasses a broad range of disciplines and means something different to each individual artist. The ethos behind this book is to explore the subject's many possibilities in a way that is most relevant to your personal approach to painting. Ultimately I hope the ideas inspire you to adapt a more expressive yet relaxed, intuitive and fluid attitude to your creative process.

Painting the most striking and flamboyant offerings of nature in mixed media is such an immersive and engaging experience. Creating art presents, of course, its own kind of stresses and dilemmas, but these are not bad stresses, and with an open mind, imagination and a variety of media and techniques, you should always be able to find new solutions and let your creativity transport you to a happy place.

I started and completed this book in 2020, during the most challenging of times for the human race, and it is testimony to the therapeutic magic of creativity. It has truly sustained me throughout this difficult time and I hope the joy I took in writing this book resonates with you and motivates you to pick up your brushes and immerse yourself in the joy of creation.

In this book you will find comprehensive information regarding different media. This is not to encourage you to buy more art supplies, but to help you make informed choices. You'll also discover demonstrations and projects to guide you through negative shape painting, colour relationships, combining media and colour mixing.

Unless otherwise stated, all the acrylics, QoR watercolours and Williamsburg oil paints are manufactured by Golden Artist Colors. Oil pastels and crayons are from Caran d'Ache, soft pastels are by Sennelier, Unison and Jackson's, watercolour papers are by St Cuthbert's Mill, and FW inks, mount boards and Langton paper are by Daler-Rowney. There are equivalent brands available for some of the products.

(Opposite page) **Pink and White Lilies**
51 × 41cm (20 × 16in)
Mixed media on watercolour paper

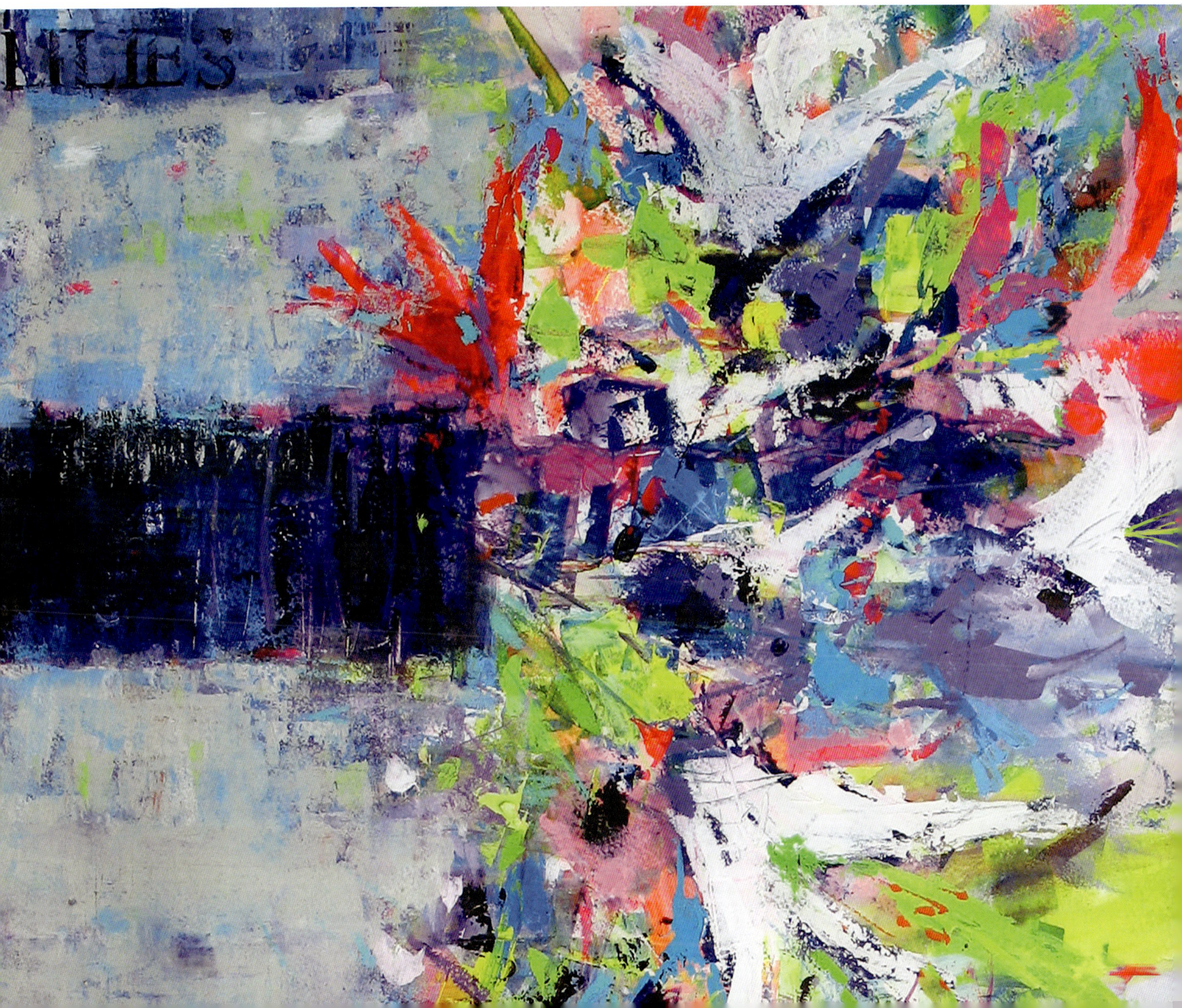

LILIES

A PERSONAL NOTE

I don't really have a profound reason for my love
of painting flowers other than that their dazzling
colours and spectacular shapes suit my colourful and
contemporary approach to painting. I paint flowers
when I am happy or sad; it is the subject I turn to when
inspiration runs dry. Painting them in mixed media keeps
creative boredom at bay as the infinite combination
of materials presents fresh surprises and exciting
possibilities. It really suits impatient, expressive and
spontaneous artists who thrive on working organically
and enjoy taking risks without the fear of failure.

My painting process has always been intuitive, but
I have learnt to analyze it more in order to teach and
write about it. When working on personal projects I am
careful not to let the analytical side stifle the intuitive
process, and successful pieces are the ones where I get
the balance right.

Writing this note a few years ago would have sounded
very different indeed. Each year of walking along the
creative path brings more 'Aha' moments, and with them
comes not only a greater understanding of the reasons
for painting in the first place but, better still, a more fluid
and relaxed attitude towards the process of creating art.
Right now enjoying the process and experiencing the
therapeutic and meditative effect of painting is at the top
of my list, and success of any kind along the way is the
cherry on the cake.

Looking at my brightly coloured paintings you will never
guess that I am mostly attracted to paintings with much
more sophisticated and understated colour schemes.
To remain true to myself, however, I hope to continue
painting with these unapologetically vibrant colours
for as long as I can. I am full of gratitude to have my
work and most treasured pastime merge so seamlessly
together and never a day goes by when I take this
privilege for granted.

(Opposite page) **A Touch of Spring**
79 × 56 cm (31 × 22 in)
Mixed media on mount board

(Below) **Birthday flowers**
51 × 51 cm (20 × 20 in)
Mixed media on mount board.

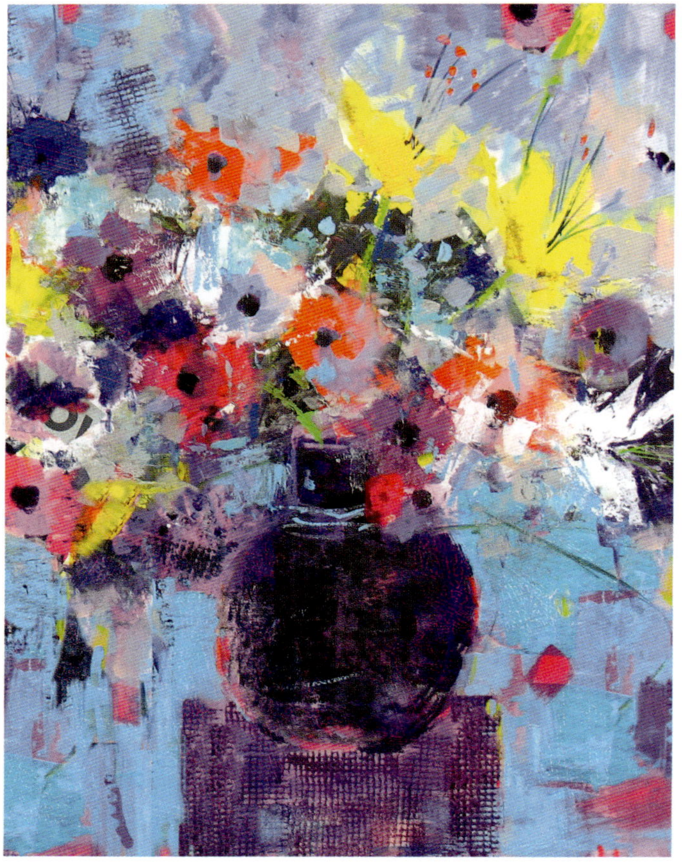

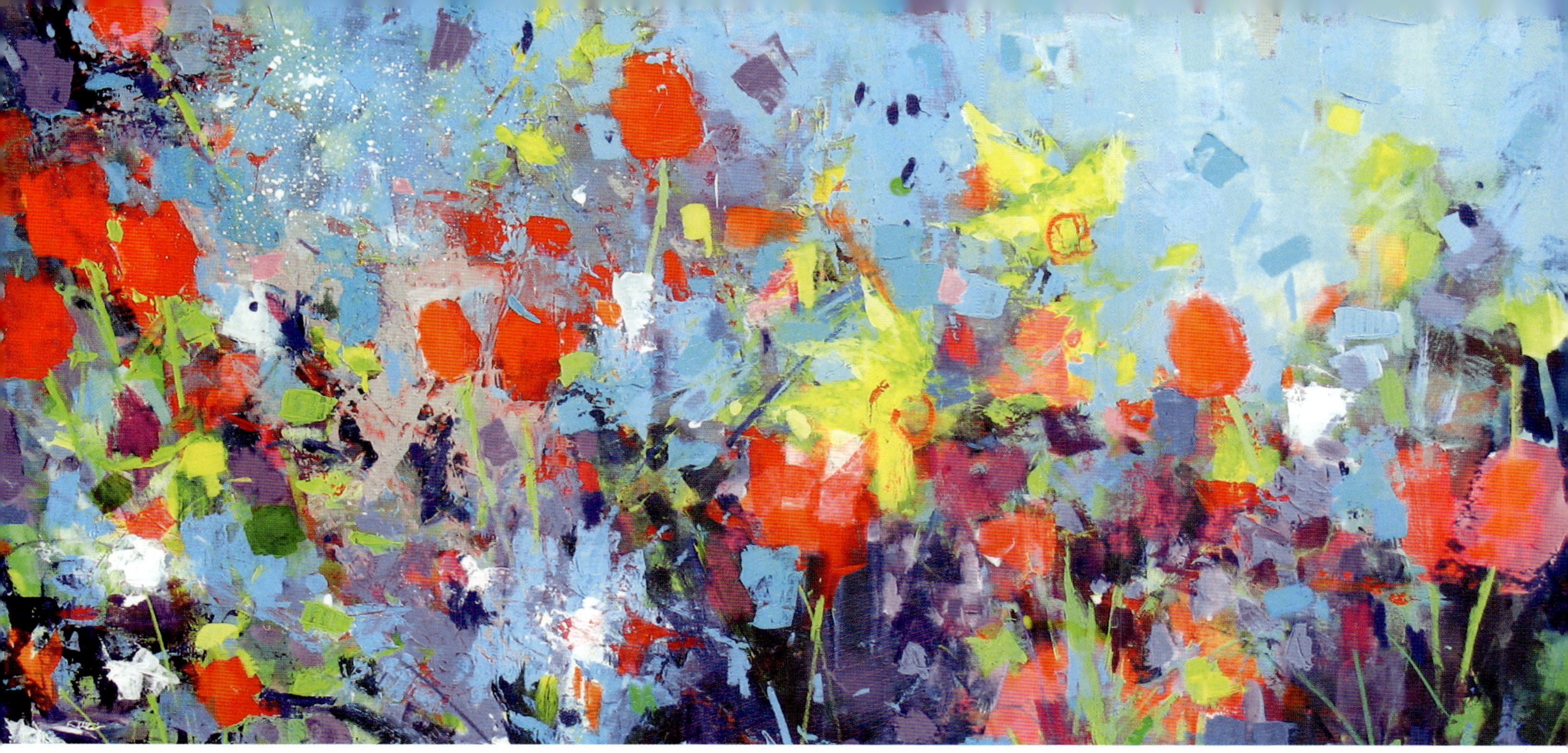

CULTIVATING YOUR UNIQUE VISUAL VOICE

The art world is overflowing with talented artists; it is your authenticity and individuality that will help you thrive in this competitive arena. Cultivating your own voice needs internal focus while progressing with the technical aspects of your painting. It is through frequent practice and by closely observing and studying the repeated patterns in your own work that you get to know who you are as an artist and what makes you tick.

If you are just starting out and dabbling in different subjects and media, pick out the few that get your heart racing and make you rush to pick up your brushes. Working in a series of your most stimulating subjects creates a body of work with a common thread rather than numerous paintings each singing a different tune. Limiting external influences to a few you truly admire helps focus your mind, and always analyze and study rather than copy. Use inspiration like the spices in your kitchen: a little sprinkle to add that extra touch of magic but not to overshadow your own individuality.

Be savvy when browsing art websites: you want to access their positive aspects without the negative distractions. Connecting with other artists globally through social media can be a positive experience, but on the flip side, being bombarded with imagery when scrolling these sites for long periods can be confusing and even promote feelings of inadequacy. Above all, it takes precious time and energy that can be spent more positively in your own creative space.

It may sound like a cliché, but ultimately it is the deep and genuine connection with your subject that will resonate with the viewer. Practice and perseverance are the two key ingredients that will help you emerge as an artist with a unique visual voice.

EXPLORING THE MEDIA

The synergy between the individual mediums combined together in one painting is at the heart of using mixed media. With no particular rule book on how to make them work well together, your knowledge of each medium is paramount. Ultimately, the aesthetic success and longevity of a painting depends on the compatibility of the materials coming together in a logical sequence.

In this chapter we shall be looking at a selection of mediums and their idiosyncrasies, and the ways in which they can be a worthwhile contributor to your mixed media art. Getting to know each medium intimately means that you can judge where and how you can incorporate it, not only to enjoy a more liberating art-making process but also to add excitement to your paintings.

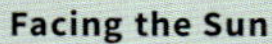

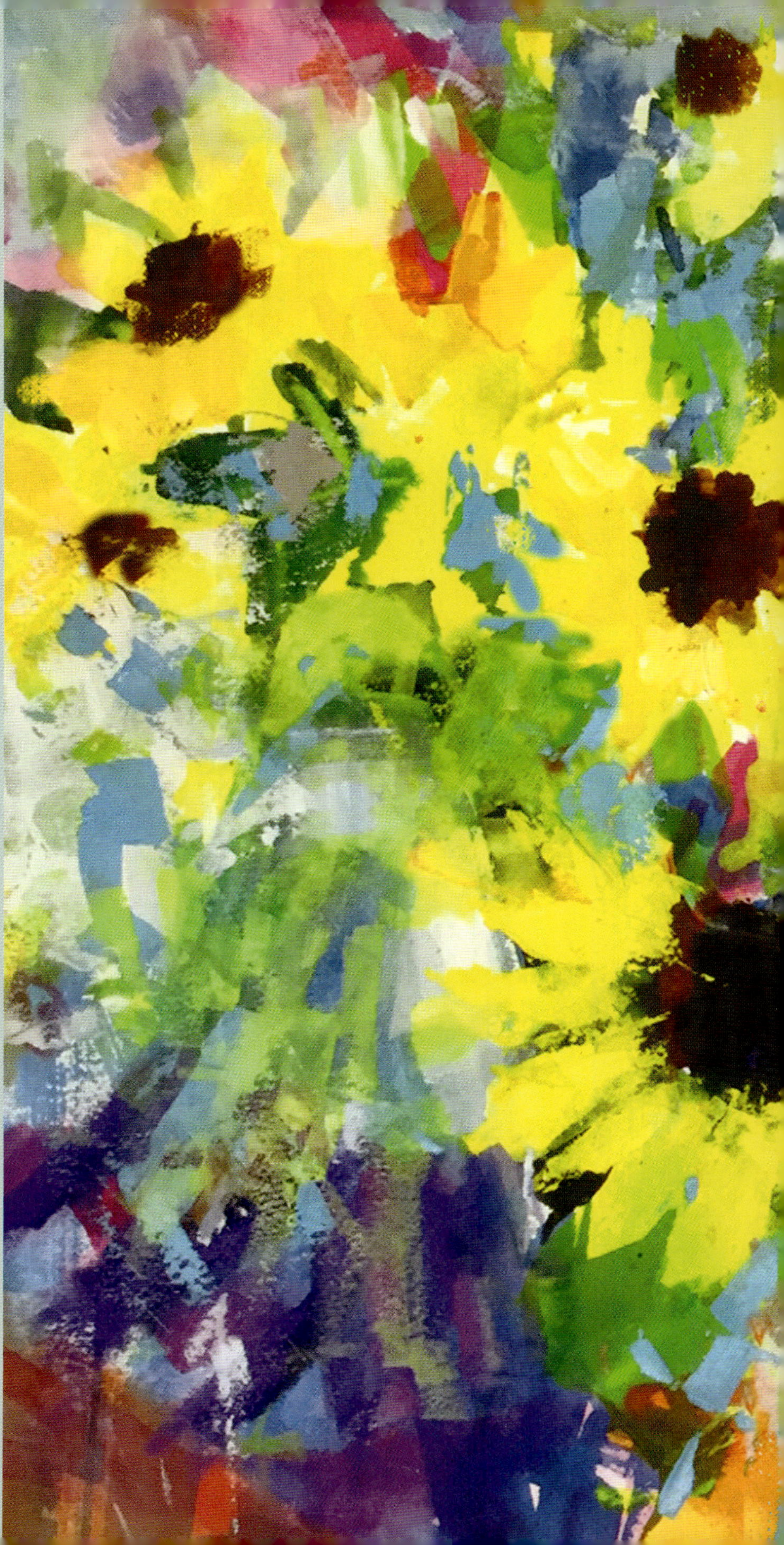

Facing the Sun
72 × 53 cm (28½ × 21 in)
Mixed media on watercolour paper

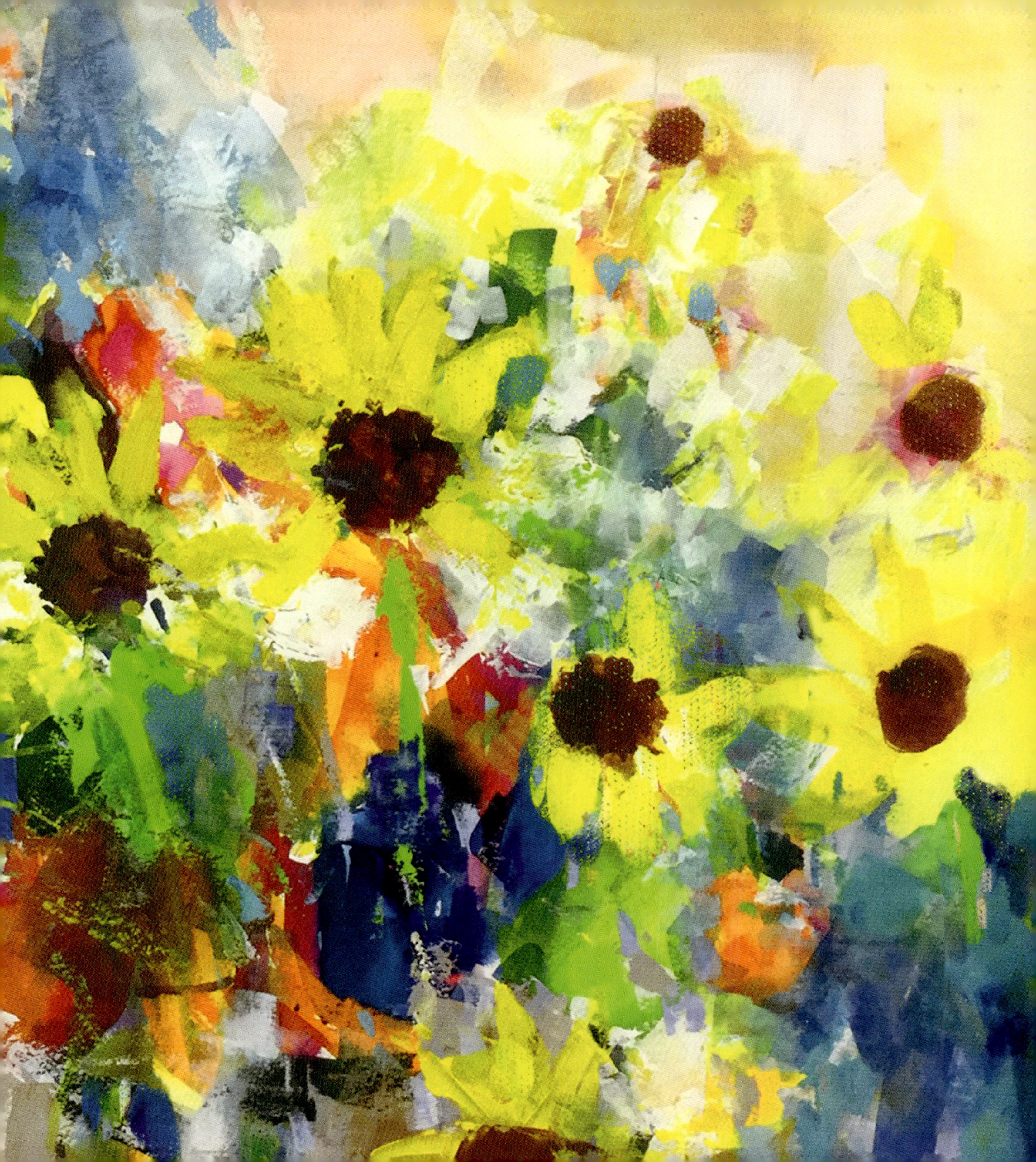

THE ROMANCE OF WATERCOLOURS

Light reflected through translucent washes of watercolour creates visual sensations unmatched by any other medium. Modern watercolours with strong, vibrant pigments and better quality binders have changed the sometimes wishy-washy image of this most challenging medium of all. Working on good quality paper will allow for lifting and washing out of colours and will help you to be more daring with this amazing medium. Primers such as Golden watercolour ground will give you the ability to make exciting and contemporary watercolours on canvases and artist's panels or to eliminate unwanted areas for correction. The light dimensional ground and cold press ground manufactured by Golden give you more opportunities to explore innovative and exciting textural approaches in your watercolour flower paintings.

The magical medium of watercolour is a great contributor to a mixed media art box, either in early washes of wet-into-wet or for glazing over acrylics to recede an area or change the tone of a colour. It can be applied for tinting a wet and dry artist's quality sandpaper or a NOT surface watercolour paper to make a tinted base for a pastel painting. So many factors come into making a successful watercolour – the quality of your paint, your surface, the brushes you use – but ultimately you, the artist, are the game-changer in the way you can stretch this medium way beyond its limited traditional image.

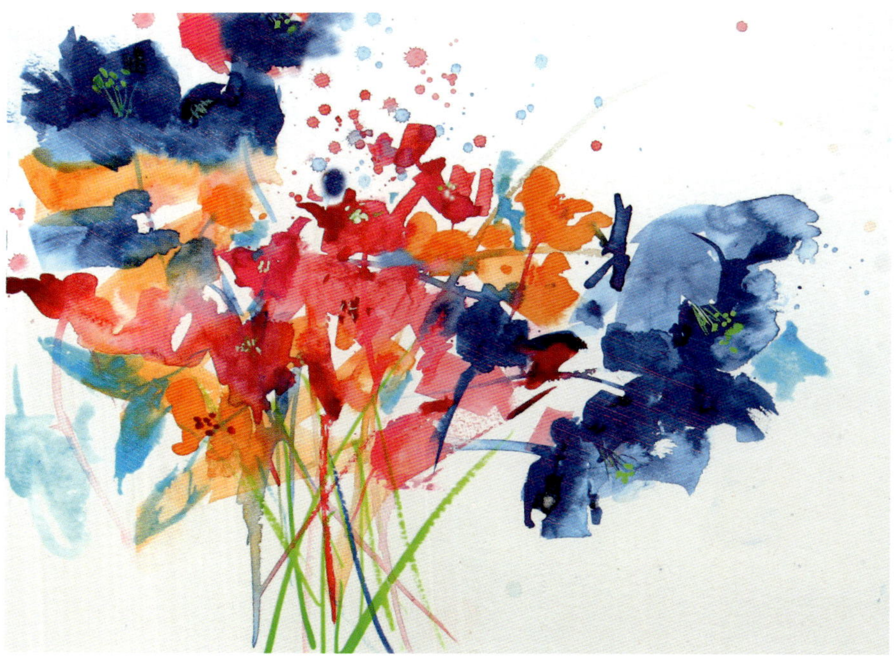

(Opposite page) **Poppies and Daisies**
53 x 53 cm (21 x 21 in)
Watercolour on paper
Knowledge of colour relationships and pigment characteristics is crucial to avoid making muddy colours and keeping your colours clean and vibrant, especially in semi-abstract styles such as mine where there are a lot of layered colours and overlapping passages. The ability to lift colour is a very appealing feature of working in watercolours for me, whether to reveal the white of the paper or a ghost of the more staining colours left behind. Above all, the luminosity of colours against the white of the paper is why watercolour is still one of the most popular mediums with artists around the world. I use Saunders Waterford High White paper for my watercolours to gain the crisp white contrast against the darker values. I love the soft edges of wet-into-wet washes against the hard edges of wet-on-dry and the texture of dry brush on NOT surface watercolour paper.

(Left) **Posy with Himalayan Blue Poppies**
28 × 24 cm (11 × 9½ in)
Watercolour on paper
A pocket-sized field watercolour box is the perfect bit of equipment to take out for quick sketches in the garden or days spent painting on location. These quick studies make great reference materials for larger future paintings.

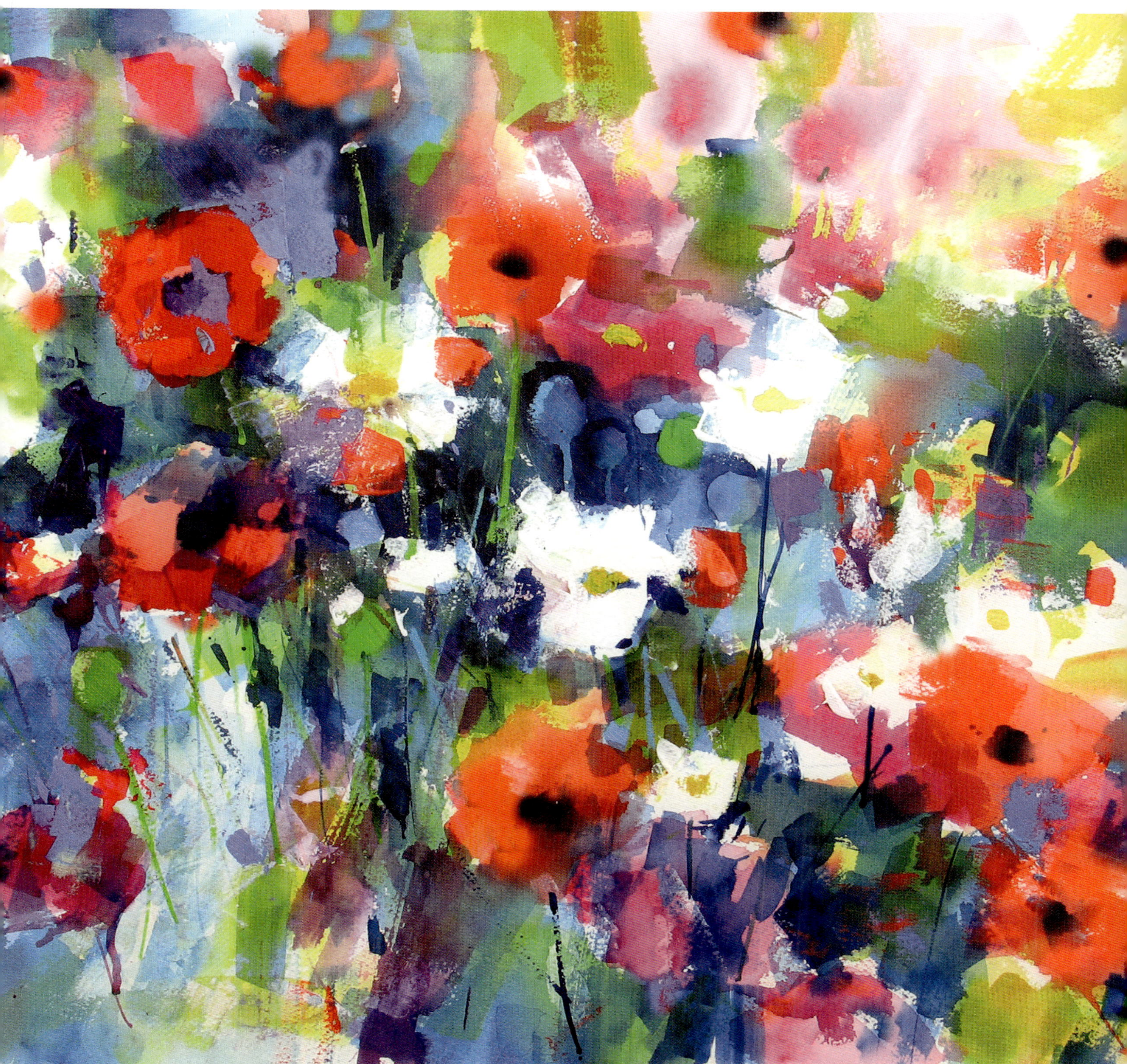

GOUACHE

Gouache, or body colour, is another versatile water-based medium with a matte finish. It has a binder of gum arabic and white to make it more opaque than watercolours. The advantages of gouache over watercolour is that it can range from transparency to opacity according to the amount of water you use and the nature of the particular pigment, and it allows you to mix opaque tints with white. The ability to apply lighter colours over darker ones and rectify mistakes by repainting easily makes gouache a more versatile and forgiving medium than watercolours, but you don't have to dismiss one in favour of the other – just use them where they can work well in your painting to create the maximum impact.

In a similar way to acrylics, gouache combines well with dry media; the interplay of transparent passages with thicker, more opaque ones can produce some wonderful effects. You can paint with gouache on a background of any colour from light to dark. The stunning range of colours and the matte finish give the medium its unique superb qualities, making it a worthwhile addition to the mixed media art box. It has a special place in my heart as I painted with it during my teenage years, and it always takes me back to a very happy place.

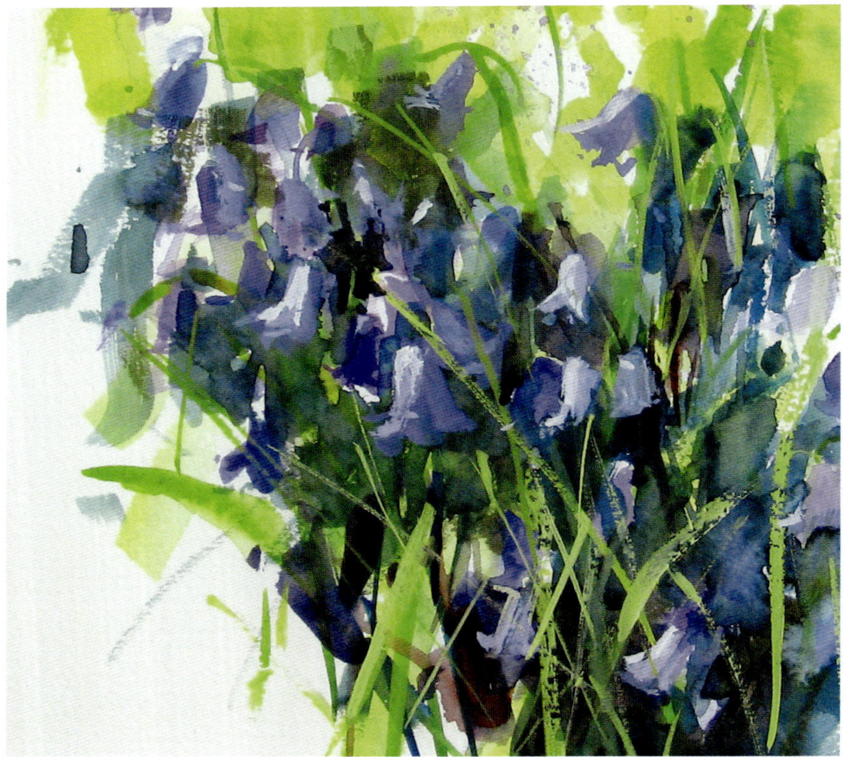

(Opposite page) **Sunlit Bluebell Study**
25 × 23 cm (10 × 9 in)
Gouache on paper
I started this painting with a light green wash made from a touch of Phthalo Blue into Lemon Yellow. I then mixed a much darker green using Phthalo Blue, Lemon Yellow and a touch of Magenta. The sunlit bluebells are a mixture of purple (made from Phthalo Blue plus Magenta) with white so that I could superimpose the lighter ones over the darker tones of the background. This eliminates the need for masking the areas for the lighter colours or working from light to dark as in watercolours. The lighter vivid green added over the top has more white in the mix to make it more opaque. The whole painting is made up of three colours plus white.

(Left) **Sunlit Bluebell Study (detail)**
This close-up demonstrates the depth you can achieve in gouache by the juxtaposition of opaque and transparent layers while still retaining the lightness of touch. It also shows clearly how lighter tones have been superimposed over darker layers, displaying the versatility of gouache as a medium.

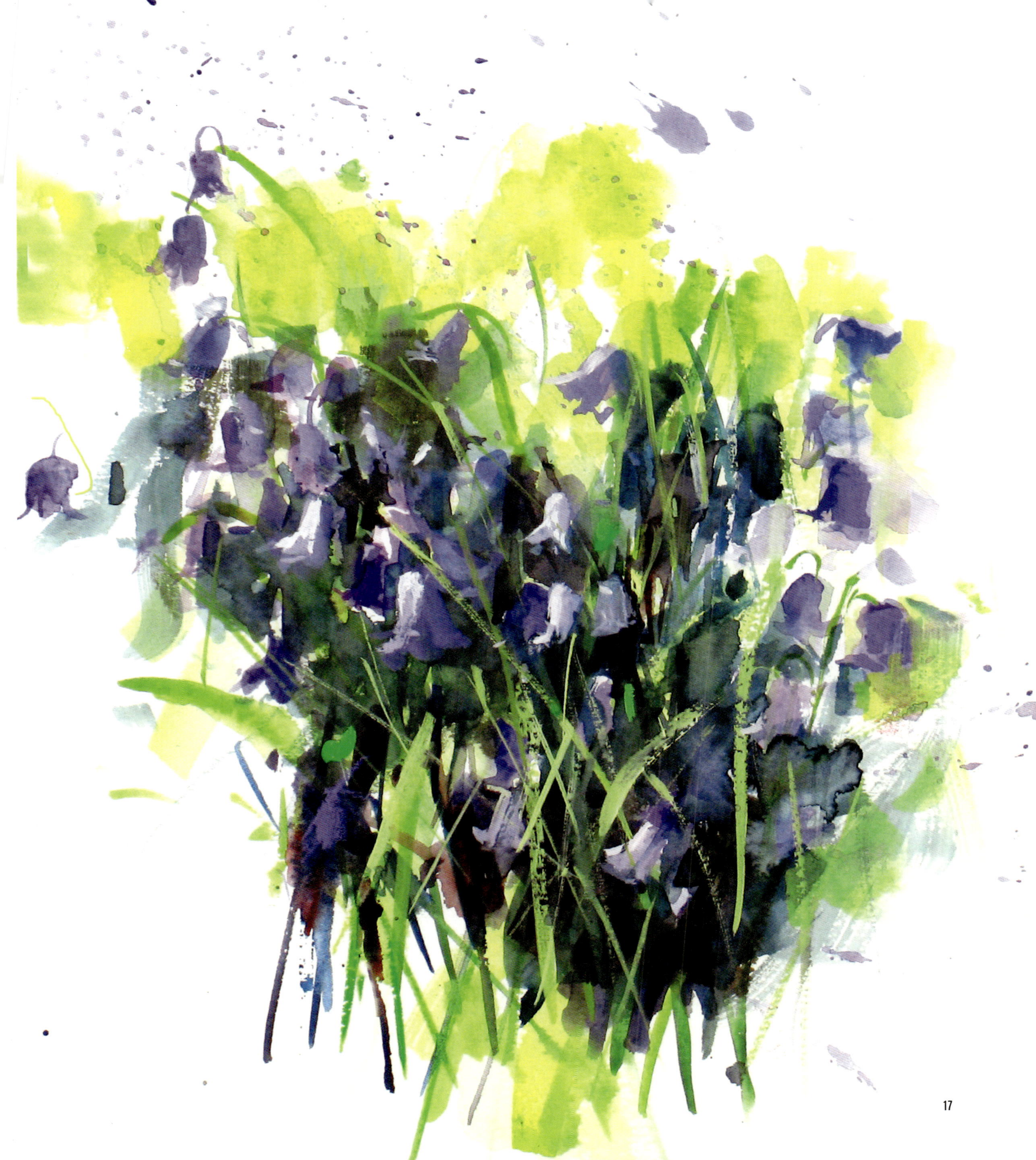

THE VERSATILITY OF ACRYLICS

Acrylic materials are by far the most versatile of all painting media. Artist's quality acrylics come in three quite distinctive consistencies: heavy body acrylics, the quite runny fluid colours and the inks, which are the most liquid form. These different viscosities help you to make the right choice to achieve the desired effect in your painting. All three viscosities are intermixable on a single surface and all are great contributors to a mixed media painting.

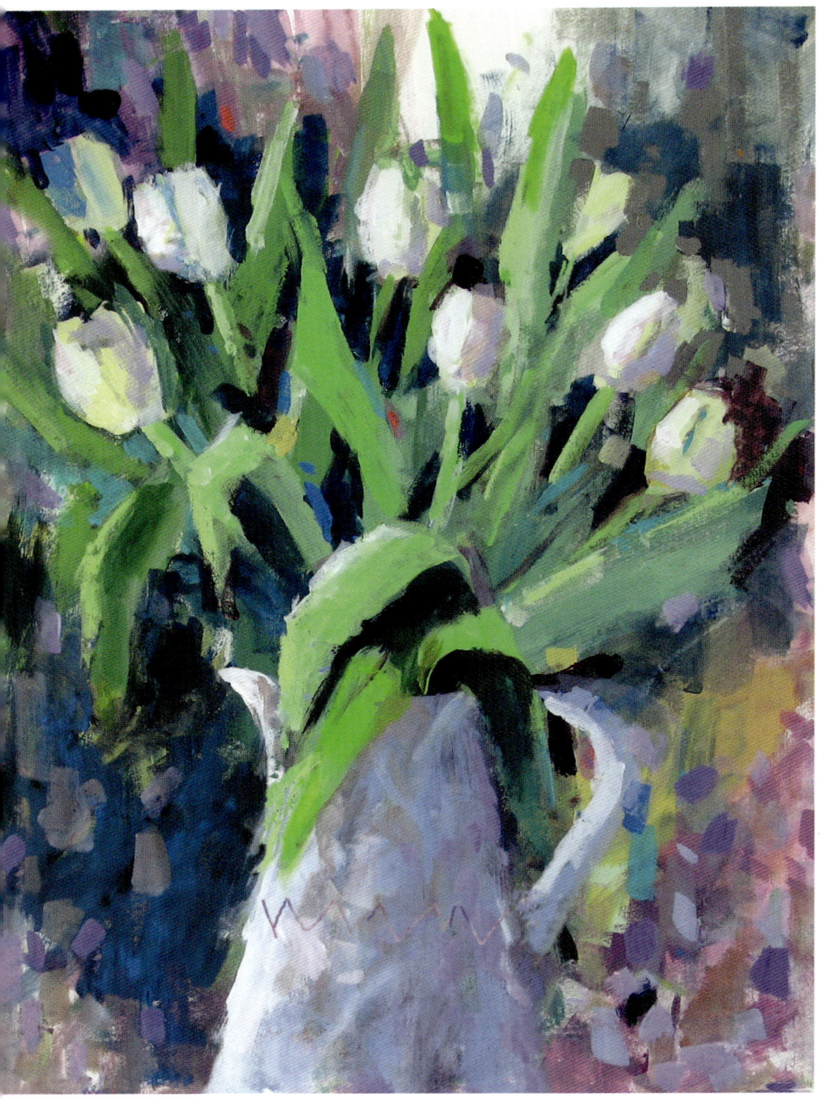

Heavy body acrylics

Also known as high viscosity acrylics, heavy body acrylics can be used in all kinds of techniques similar to oil painting, with the advantage of fast drying times for the rapid application of many layers. You have the option of applying the paints in thick impasto layers right from the start or slightly diluting them for more translucent, thinner layers building up to thicker applications. You can also glaze thinner layers over the heavier ones. There are no particular rules and as an artist you can make your own choices as to how you wish to use this most forgiving medium. Heavy body acrylics can be applied using acrylic brushes with stiff hair, your fingers, palette knives, rollers, pieces of card, and many other implements. As long as you avoid a greasy or shiny surface you can choose from a wide range of supports – paper, board, canvas, wood, metal and many more.

White Tulips
51 × 36 cm (20 × 14 in)
Heavy body acrylics on mount board
I find painting with heavy body acrylics
incredibly therapeutic, using brushes, a palette
knife and sometimes even my fingers or other
implements. I work in layers that are applied in
quick succession, so I find the fast drying time
an advantage for my painting process.

Artist's quality acrylics are made with high
quality pigments and binder, making the
painting process a joy rather than a struggle.
If you have a limited budget, buy the necessary
basic palette of the six warm and cool primary
colours plus white and learn to mix an infinite
number of secondary and tertiary colours.

Acrylic mediums

Acrylic gloss and matte mediums give you the
option to extend the paints or change the sheen
of the surface by mixing them with the paint
or adding them as a final layer. The mediums
can also be used to stick down collage or as a
primer to seal your support. You can also apply
a coat of medium as an isolation coat before
varnishing your painting.

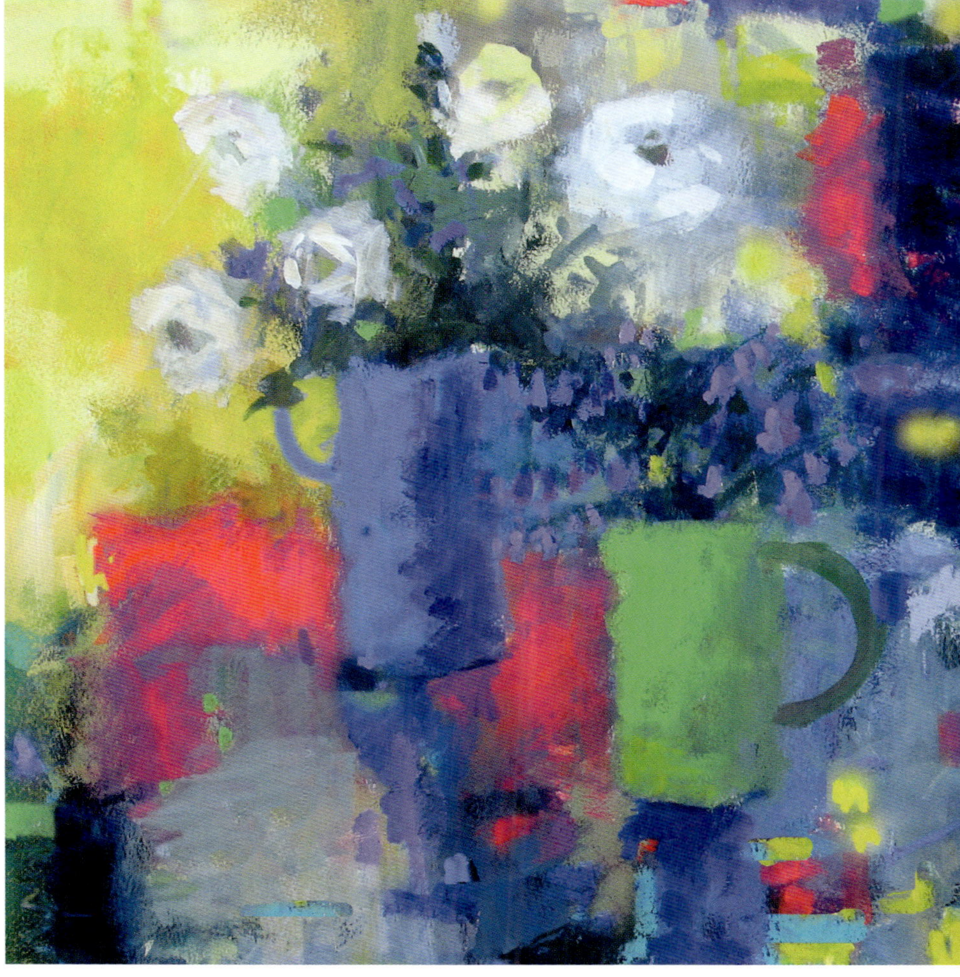

White Roses and Bluebells
51 × 51 cm (20 × 20 in)
Open acrylics on
watercolour paper
Open colours have a lovely
creamy texture and my
paintings often have a softer
look when I paint with
them. They are great for
blending techniques that
can be rather difficult with
fast-drying acrylics.

Acrylics with extended open time

If you find the relatively short working time of standard acrylics frustrating, you may find
Golden Open acrylics a much better alternative. These stay wet for a longer period, so
you have more time to push them around the paper or canvas. They are great for all types
of oil and acrylic painting techniques, especially blending, and are the best option for
plein-air painting with acrylics, particularly in hotter climates. You can also use them for
print-making as an alternative to oils.

Open acrylics have their own gels and mediums to retain the same working time. However,
you can also cut down the drying time by mixing them with standard acrylics, mediums
and gels – the drying time will depend on the mixture's ratio. You can also dry Open Acrylics
with a hairdryer. If you intend to use both Open and fast-drying acrylics in one painting, it is
best to use the fast-drying colour in the first few layers to avoid cracking of the surface.

FLUID ACRYLICS

Wherever I need highly intense colour with a flowing consistency that is not quite as thin as inks I turn to Fluid colours. You can't turn the heavy body acrylics into Fluid colours by adding water, as these are highly pigmented artist's quality colours with no filler or extenders, which are especially made with this particular viscosity, similar to double cream. A small drop of Fluid acrylics gives you an explosion of heart-stoppingly beautiful colour. If you wish to paint with no visible brush marks, the levelling quality of Fluid colours is the right paint for the job. By adding airbrush medium, you can spray your support to stain it or paint through stencils to create apparently spontaneous abstract marks.

Fluid colours are the ideal paints for pouring techniques as well as adding fine linear marks and small details to your paintings. They blend beautifully with all acrylic colours, gels and mediums, especially with pouring medium for producing amazing abstracts.

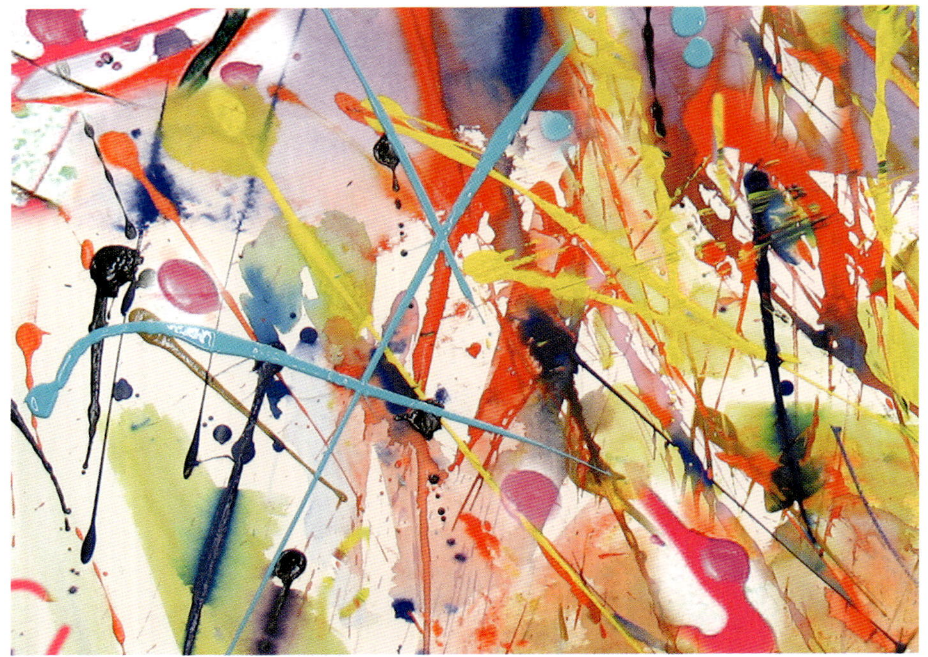

Fluid colour drizzles
Fluid colours have a heavier consistency than inks, so are very suitable for flicking strands of colour across the paper or canvas that dry with a slightly raised profile, and are quite different to marks achieved with the thinner inks.

(Opposite page) **Dahlia Impressions**
53 × 72 cm (21 × 28½ in)
Fluid colours on watercolour paper
The flowing consistency of Fluid colours allows for flicking strands of colour as well as dripping, drizzling and splattering. This is ideal for making incidental and random marks, as displayed in this semi-abstraction of some dahlias. You need to allow a little more time for drips and drizzles to dry than is required with inks, as Fluids have more body. They dilute easily for wet-into-wet applications – the highly saturated colours can withstand dilution and still retain their intensity.

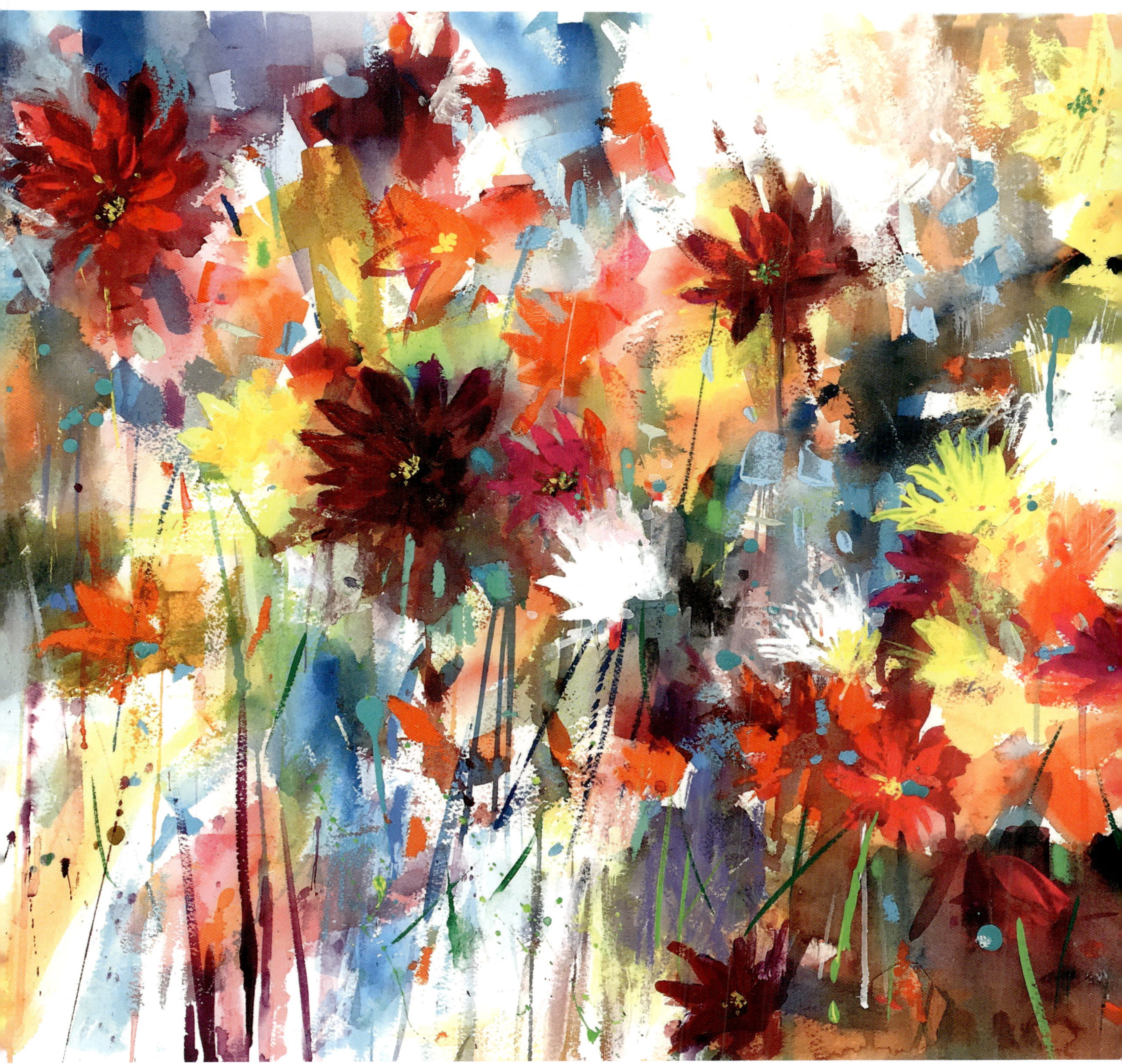

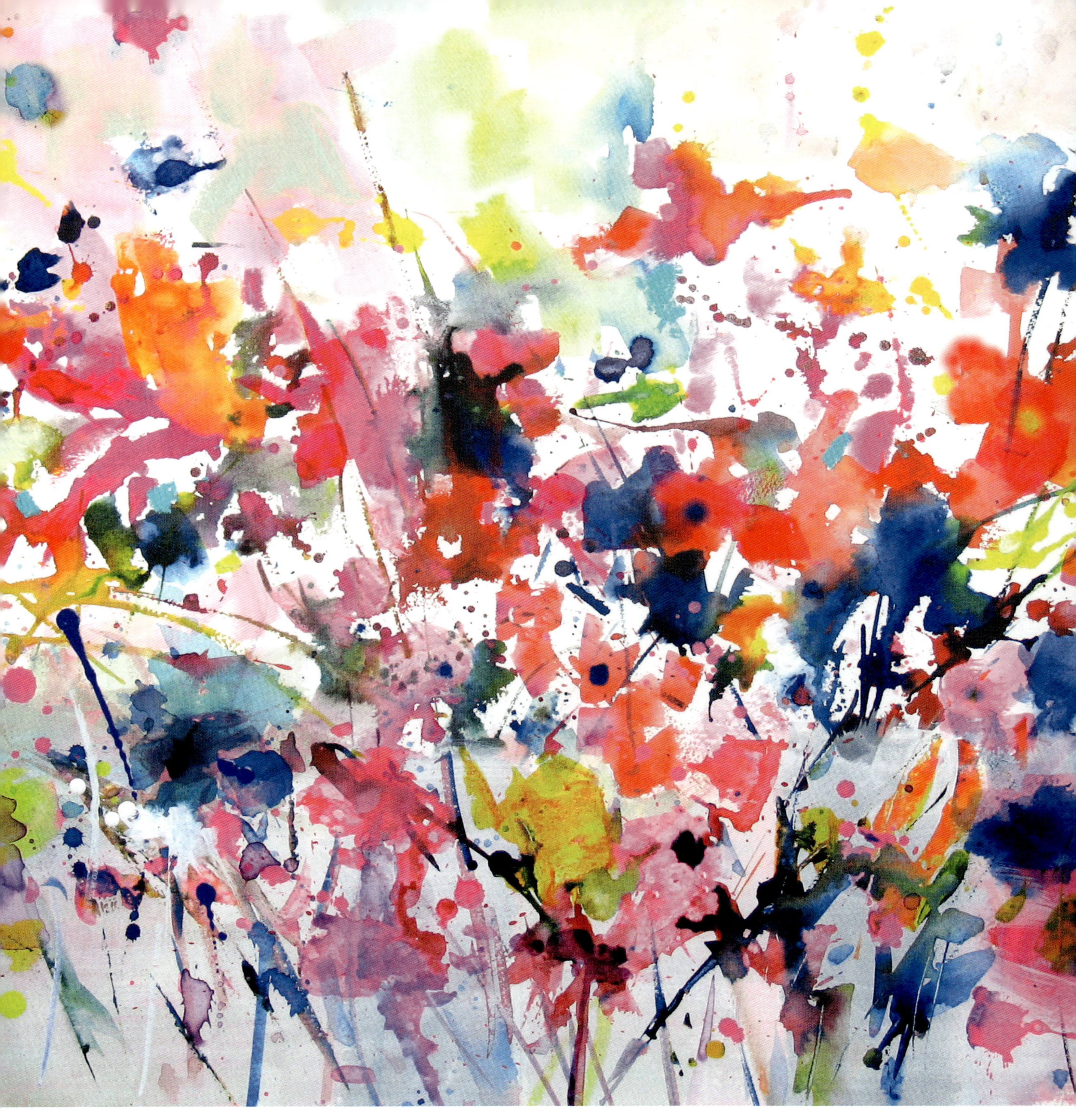

ACRYLIC INKS

Discovering these inks back in the late 1980s was such
a turning point for me. They provided the fluidity and
transparency I needed but with a great deal more versatility
than watercolours, especially as the latter were comparatively
limited in variety back then. I soon learned how to lift colour
with necessary speed, and how the polymer binder affected
the working properties, and I truly fell in love with them. It
almost seemed as if I could do no wrong, and the freedom of
applying many washes without making muddy colours was
such a revelation. The vibrant and saturated colours already in
fluid form meant I could be more spontaneous and they suited
my style of layering rapid washes of colour.

Just like watercolours, inks work best on absorbent surfaces
such as watercolour paper, but using them on primed
canvases or gesso-primed watercolour paper can bring
some surprising and wonderful effects. They are excellent
used on their own, but combine well with other media as
a base colour or glazed over other layers including collage,
and they contribute a great deal to a mixed media painting.
They work best with watercolour brushes for creating the
more mainstream watercolour techniques of wet-into-wet
or wet-on-dry but can be splashed, dripped, drizzled and
manipulated with other implements for more spontaneous
and energetic marks too.

(Opposite page) **Colourburst**
71 × 54 cm (28 × 21¼ in)
Acrylic inks on watercolour paper
This playful abstract inspired by a mixed
bouquet shows the vibrancy and the wide
range of mark-making possibilities with acrylic
inks. They are great for wet-into-wet, dry brush,
flicking, splattering, staining and fine detail and
linear marks – all the applications that can be
rather clumsy with heavy body acrylics.

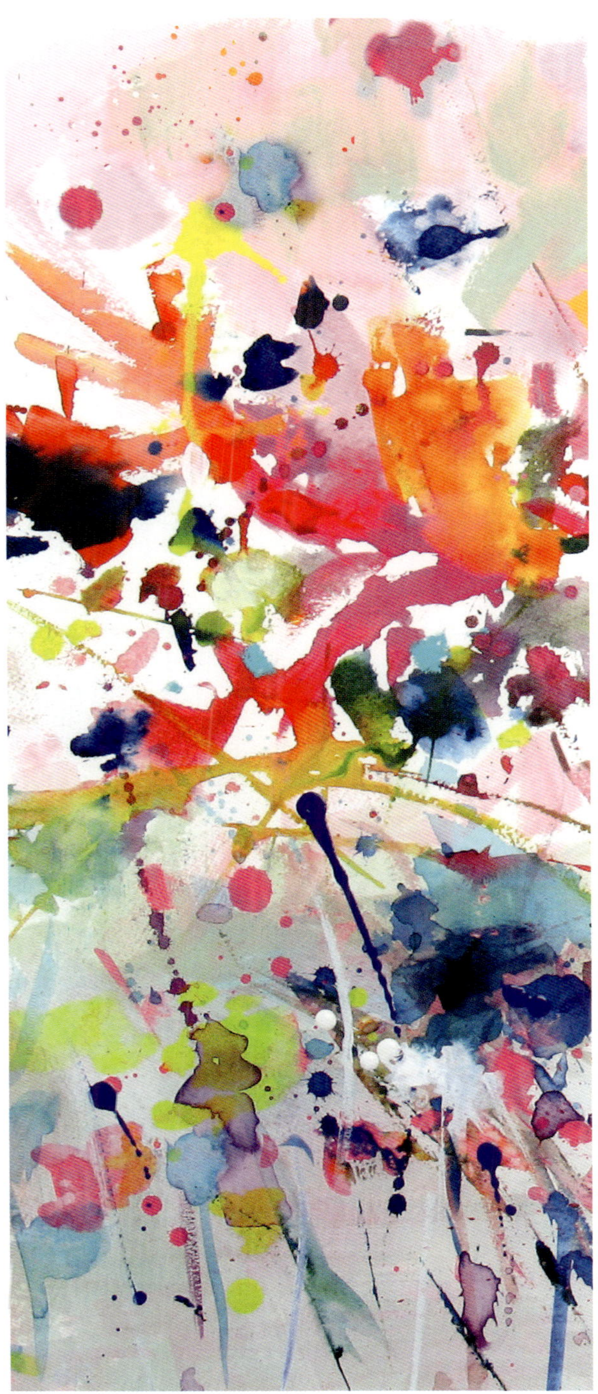

Colourburst (detail)
I love the vibrancy of acrylic inks and the
ability to make energetic overlaying of
colours without the fear of muddiness.

DRY PAINTING MEDIUMS

Painting with dry mediums takes away the need for colour mixing and makes the whole process more spontaneous. Soft and oil pastels, wax crayons and other dry mediums add an extra touch of magic that can lift the whole painting to a new level. They are great for intuitive drawing exercises, as your direct contact with the medium releases a different kind of energy that can lead to some exciting discoveries and interesting mark-making.

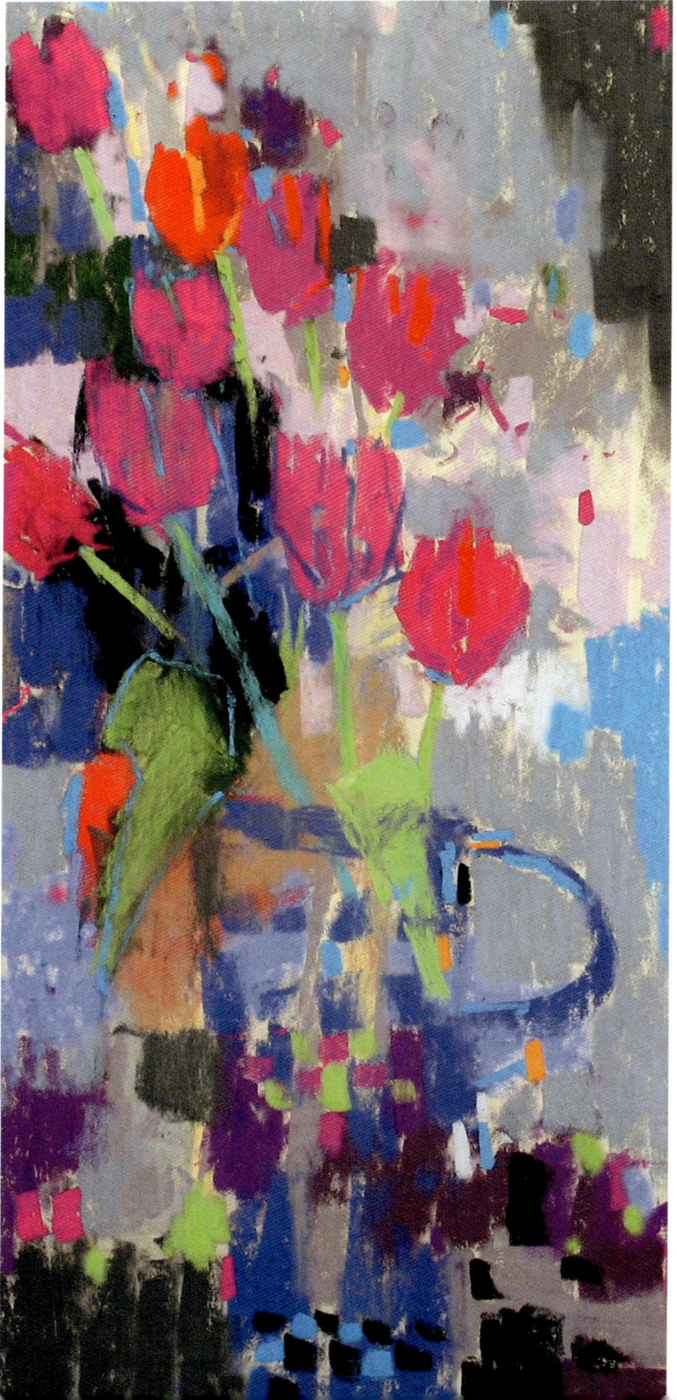

Soft pastels

A tactile and immediate medium, soft pastels can add a touch of sublime colour that is sometimes impossible to replicate in wet mediums. There is often a noticeable colour shift in water-based mediums – acrylics tend to dry slightly darker, watercolours and ink slightly lighter. Artist's quality soft pastels are almost like pure pigment with very little binder or filler, so the colour remains vibrant and retains its tonal value.

Unlike water media, there is very little scope for mixing colour, so when working with pastels on their own, you will need your lightest light and darkest dark in each spectrum, plus all the tones in between. When you paint with pastels in mixed media works you have the benefit of other opaque mediums, so any colours missing from your pastel box can be replaced with acrylics, gouache or other types of crayons. Pastel pencils can be useful for linear marks or any small details you may wish to add.

Pink Tulips in Spanish Jug
41 × 18 cm (16 × 7 in)
Soft pastel on card
This painting was done with Jackson's luscious handmade soft pastels on card primed with Golden pastel ground. I used a range of cool greys in the background, plus Dark Violet, Fade Violet and Lilac to magnify the impact of the vivid pink-purple of the tulips. Accents of sky blue, black and violet-blue bring added interest to the abstracted background. I love this range as you can buy all the values of each colour spectrum in one box.

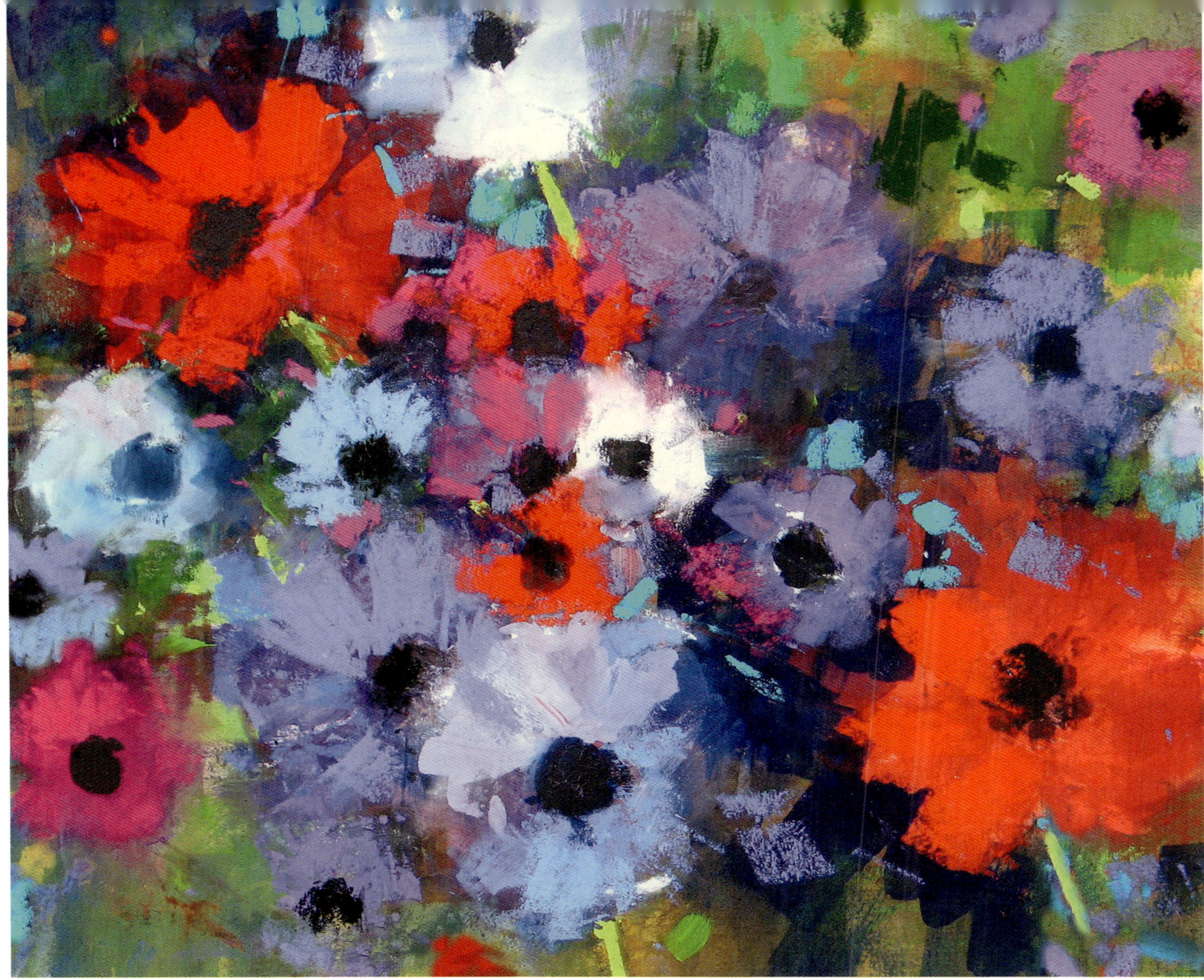

Combining transparent and opaque materials

The transparency or opacity of your materials plays a big role in creating interesting passages in your painting. Almost all water-based mediums have a range of both transparent and opaque colours. Dry mediums such as soft and oil pastels are opaque, meaning a layer of colour will cover the one below. Watercolours and inks are generally thought of as transparent mediums, but they also have some opaque and semi-transparent colours. Knowing the characteristics of your mediums in this respect will help you to create beautiful translucent backdrops, glaze over areas with translucent colours, create impasto and textured layers or simply cover various parts when needed with opaque colours. It will also help you a great deal in mixing colours with clarity.

Colourful Anemones
33 × 33 cm (13 × 13 in)
Soft pastel and ink on sandpaper
Here I used soft pastels on a wash of ink on artist's quality wet and dry sandpaper. Inks, watercolours, gouache and acrylics are great for creating the perfect base and background mood for a pastel painting. Not only is the result beautiful, you also avoid potentially inhaling a lot of pastel dust. Leaving some of the background colours will make for an atmospheric painting.

OIL PASTELS

Possibly one of the most under-used mediums, oil pastel hasn't had the exposure that other mediums have had through books and articles. The artist's quality versions of this fabulous medium can contribute a great deal to your mixed media artwork. They come in a range of beautiful colours with rich and luxuriant texture to use as resists under washes of watercolours, gouache or acrylics, or to be added as highlights to enhance other mediums. They are made from pure pigment, inactive oils and mineral waxes, so they have a tacky surface. To eliminate unwanted applications from an area, I usually scrape off the surface with my palette knife and then paint over the area with heavy paint. They accept thicker colour easily.

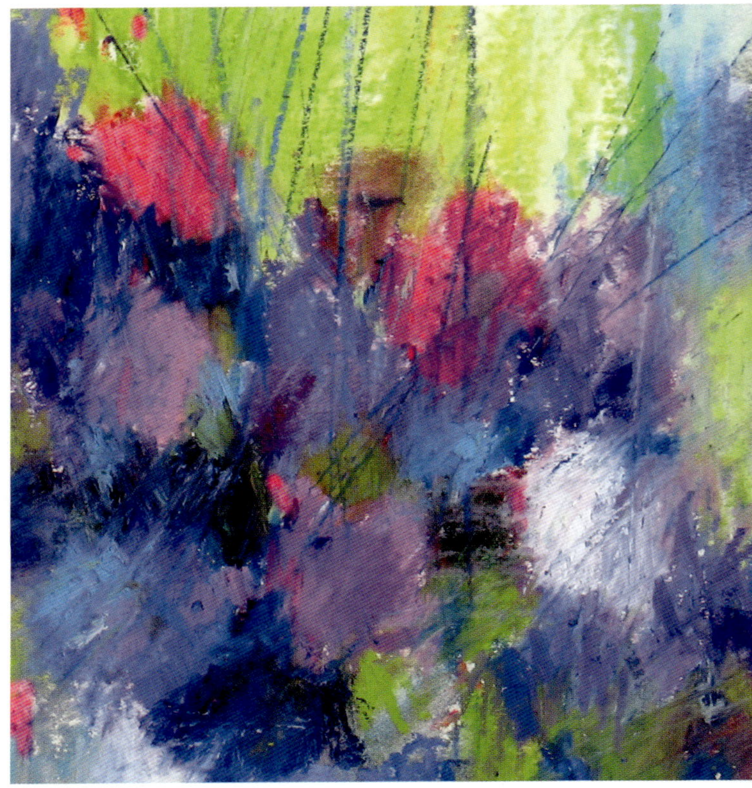

This sample board shows the build-up of oil pastel applied then softened with a rag dipped in low-odour thinner. Once dry, it was overlaid with more oil pastels to create a rich surface and allow the various shapes within the painting to gel together.

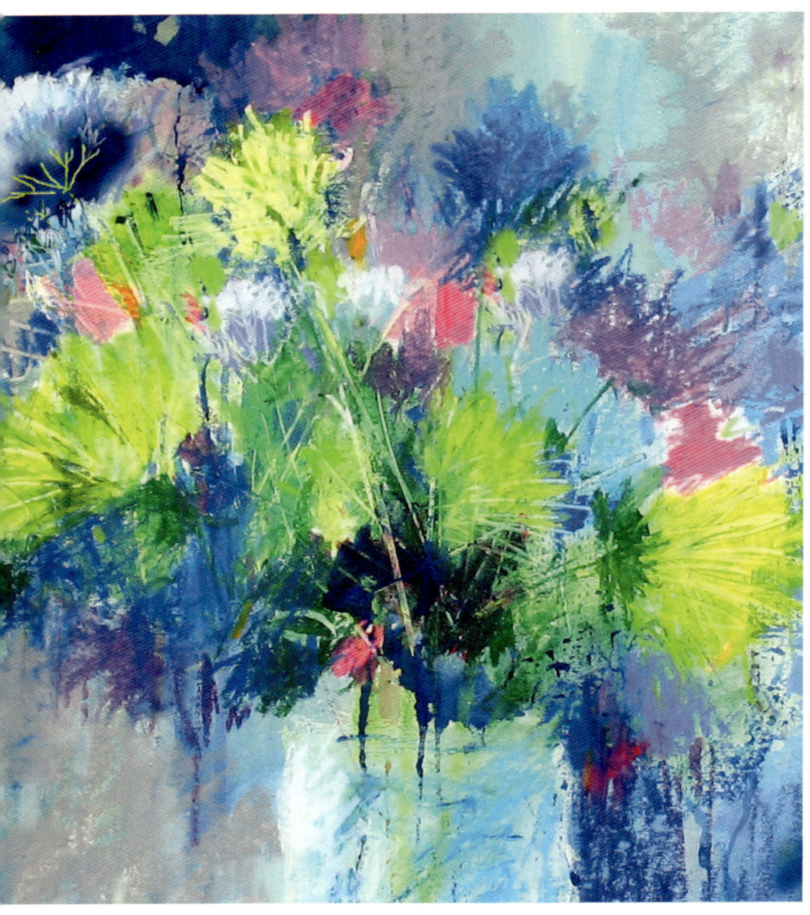

Yellow Chrysanthemums
36 × 36 cm (14 × 14 in)
Oil pastel on mount board
By layering oil pastels and scratching into them it is possible to achieve some lovely visual effects that convey flower textures, as shown in this image of yellow chrysanthemums. I spread the oil pastel using solvent with a brush to create a wash effect in the background. I added some inks afterwards to get some lovely dark values – I liked the dribbles, so I left them to dry on the surface.

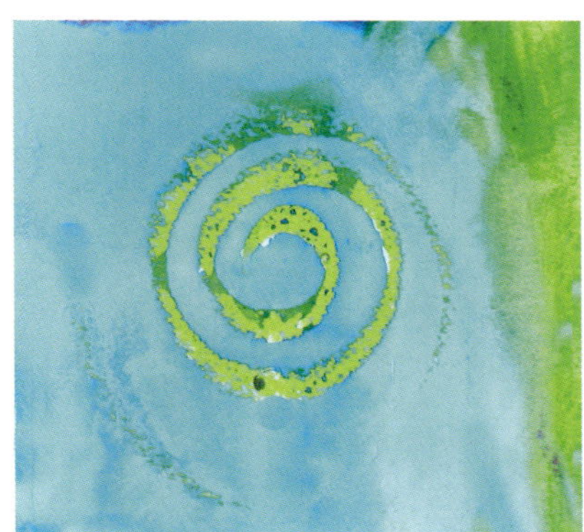

Apart from bringing some beautiful accents of colour, oil pastels can be used under washes of watercolour, acrylic inks and diluted gouache (but not heavy body acrylics or Fluid colours unless very heavily diluted) to create a resist.

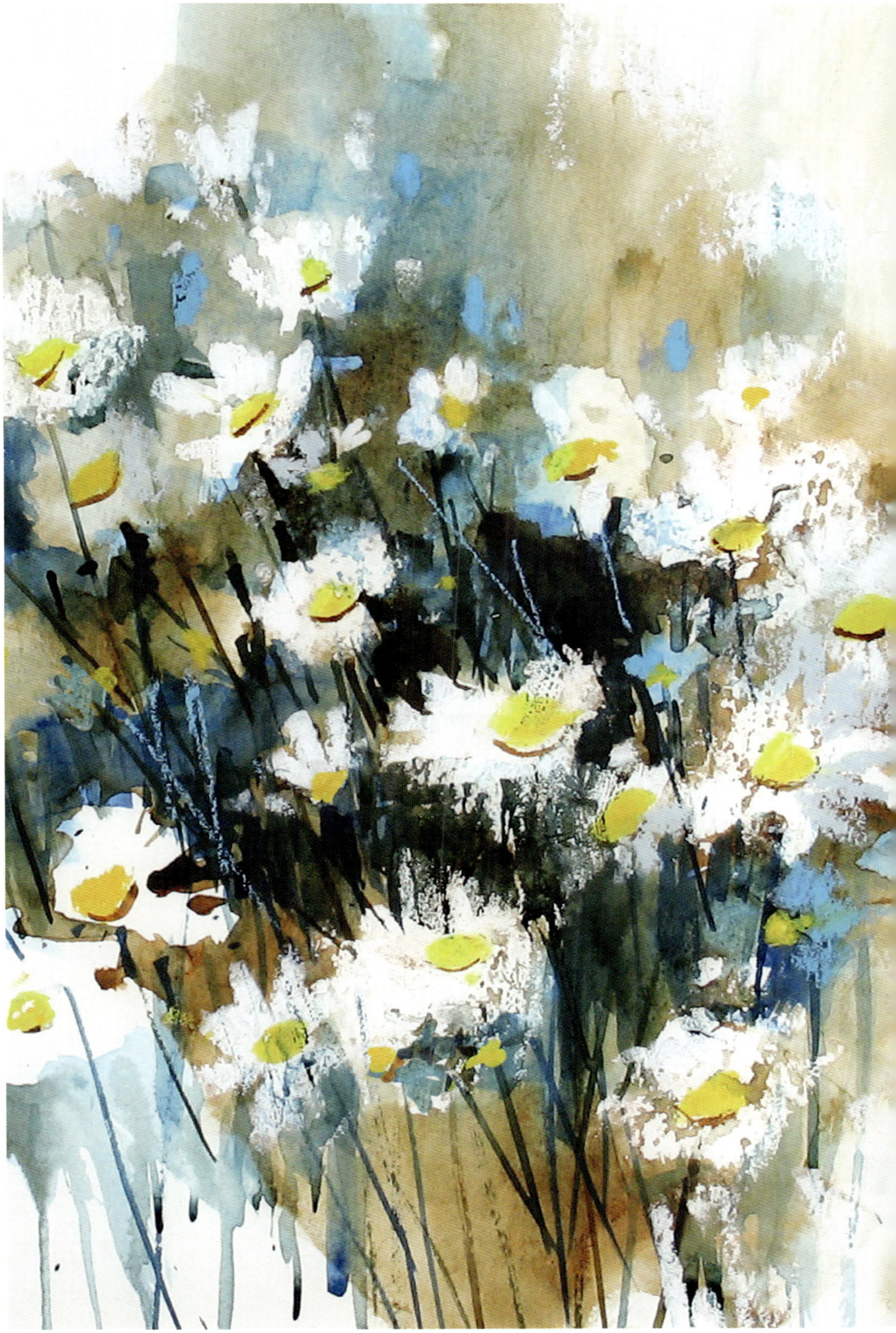

White Daisies

32 × 24 cm (12½ × 9½ in)

Oil pastel and ink on watercolour paper
This image clearly shows the very effective way in which the oil pastel resist can work in your floral paintings. I used white and soft grey for the shadows of these lovely daisies and then flooded the surface with strong washes of ink in Sepia High Flow, FW Process Cyan and Payne's Grey. I then added the stems, using oil pastels for some and ink and a rigger brush for others.

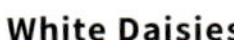

OIL PAINT

Of all the mediums an artist can use, oil paint is one of the most highly regarded by painters, galleries and collectors. Not only does it have a sumptuous consistency, the longer drying time and the ability to move the paint around the support is one of its attractive features for artists. Some oil painters love the smell of the thinners and mediums, but for those who are either allergic to traditional ones such as turpentine or don't like the smell, there are alternatives like low-odour thinners and Zest-it, which has the scent of orange.

The drying time of oil paint makes it a tricky medium to bring into the mixed media box, but as long as it is used sensibly and in layers where it is allowed to dry, the beautiful, lush colours can contribute a great deal. You can paint with oils over a dry acrylic base, but acrylic paint may peel off if painted over a dry oil painting and the two paints do not mix together. I use oil sticks and oil pastels over dry oil paintings for highlights and accents of colour and often block in the first couple of layers with acrylic paint.

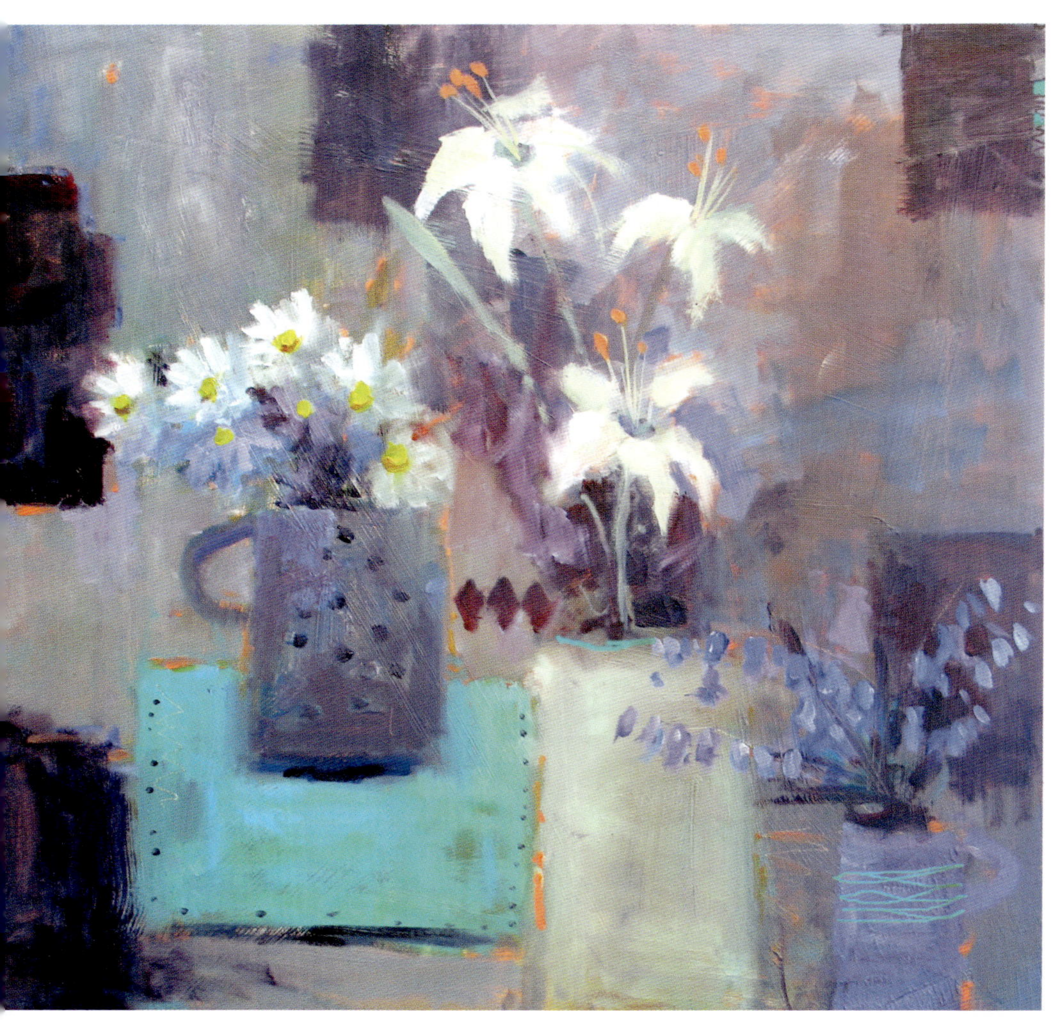

Daisies, Lilies and Bluebells
51 × 51 cm (20 × 20 in)
Oil on panel
For some reason I tend to use a totally different palette for my oils – they are often softer and more sophisticated colours. This painting was done on a gesso-primed artist's panel, which is a lovely rigid surface for oils. I used a drop of Cadmium Orange Fluid acrylic in my gesso to unify the painting.

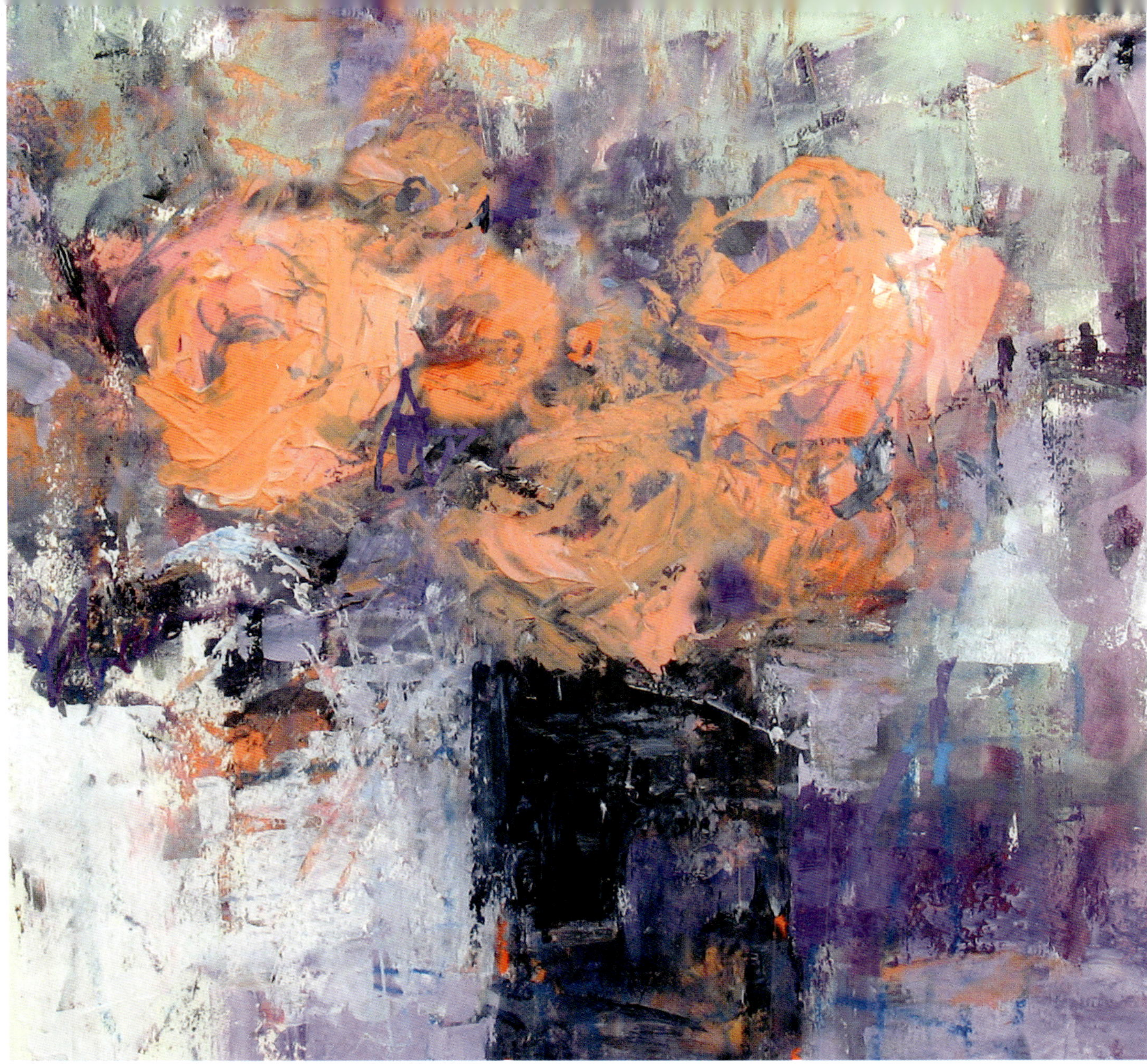

Cold wax

A semi-solid mixture of wax and solvent, cold wax adds a sculptural quality to oil paint. I use Williamsburg oils for their buttery texture and add cold wax to give the paint an even more solid feel to fuse layers together. It adds a great tactile quality when I am moving it around and is a very enjoyable way of using oils.

Peach-coloured Roses
35 × 35 cm (13¾ × 13¾ in)
Oil and cold wax on artist's wooden panel
This painting started in acrylics overlaid with oils and cold wax, allowing some of the initial colour applications to show through. It is an ideal way of using oils for me as it suits my free style of working and layering colours. A little patience is needed to allow some layers to dry but it is a small price to pay for the very enjoyable process.

PAINTING WITH ALTERNATIVE IMPLEMENTS

Despite being a self-confessed brushoholic, I do enjoy the liberating and joyful experience of painting with other implements. I think any exercise that takes you out of your comfort zone gets you a step closer to adopting a more relaxed and free style of painting. You can be very creative with finding alternative materials to paint with, for example, brushes made from twigs and other rough-surfaced materials, all kinds of rollers, pieces of card, sharp objects for sgrafitto and so on – all come with a certain amount of unpredictability. The lesser degree of control when using these implements leads to some wonderfully random and seemingly incidental marks that make the results look both playful and effortless.

This is just a very small collection of some of my mark-making tools apart from my vast collection of brushes. Some, such as Catalyst blades, are designed for artists, but others I find in DIY or kitchen stores or children's toy shops. They all bring different marks to the painting which can be more difficult to make with a brush.

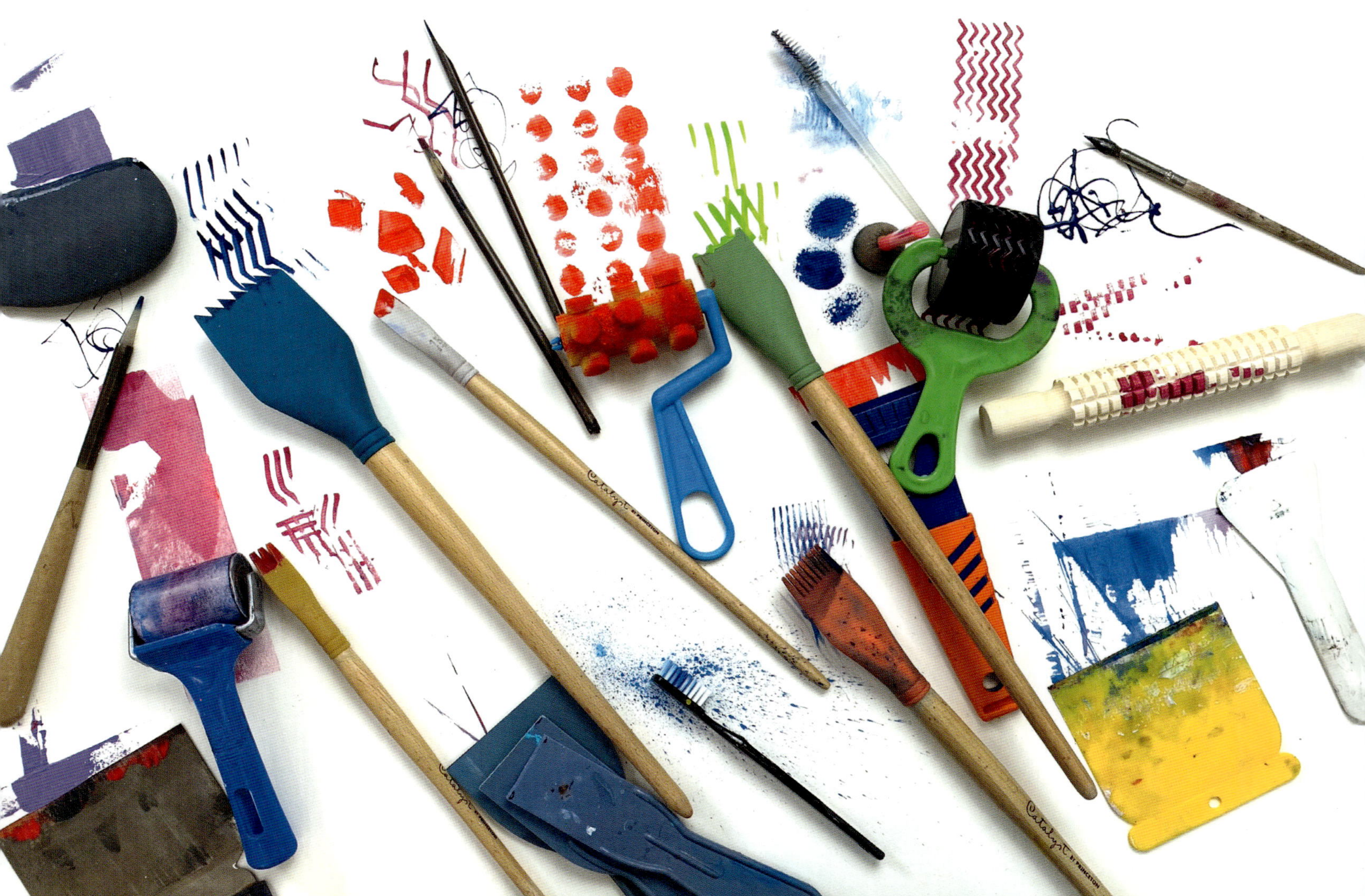

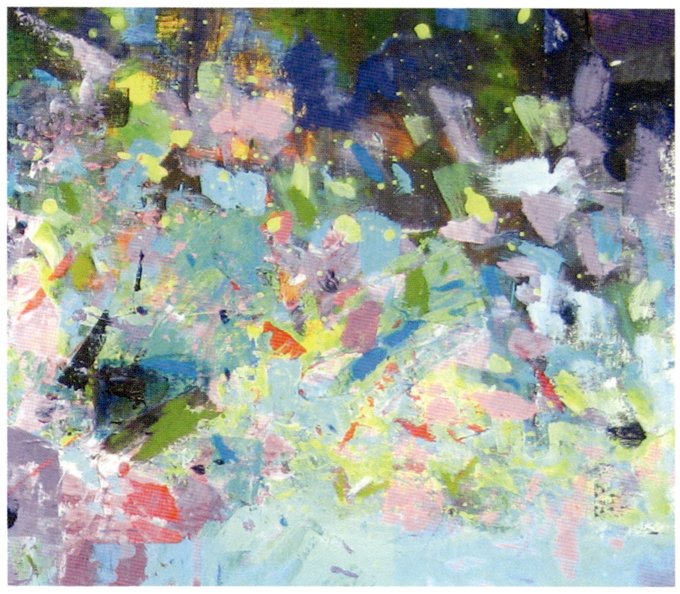

Broken-colour marks made with cut-up credit cards dipped in paint.

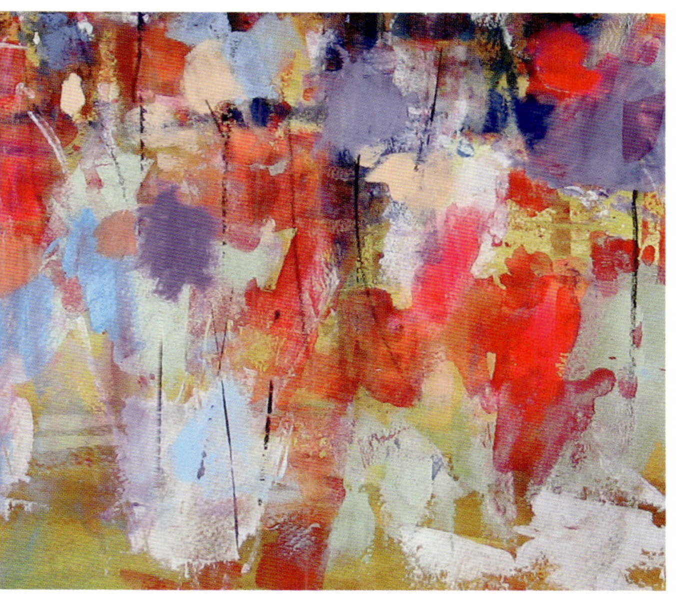

Dragging the paint with a spatula and making fine lines with a pen dipped in ink.

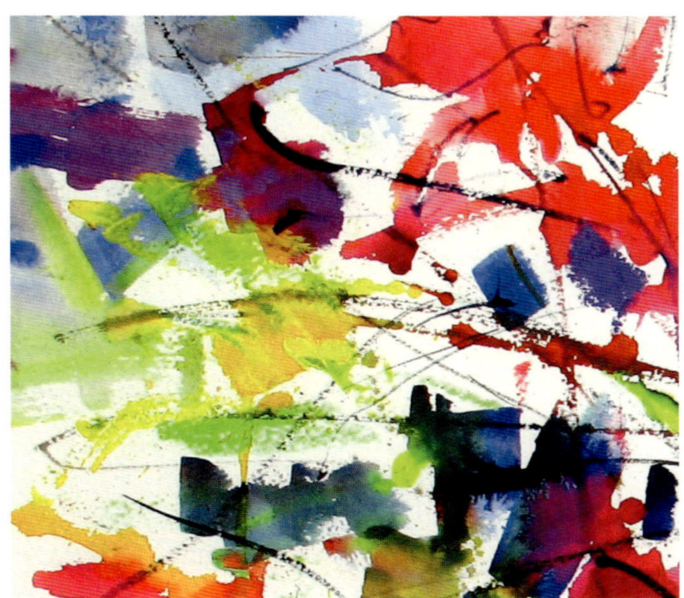

Dragging the inks with Catalyst tools and using twigs for linear marks.

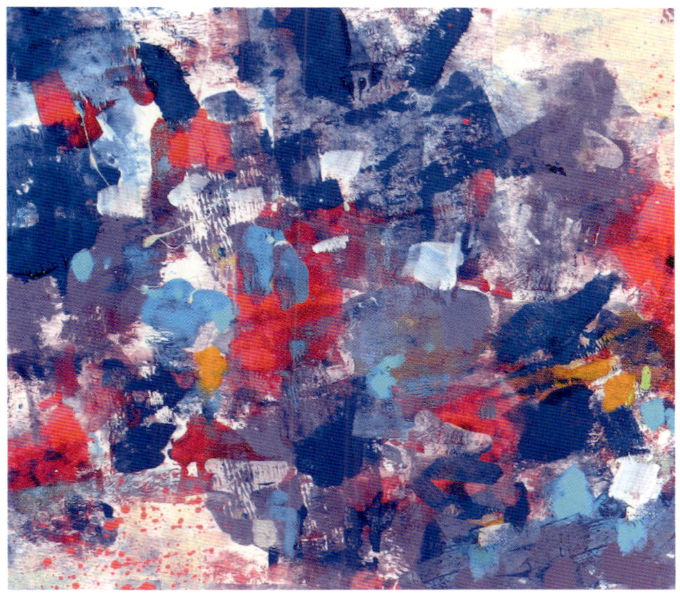

Using various rollers from soft to hard rubber and sponge rollers all give you different marks. These alternative tools make the marks appear more playful and give the painting a more spontaneous appearance.

ALTERNATIVE MARK-MAKING MATERIALS

Art shops are packed with an array of materials so tempting we often buy some extras, only to find them still unopened on the studio shelf months or even years later. Working in mixed media is the ideal time for incorporating such materials into your work. Coloured pencils, water-mixable wax crayons, pure wax crayons, marker pens, spray paints, charcoal, and watercolour sticks and markers all have their own unique way of mark-making that can be used for fine lines or broader marks, glazes, background colour, staining and much more. Delve into your forgotten store of materials and put them to good use in your mixed media painting.

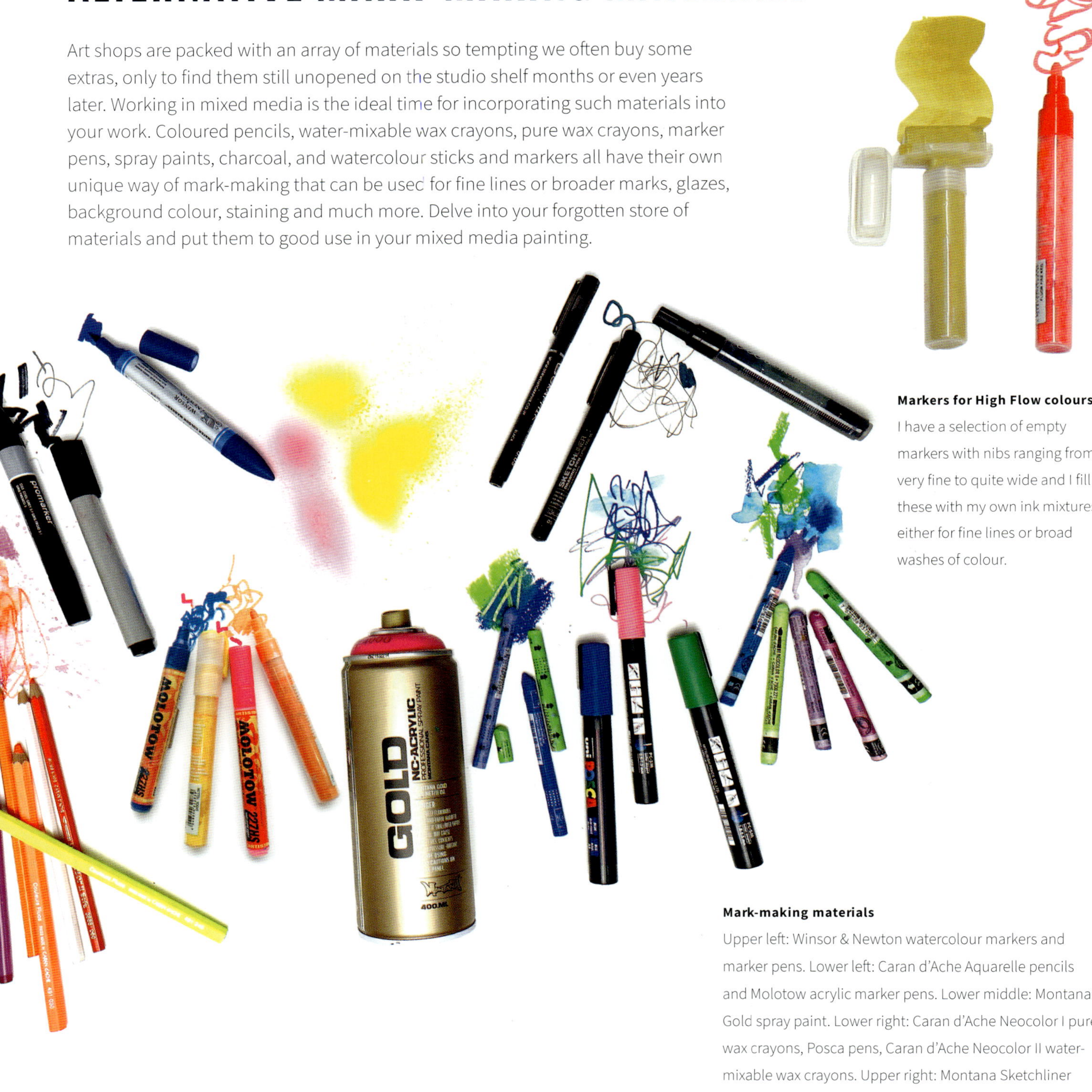

Markers for High Flow colours

I have a selection of empty markers with nibs ranging from very fine to quite wide and I fill these with my own ink mixtures, either for fine lines or broad washes of colour.

Mark-making materials

Upper left: Winsor & Newton watercolour markers and marker pens. Lower left: Caran d'Ache Aquarelle pencils and Molotow acrylic marker pens. Lower middle: Montana Gold spray paint. Lower right: Caran d'Ache Neocolor I pure wax crayons, Posca pens, Caran d'Ache Neocolor II water-mixable wax crayons. Upper right: Montana Sketchliner drawing pens; empty marker pen filled with black ink.

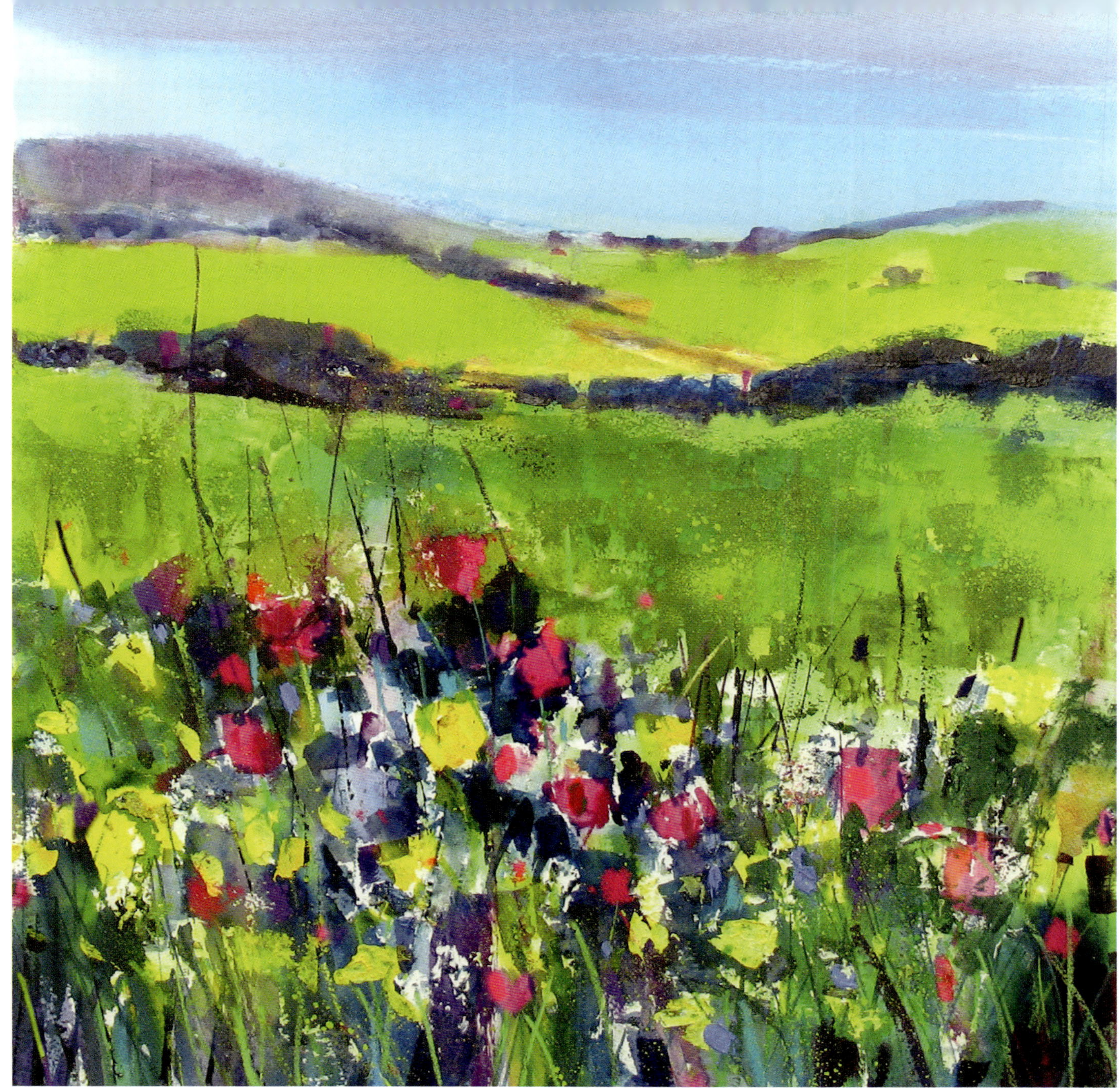

Wildflower Hedgerow

46 × 46 cm (18 × 18 in)

Paint, pastel, pen and watercolour on watercolour paper

Here I used a soft blue transparent spray paint for the sky and a vivid lime green for the fields. The foreground colourful flowers were painted with yellow oil pastels and magenta Neocolor II, and most of the greens are done with Neocolor I and II. I also used Posca pens for fine lines, marker pens for the edge of the field, and watercolour markers for the distant hills. I love the direct connection with the artwork when painting with these kinds of materials; the water-soluble ones are great for providing broader areas of colour. Caran d'Ache Neocolor II wax pastels are among my favourites as they offer wonderful lush pigments that mix with water and provide strong passages in the painting.

COMBINING DIFFERENT MEDIA

This project is especially useful if some of the materials in this chapter are new to you. Making small practice pieces comes with far less pressure than combining media in a bigger and more complex painting, and they make wonderful reference guides stuck in a sketch book or even drawn in a concertina sketch book. These are some of my samples that help me explore interesting textural effects to use in future paintings.

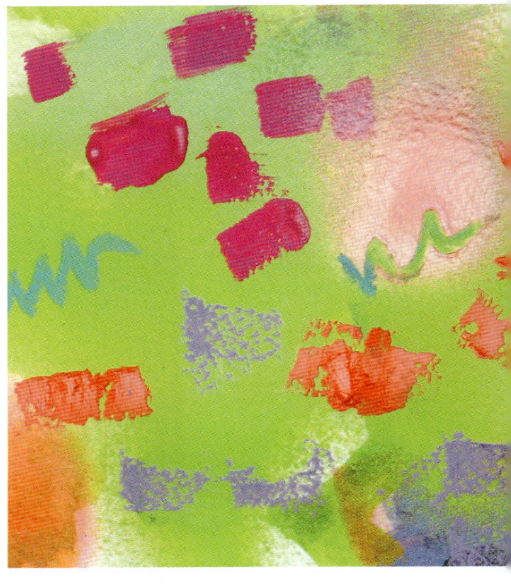

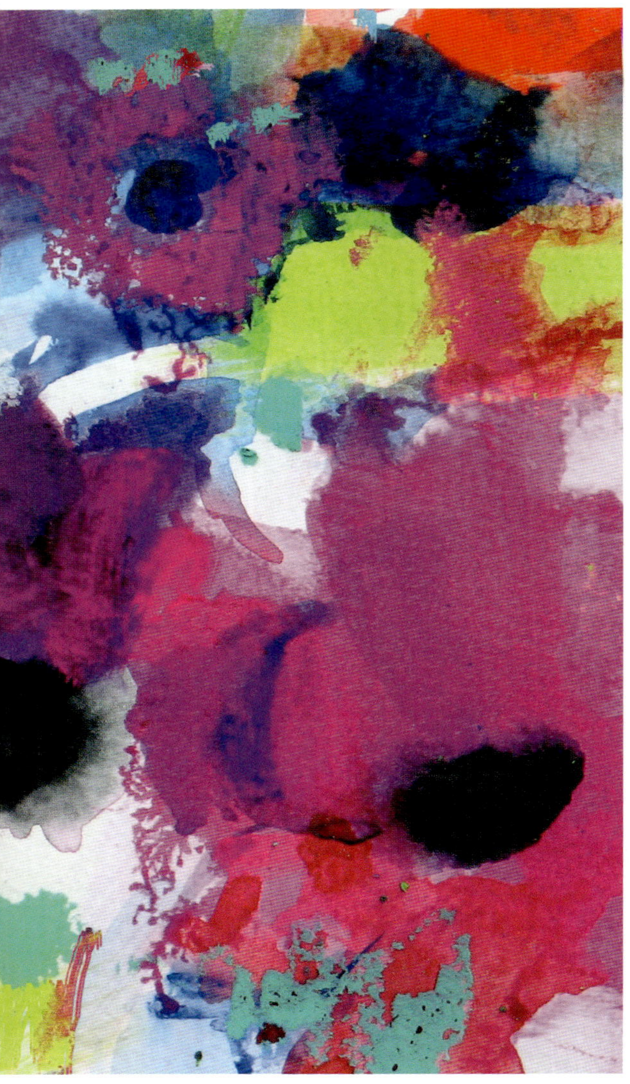

1

Here I used oil pastels as a resist underneath vibrant washes of acrylic inks.

2

Spray paint makes a great ground for gouache, heavy body acrylics, oil and soft pastels and watercolour pencils.

3

Gouache provides a wonderful matte surface for soft pastels. The pastel has picked up the pattern of the NOT surface of the watercolour paper, making an interesting textural effect.

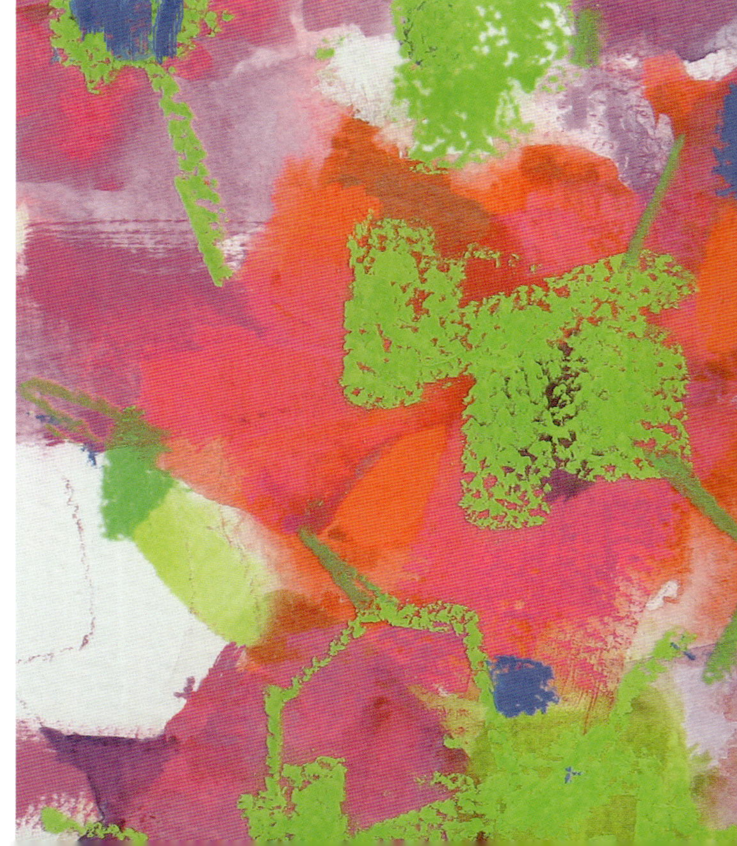

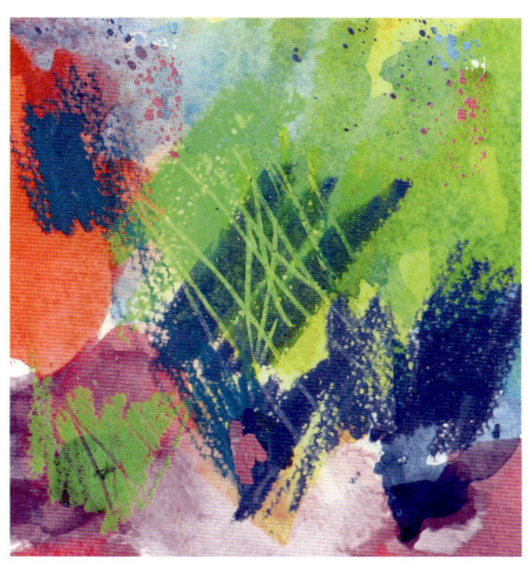

4

I used the sgraffito technique here, applying darker blue Neocolor I wax pastel over lime green, and scratching into it to reveal the colour underneath. I also used washes of watercolour over Neocolor I which, as wax, resists washes of colour.

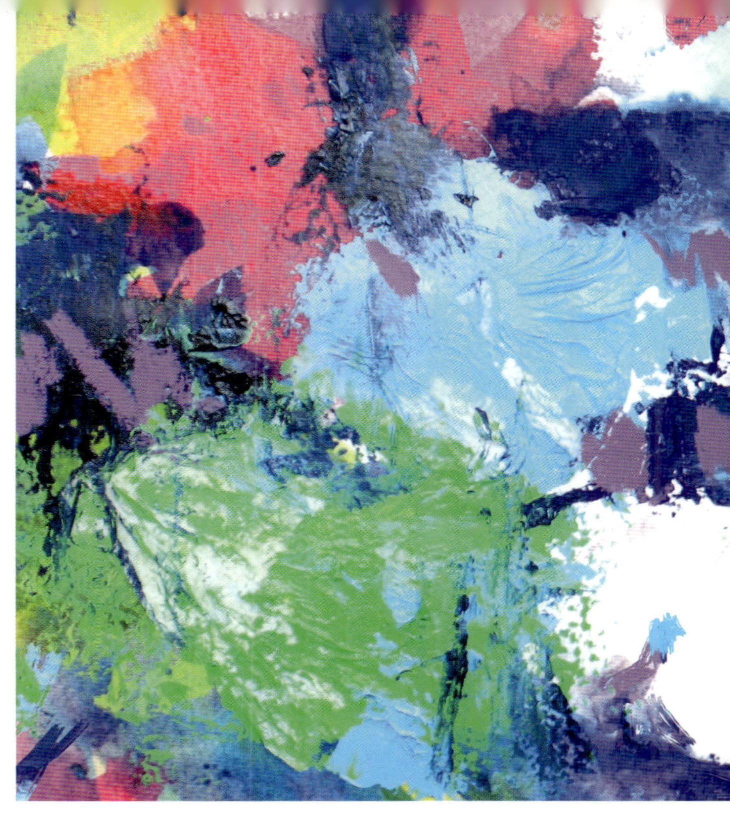

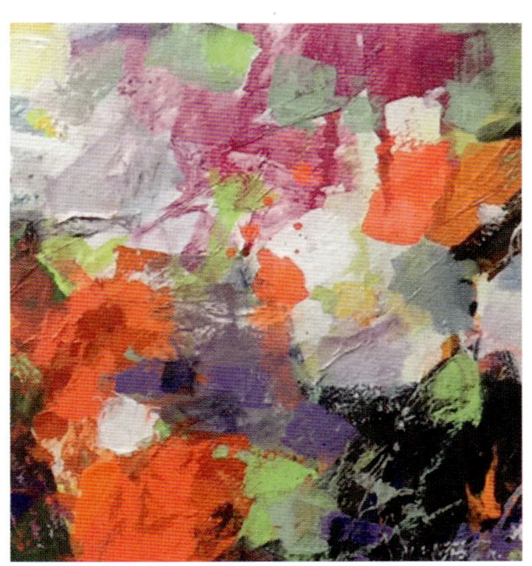

5

This is a detail of a painting where I used tissue, oil pastels, inks and heavy body paint together on a surface primed and textured with regular gel.

7

This sample has pieces of handmade paper, inks and heavy body colours overlaid with Neocolor II watercolour pencil.

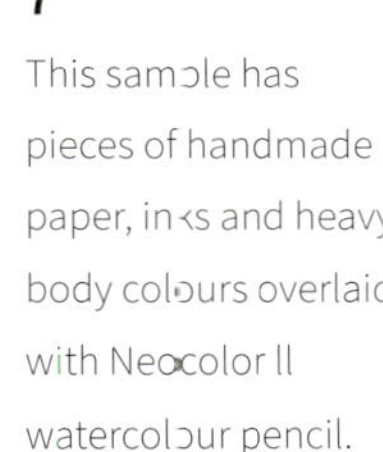

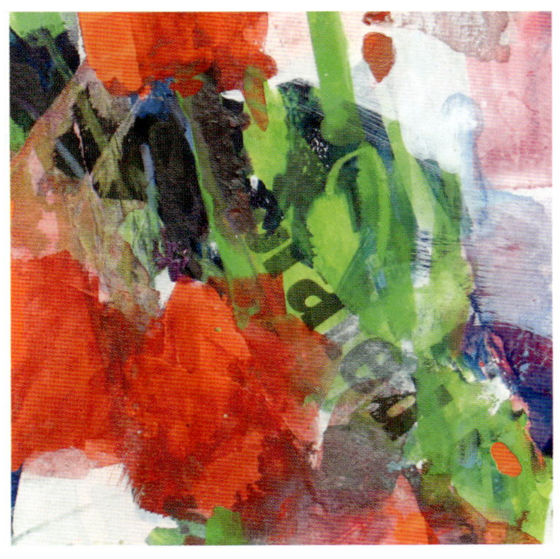

6

Here ink, heavy body acrylics, oil and soft pastels have been applied over a gesso-primed surface and collage pieces.

8

Oils and cold wax medium are a great combination – the wax gives the oils even more of a buttery texture. Once the surface has dried it can be enhanced with oil pastels or oil sticks.

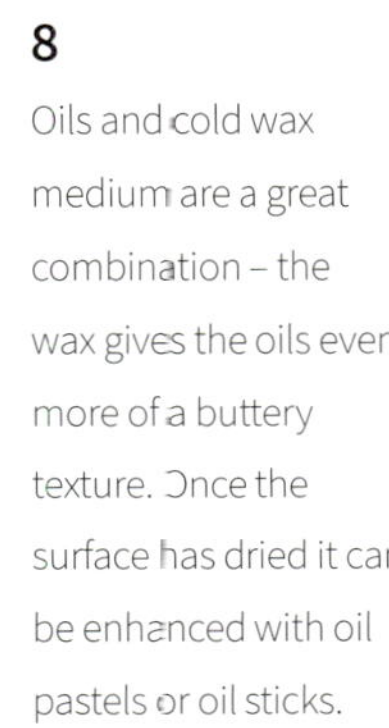

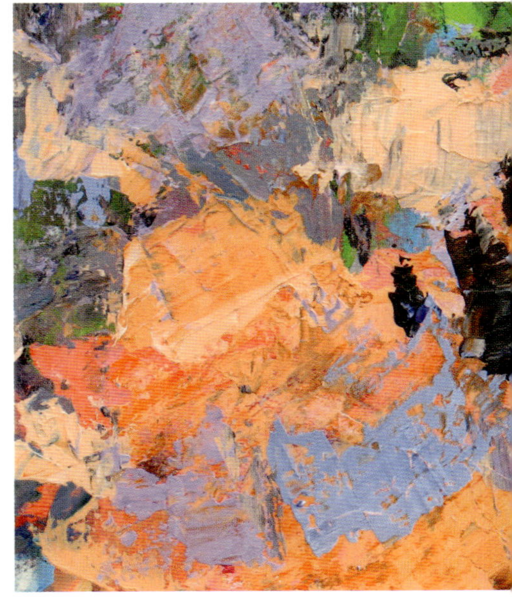

DYNAMIC DESIGN STRATEGIES

The first crucial step in the creative process is the design and composition of your subject matter, for without a sound, imaginative and well-balanced composition the painting is doomed to fall at the first hurdle.
A tremendous number of factors come together to make a successful painting. In this chapter we shall be looking at ways of using the elements and principles of design to interpret the visual information, not only to make a more fluid creative process, but also to create art that fully engages your audience.

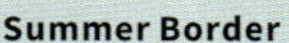

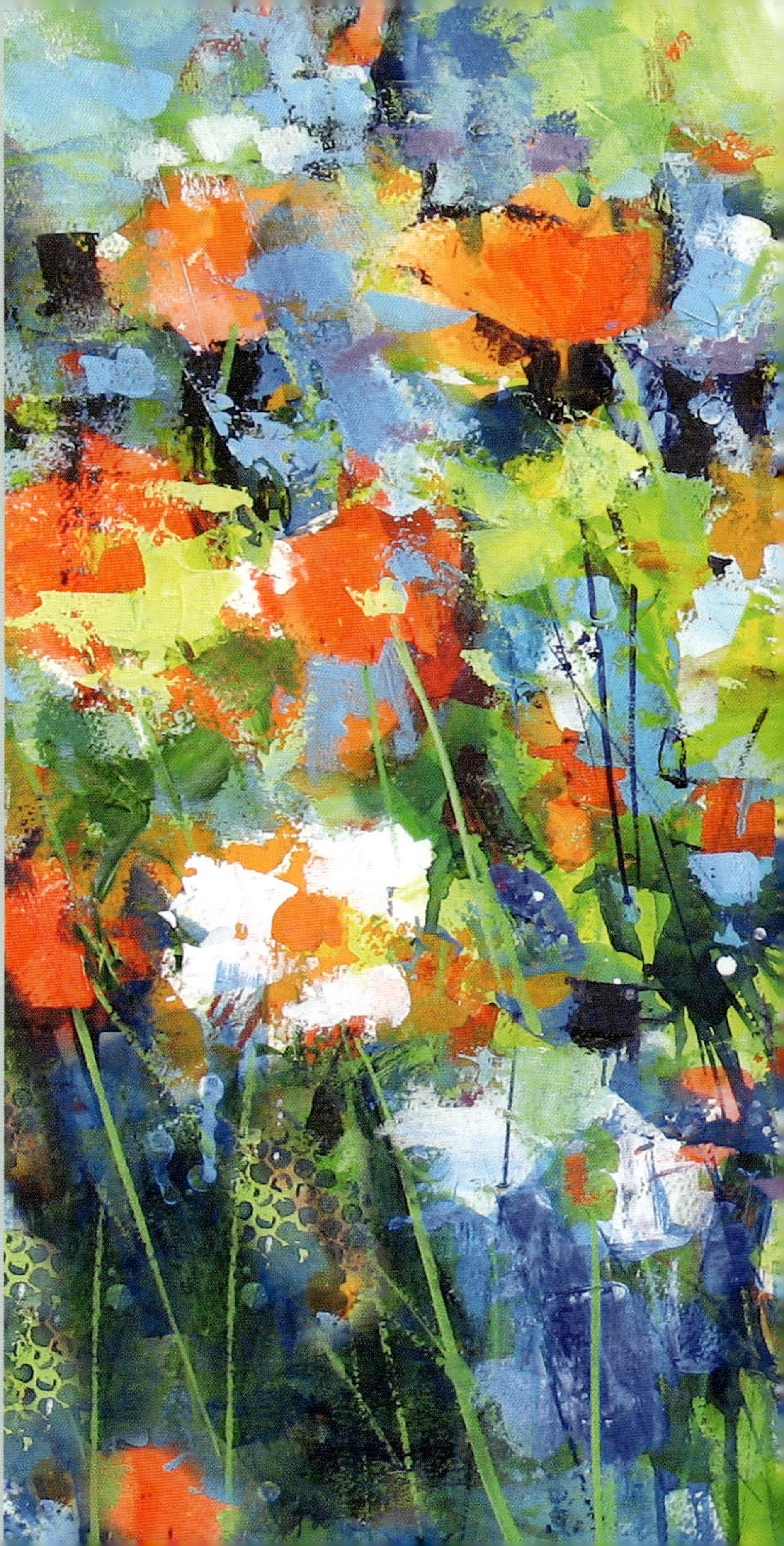

Summer Border
72 × 53 cm (28 × 21 in)
Mixed media on watercolour paper

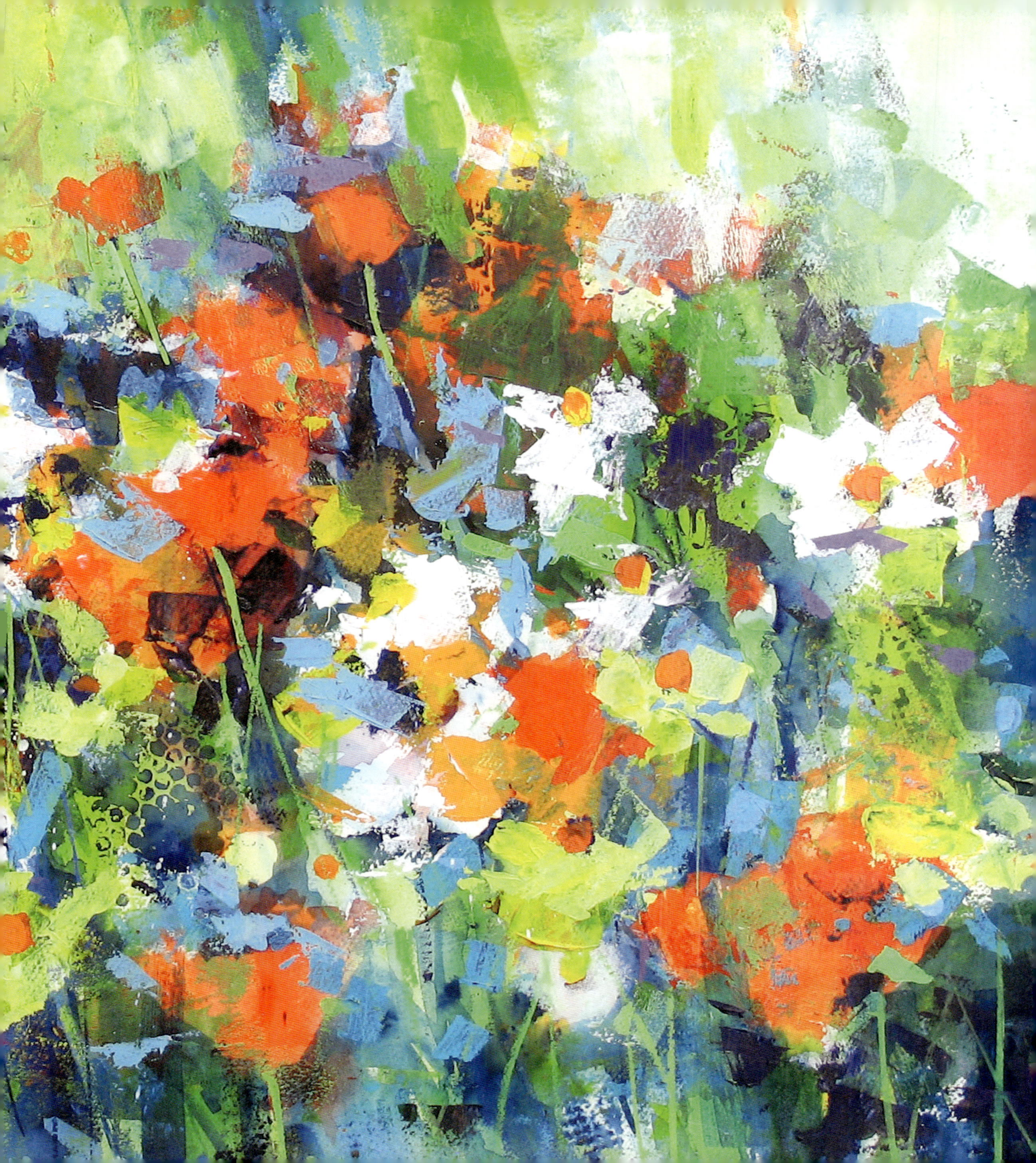

COMPOSING YOUR PAINTING

Composition is the aesthetically pleasing arrangement of the components of your subject matter, using the elements and principles of design. A well-balanced composition is crucial to the success of your painting. Flower painting composition will generally adhere to the same kind of design strategies as any other subject matter, but the intricate shape of flowers may add another layer of complexity to the design process.

Most artists possess an inherent instinctive ability for composing their paintings, but there are some very useful practical guidelines that can help newcomers to painting to gain more confidence with their composition. You may come across paintings that break some of these rules and still have great integrity and charm, but often every broken rule is compensated for in some way by another element or principle of design to make the painting work.

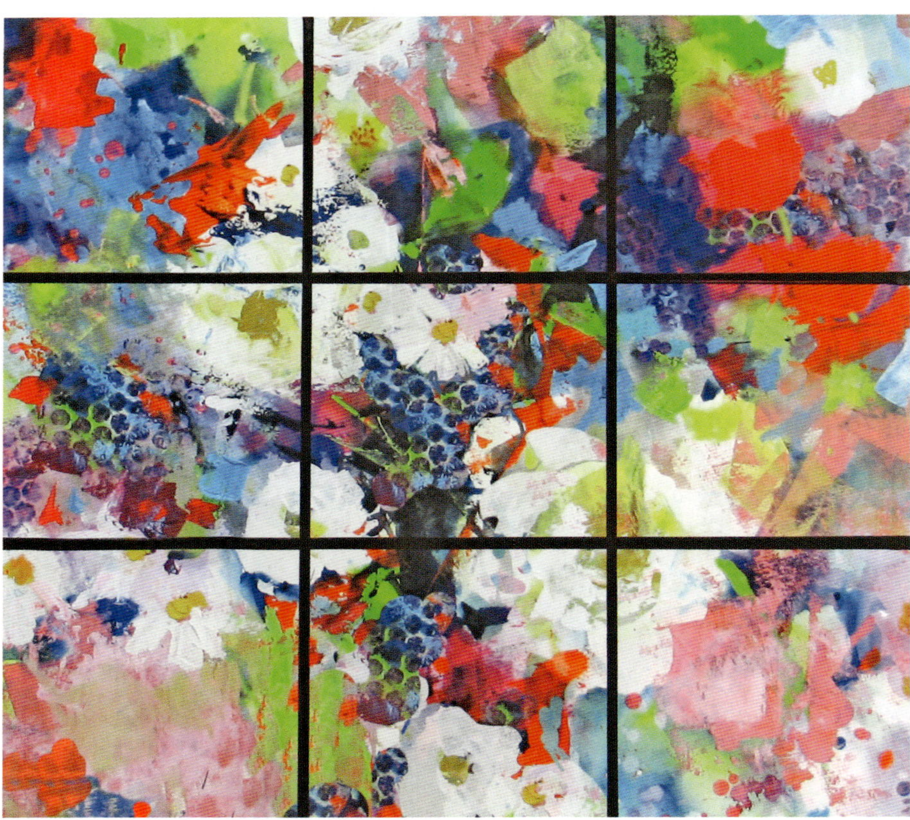

Abstract Roses and Daisies
Divide each side of your support into thirds and join the lines. Each intersection is a good place for your focal point. In this case the focal point is the largest white rose.

The rule of thirds

Following the rule of thirds is the easiest way to find the most striking position in which to place the focal point of your painting. Once you have decided on your format, divide the picture plane into three equal sections, both vertically and horizontally. Each of the four areas where they intersect could be the sweet spot for the focal point of your painting. This might be your largest flower head, or mass of flowers, the bloom with the brightest colour or the most dramatic lighting. Paintings without a clear focal point often have other elements such as movement and rhythm to compensate for the lack of it. The rule of thirds is a simplified version of the historic golden section or golden ratio and a great way to help you create the most impact in your composition.

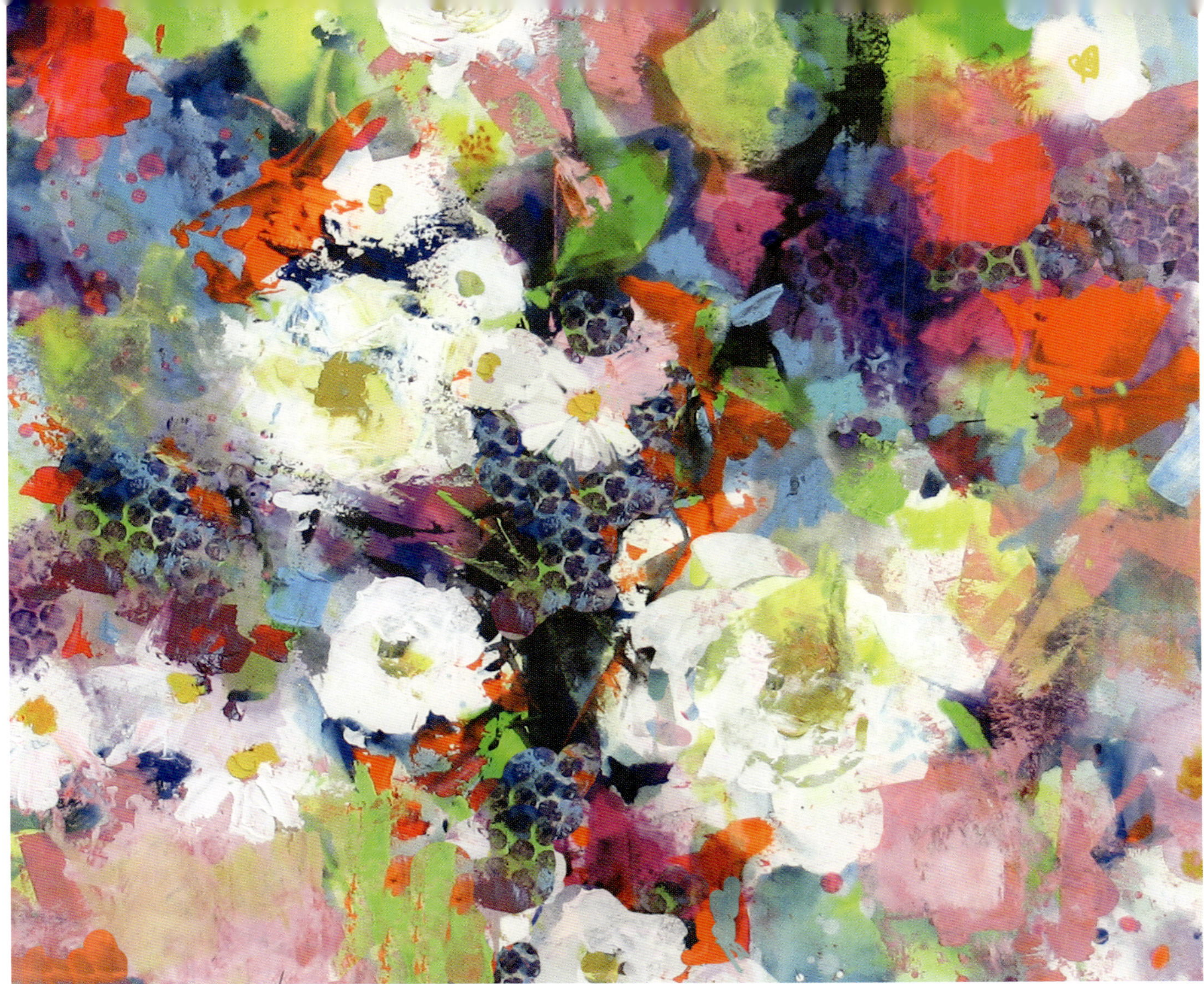

The path to the focal point

In most compositions, the elements of design are arranged to take the viewer on a path of visual exploration that leads to the focal point. Of course this point should always be supported by other interesting elements in your painting, so the design needs to work as a cohesive whole. The focus of the painting can be arresting and dramatic or understated and subtle, chosen from similar shapes or something that acts as a foil to the other shapes in the painting.

Not every painting needs a prominent focal point as long as your arrangements create a pleasing rhythm for the eye to be able to trace through the painting – for example, a path indicated by interesting linear marks or repeated pattern or colour that leads the eye around the image.

Rhythm and movement

Visual rhythm can be achieved through the repetition of an element such as line, shape, edge or colour in your painting. You can think of rhythm as the bass player of your image. This is the principle of design that creates movement and energy and helps the viewer's eye to meander through the painting.

Lavender Pattern

21 × 15 cm (8¼ × 6 in)

Acrylic inks and oil pastels on watercolour paper

In this image the fragments of the red underpainting representing red background flowers creates a gentle rhythm through the painting and helps the viewer to move through the patterns created by the flower heads and the stems.

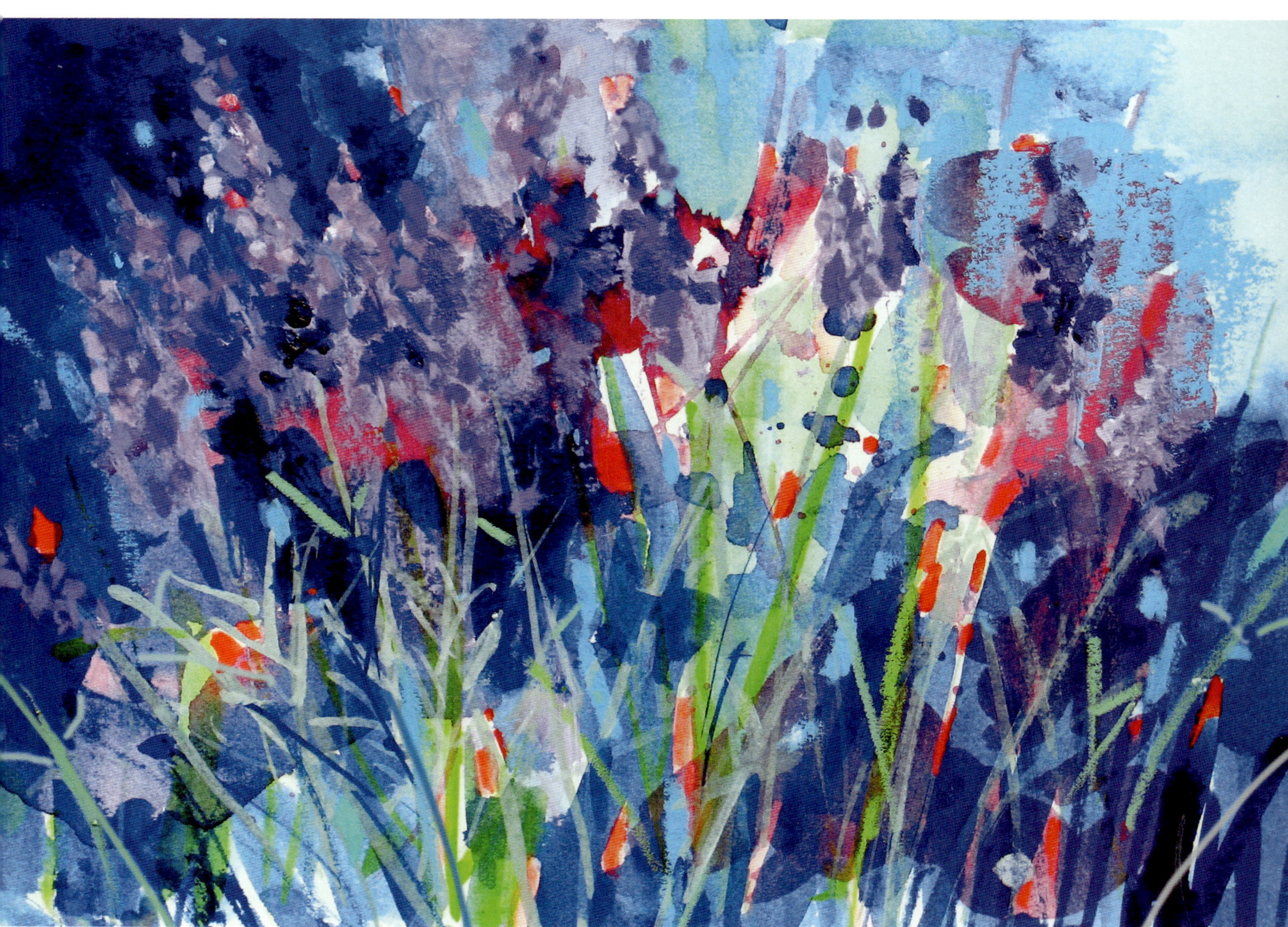

Simplification

Floral subjects by their nature tend to present an overwhelming amount of information. Learning to simplify your source material is a very important step towards a more loose and free style of painting that sends a clear message to the viewer. What you leave out is often just as important as the components that you include, so once you have settled on a subject, take a few moments to identify the aspects of the scene you found most attractive – for example, was it the light, the colour contrasts or the pattern? This will help you to pare down the subject to the most important elements.

In practical terms, one of the most effective ways of simplification is squinting at the subject, as this process naturally reduces the subject to the most basic shapes, colours and tones. If you are new to painting, a limited palette will also help you to assess the colour values more easily and simplify your colour scheme. Breaking down the subject into the structure of lights, darks and mid-tones focuses your attention as to what is necessary to include – photographing your source material and turning it into a black and white image can be very helpful in showing you the tonal structure. In time your eyes will become used to eliminating the unwanted details, helping you to create images with coherence and balance without bombarding the viewer with unnecessary and confusing details.

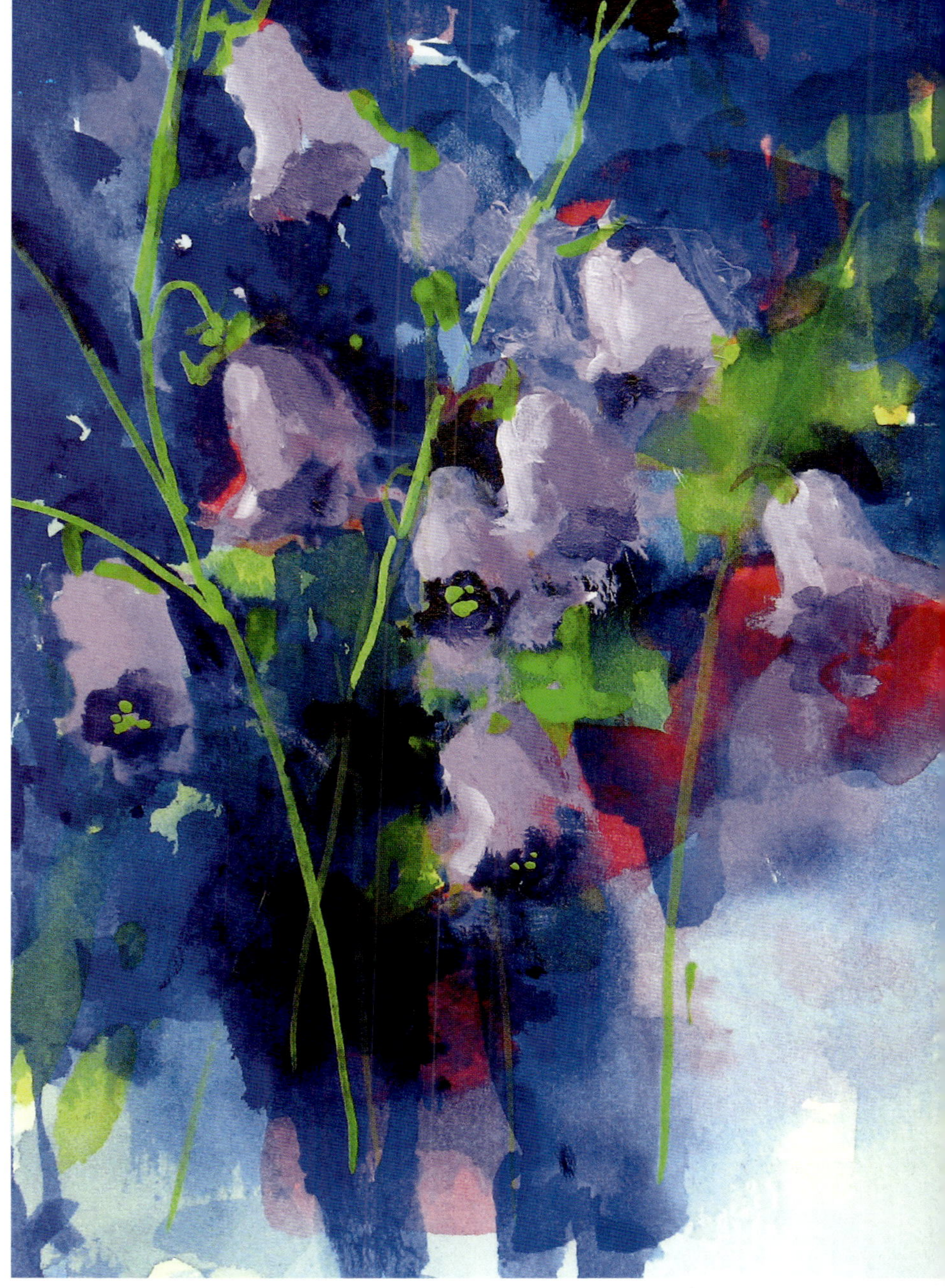

Canterbury Bells
21 × 15 cm (8¼ × 6 in)
Watercolour and gouache on watercolour paper
This small study is a preliminary sketch for a bigger piece and my way of working out some compositional issues within a manageable scale. In this case I was taken with the pattern of light on the flower heads, so I eliminated the fence behind and other flowers and foliage from around the Canterbury bells, leaving them as the main focus of attention.

"

Balance, harmony, unity and variety

Engaging images have a great sense of balance, meaning that the visual weight of the elements of art, such as line, shape, colour, tone and texture, relate to one another in such a way that creates visual equilibrium. Symmetrical balance promotes a more tranquil feeling than the livelier and more energetic tension of asymmetrical balance.

Harmony brings cohesiveness to the composition by highlighting the similarities that exist between various components of the subject – for example, analogous colours in a painting create harmony through having a primary colour in common and a close chromatic connection as neighbouring hues (see p.71).

Unity is a complex concept and one that is often hard to grasp, although the lack of it in any painting is quite conspicuous. To create unity, the artist needs to use all the elements and principles of design in such a way as to make the composition come together as a whole. Certain kinds of brush marks, texture, a repeated pattern or an underpainting that shows through the top layers can all be unifying factors that help make the whole image hang together. Harmony and unity are two important principles of design that often become muddled; although there are similarities between the two, it can be said that harmony enhances unity, but they are not the same thing.

Variety is the principle that brings contrast and diversity, adding the necessary interest. For example, in paintings made up of very similar flower heads, the juxtaposition and variation in size of the blooms brings variety as opposed to the similarity in shapes that brings unity. All principles of design work together as a team, each with their own unique contribution to make your composition work and help you to create strong images with great balance and harmony.

Alliums and Feverfew

73 × 52 cm (29 × 20½ in)

Mixed media on watercolour paper

Analogous colours and similarity in the flower shapes create harmony, while the varied sizes of the blooms and linear marks against the curved shapes bring variety. The glow of the green and gold underpainting and accents of rose bring the unifying factor and the distribution of shapes and colours makes for a balanced composition.

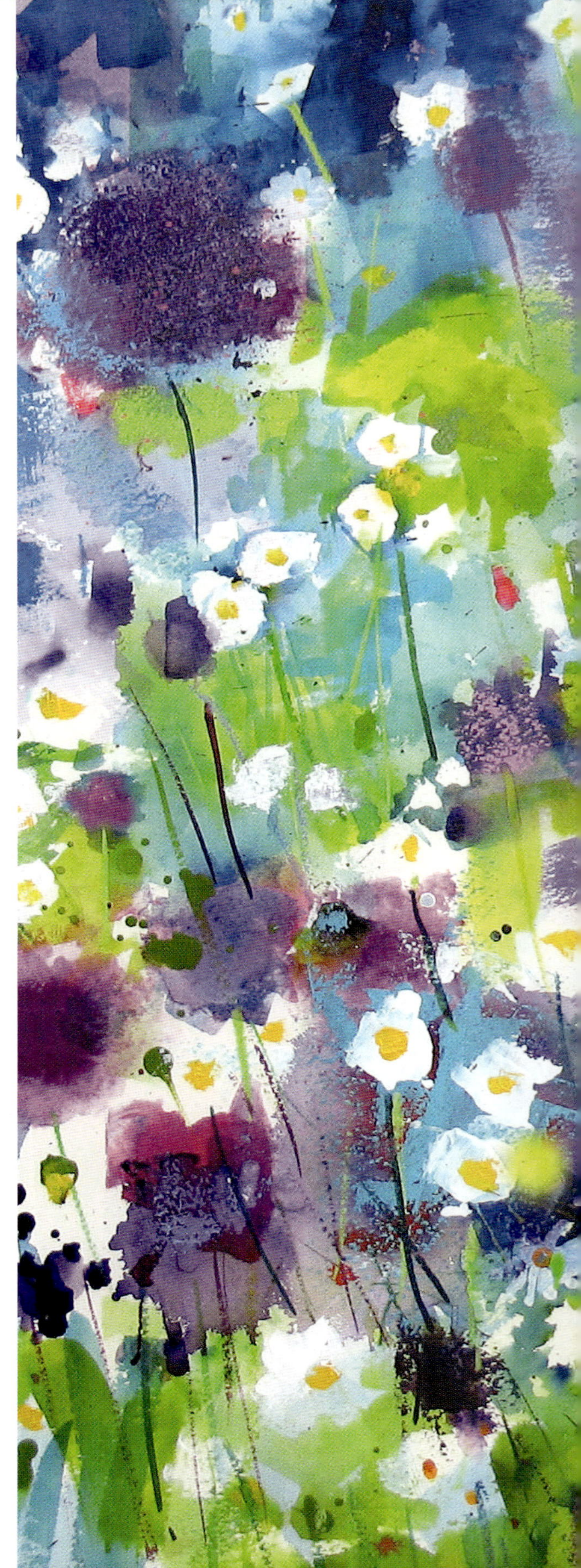

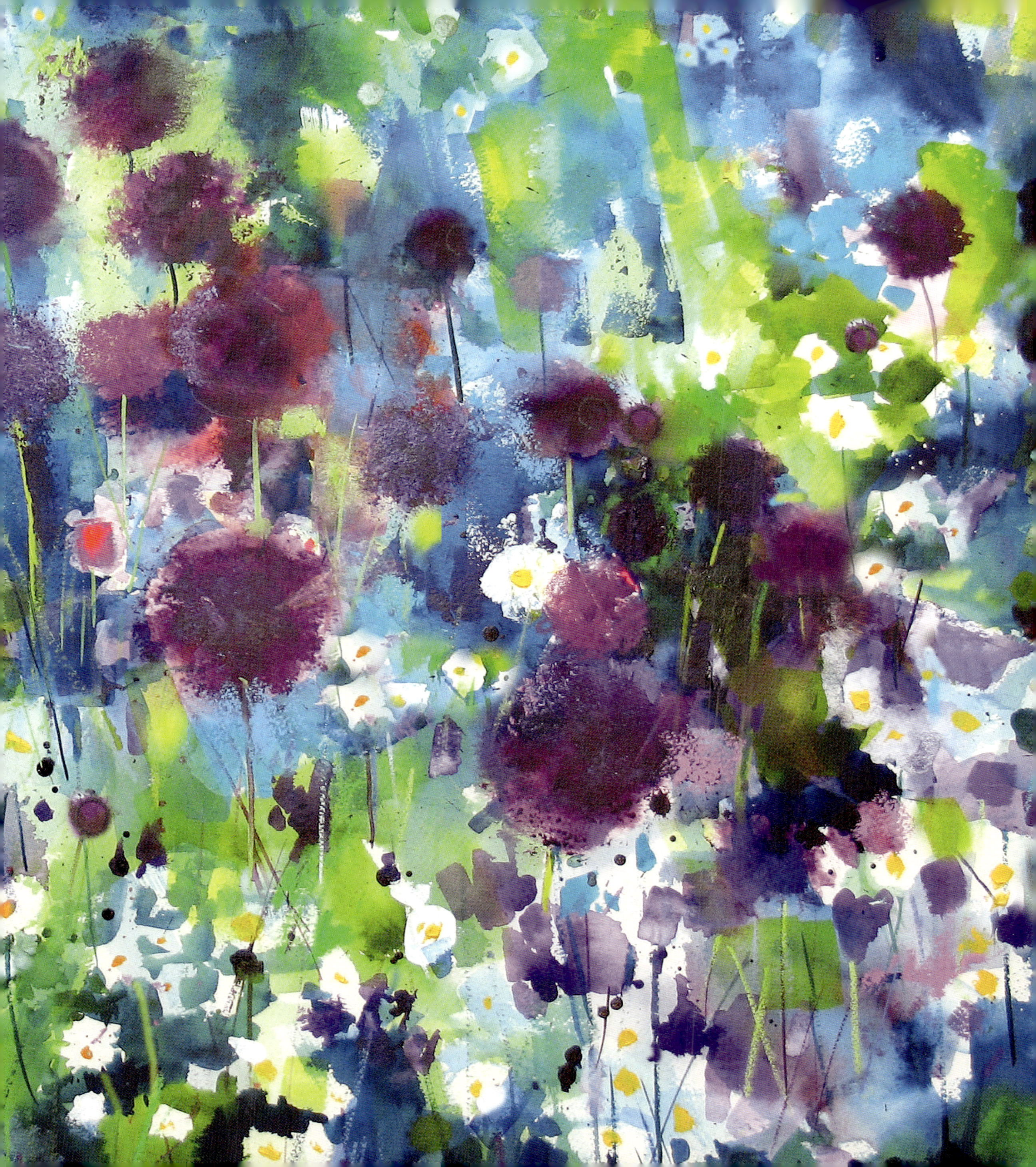

LOST AND FOUND EDGES

Aiming towards a loose and painterly style requires paying close attention to the treatment of edges between the various components of your subject matter. Try to strike a balance between soft and diffuse edges and well-defined sharp ones to create ambiguity and fully engage the viewer with your painting. Additionally, edges can convey the feeling of movement when the soft edge disappears into the background but reappears along another boundary. The lost and found concept makes a painting more intriguing, the mellow contours tending to tease and delight as well as providing a resting point for the viewer.

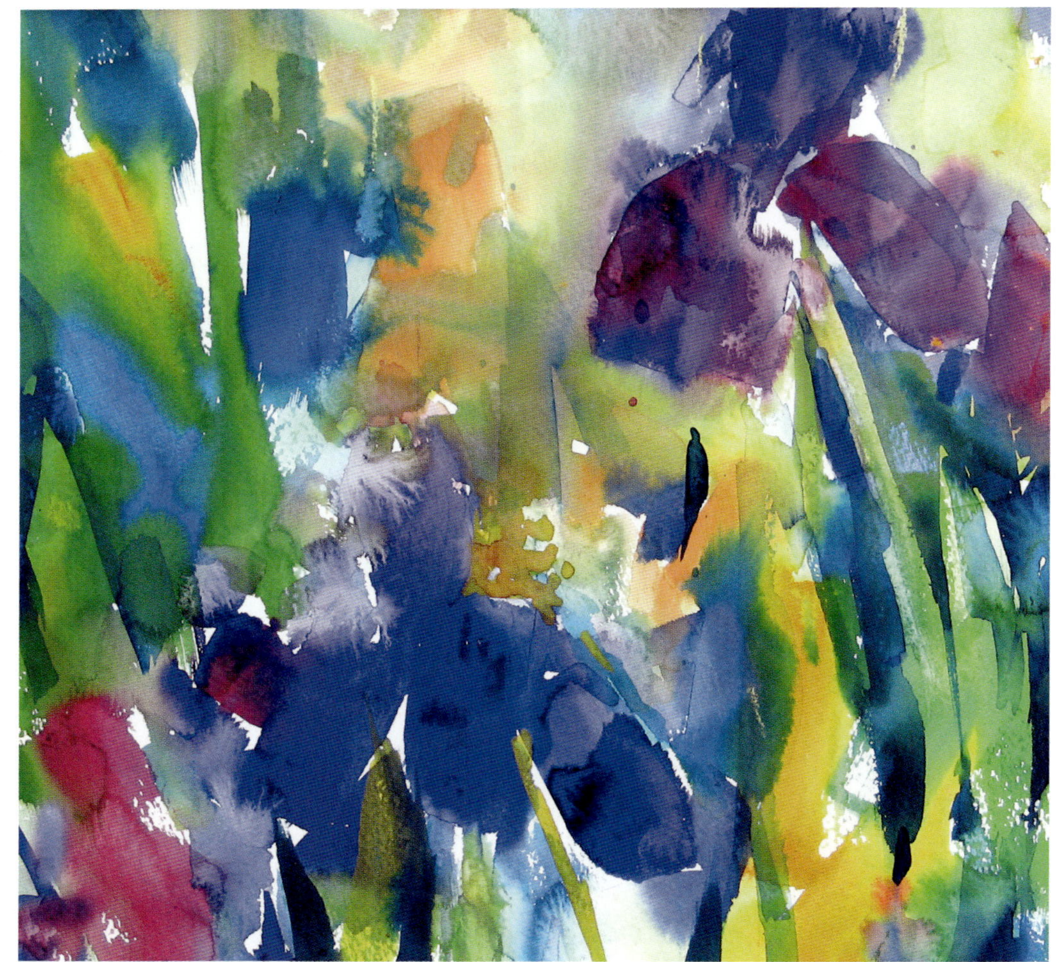

Iris Fusion

30 × 30 cm (12 × 12 in)

Acrylic inks on watercolour paper
Painting with water-based media lends itself to applying wet-into-wet washes of colour, as in the treatment of the background and the left-hand side of this painting. As well as wet-into-wet technique, I used the concept of analogous colours on the left-hand side with the soft transition of blue to green to soften the contours even further. The iris shapes vary as some edges have run into the background while others are sharp and well-defined.

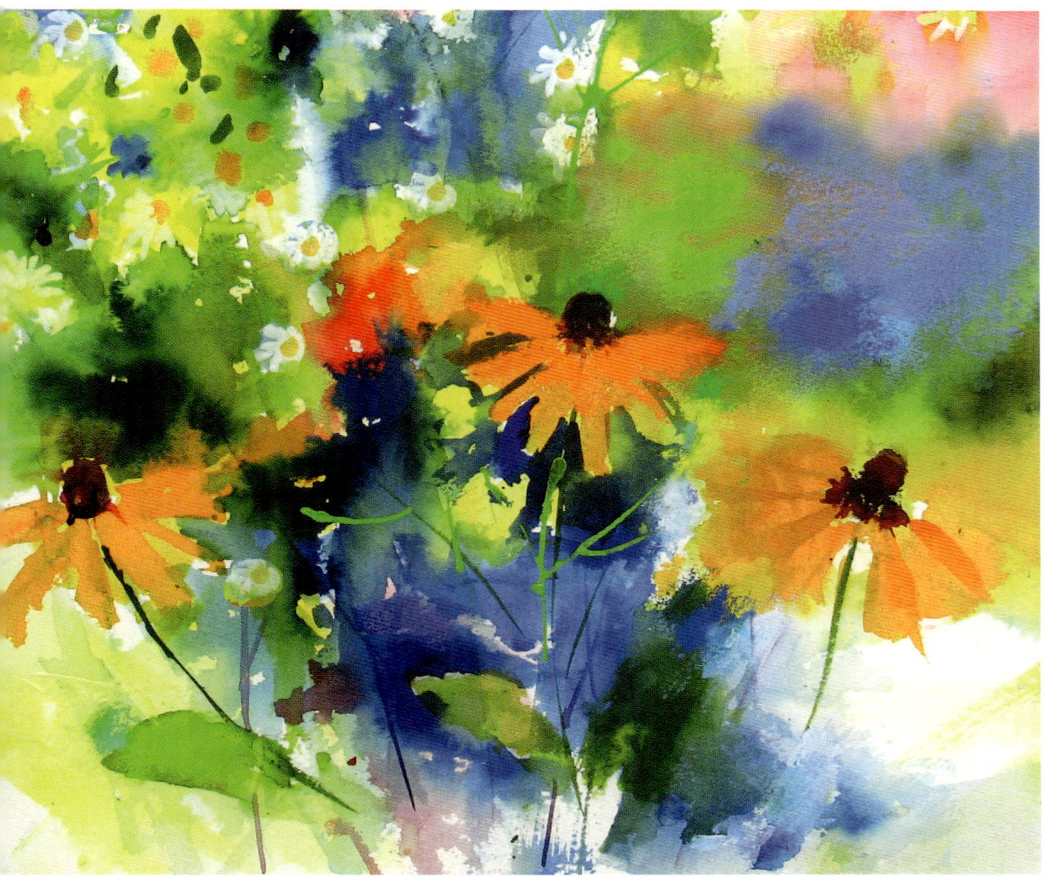

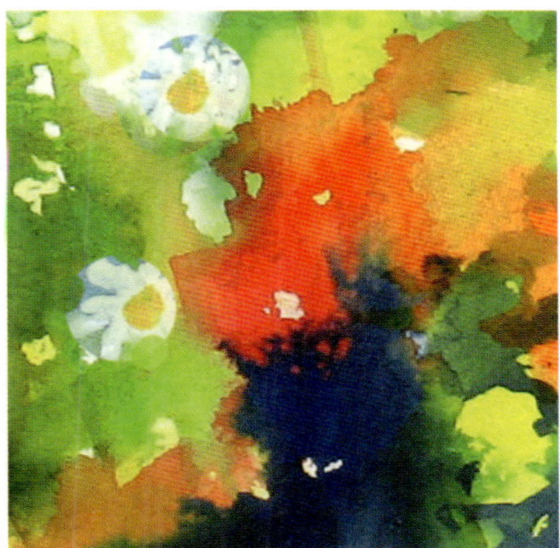

Soft edges (details 1 and 2)
The image above displays the sharp contrast of red and blue plus red and green, despite a soft edge. Below, soft transition is achieved by the analogous colours blue and green.

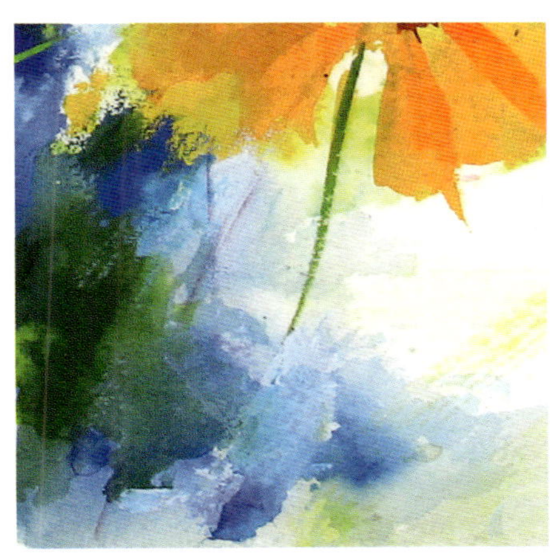

Painting diffuse edges

There are many different ways of rendering diffuse edges, wet-into-wet washes of ink or watercolour being one of the simplest. You can also soften a newly applied wash of ink or watercolour on dry paper by spraying it with water, which often results in some lovely patterns.

Speedy action is required for blending techniques in fast-drying acrylics. The thicker the paint the easier it is to blend the boundary of the two shapes. There are ways of prolonging the drying time of your acrylics, such as adding acrylic glazing liquid or a carefully measured amount of retarder to your paint, but using Golden Open acrylics will give you more time for creating diffuse edges easily.

Blending techniques in oils and pastels can also help you achieve beautifully hazy and soft edges. Soft pastels are very effective for rendering softer colours. Applying different colours of the same tone for two neighbouring shapes or a shape and its background also creates a visually softer contour.

PAINTING THE NEGATIVE SHAPES

The intrinsic complexity of floral subjects requires getting to grips with the concept of negative space painting in order to create a pleasing visual equilibrium. Negative spaces are all the shapes that are in between the main components of your subject matter (in this case the flowers, stems, foliage and bud shapes), and also spaces between the subject and all the edges of the picture plane. Floral arrangements made up of different flowers in particular can create myriad complicated shapes, and focusing mainly on the positive shapes may potentially lead to many awkward and unsightly negative shapes that can compromise the success of your painting. In a well-balanced painting the negative spaces should be just as engaging as the main elements of the subject matter.

Quick thumbnail sketches are the simplest way of working out your compositional issues before you commit to the main painting. Within these small sketches you can distribute the shapes to achieve a good balance of pleasing positive and negative shapes that fit together. In paintings of multiple flower heads, make sure there is variety in the size of the blooms. Also beware of neighbouring shapes – overlapping some of the blooms works better than connective shapes that are just touching where the edges meet or have a narrow and awkward shape between them.

The subject needs to fill the space comfortably – not so small as to become insignificant nor so big that you cannot fit in all the necessary elements. However, by taking a shape half out of the picture you can suggest life beyond the confines of the picture plane. The thinking process about this will become much more instinctive through practice and will help you to create visually balanced images.

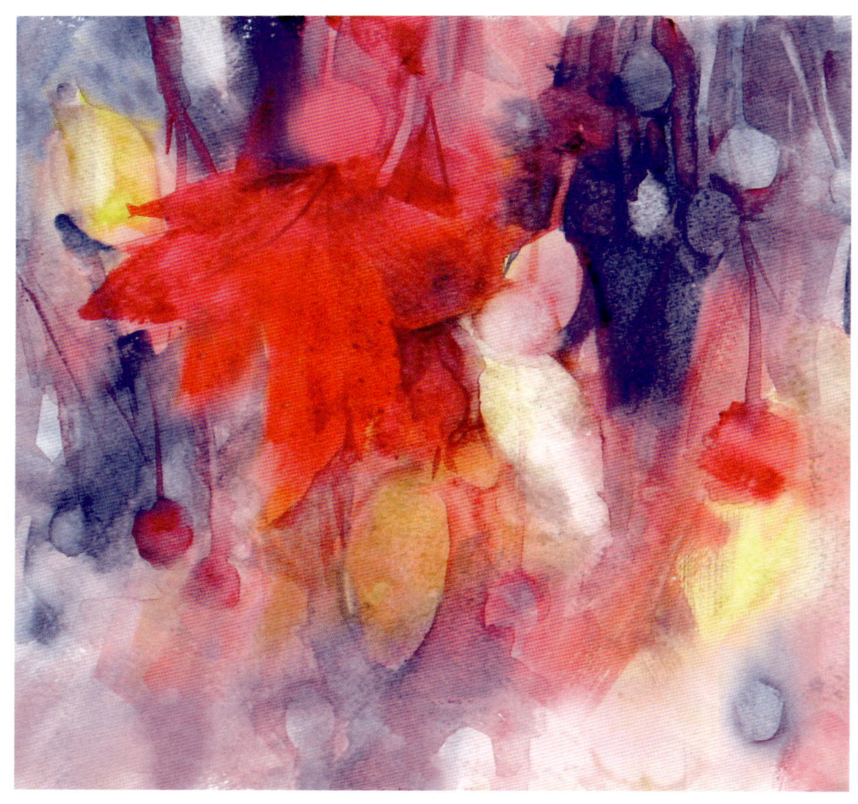

The Maple Leaf and Autumn Berries
20 × 17 cm (8 × 6¾ in)
Watercolour on paper
This small watercolour is composed of several layers – by constantly painting into the negative shapes I could achieve great depth. The early layers recede beautifully and give the illusion of being suspended within the picture plane.

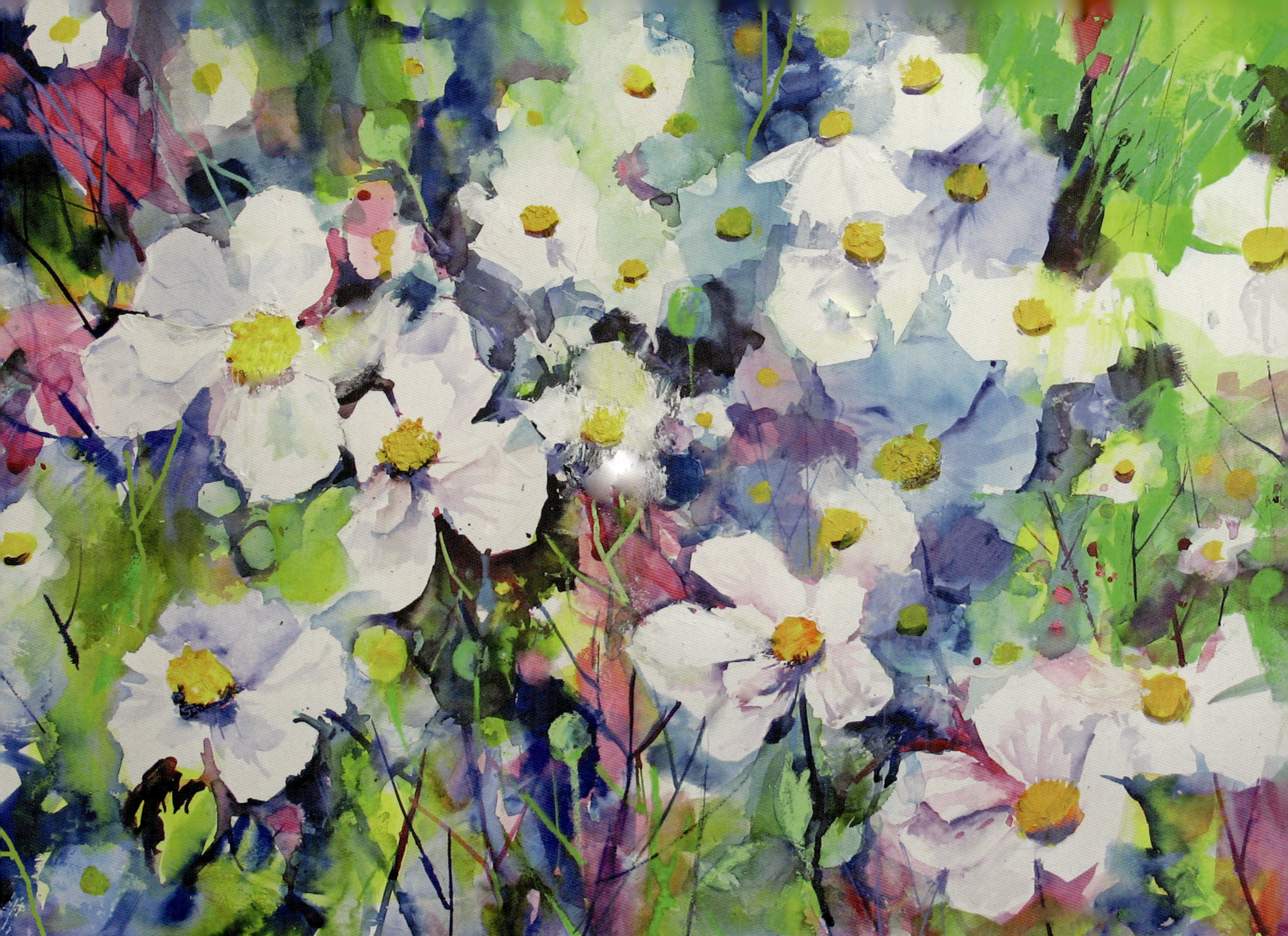

Matilija Poppies

72.5 x 54 cm (28 x 21¼ in)

Watercolour on paper

In watercolours, painting white flowers is largely a painting of the background. I love the magical way the flower shapes appear as the tonal values build up around them. In impressionist paintings you have a free rein as how imaginative and abstract you wish to be in the background, still using some of the key shapes such as foliage and buds to make an interesting backdrop that shows off the flower heads to their full potential. It is worth remembering that any white object, be it a flower head or any other shape in your composition, will only appear pure white where it is represented as fully lit; elsewhere there are always nuances and reflections of other colours and, of course, shadow colour. These need to be applied sensitively so that the delicate petals don't appear too bulky.

In the background, you are free to choose the kind of mood you wish to convey in the painting. In mixed media you can combine preserving the white of the paper for some of the flowers while painting others using titanium white. The contrast between the textures will create depth and interest in the painting.

WILD PRIMROSES

Painting white or pale-coloured flowers is an effective way of getting to grips with addressing the negative shapes of the subject matter right from the start of the painting as the initial stages are mostly concerned with painting the background. This helps enormously towards growing accustomed to paying equal attention to the negative spaces rather than concentrating too much on the positive components of the your subject.

Materials

High Flow inks
Benzimidazolone Yellow Light
Green Gold
Permanent Violet Dark

Daler-Rowney FW inks
Indian Yellow
Prussian Blue (hue)

Oil pastels
Orange Yellow
Brilliant Blue
Ultramarine Blue
Light Purple

Wax crayons
Raw Sienna
Light Umber

Support
200lb Saunders Waterford paper, NOT surface, 65 × 50 cm (25¾ × 19¾ in)

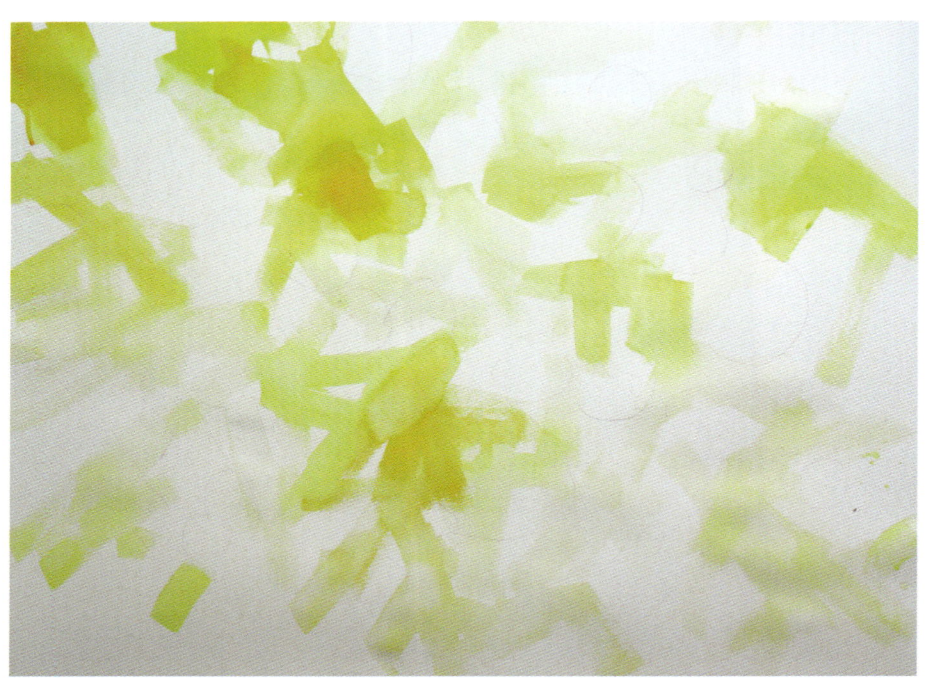

Stage 1

Using a water-soluble pencil, I loosely mapped out the position of the clusters of primroses to make sure I preserved the white of the paper for some of them. Of course, in mixed media, the option of painting a few of them positively as well using either inks or heavy body colours at a later stage is always open. I then added a very light and patchy wash of Benzimidazolone Yellow Light around the flower heads. I followed this with a second wash of the warmer Indian Yellow. Although for every painting I give some thought to where I apply the washes, there is always an element of surprise and no two washes are ever the same.

Stage 2

Inks often dry lighter, so I went back with some stronger washes of Benzimidazolone Yellow Light and Indian Yellow to strengthen the tones. I followed this with a wash of Green Gold and finally slightly diluted Prussian Blue. All the tones are quite light at this stage, as I am often still thinking about my composition and prefer not to commit to many strong colours at this stage.

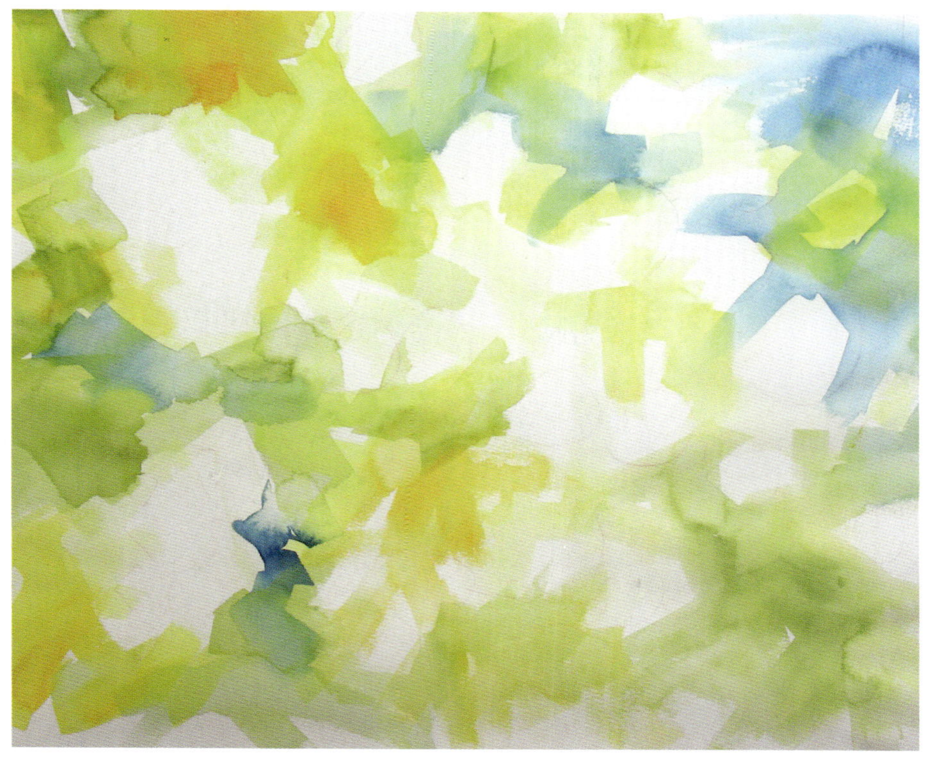

Stage 3

After some stronger washes of yellow and green I then applied saturated washes of Permanent Violet Dark. The reason for choosing this colour was that the slight hint of yellow on the primroses would be complementary. I also intend to use the same purple with Indian Yellow to make the rich brown of the earth around the flowers. I used highly saturated colour around the flower heads especially to make them come forward. I added more washes of Prussian Blue around some of the foliage shapes that happened accidentally through the first washes – your eyes will become trained to recognize these shapes once you start working this way regularly, but if you miss them you can always use a water-soluble pencil to draw some shapes for the foliage. I added a provisional centre for some of the primroses so that I could start differentiating between various flower heads. With a Raw Sienna wax crayon I applied some of the stems and also bits of dried grass that surrounded the flowers.

Stage 4

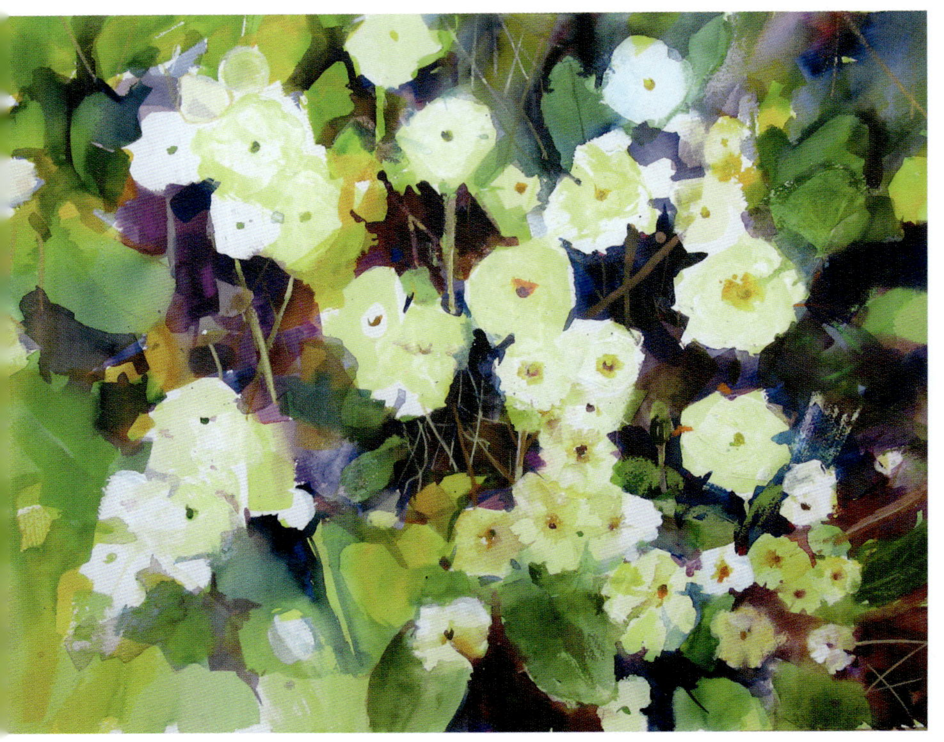

I began to define the flowers, starting from the cluster at the bottom right-hand corner. I strengthened the centres and went around the shapes with a dark mixture made up of Permanent Violet Dark High Flow ink and FW Indian Yellow. I always try to leave some lost and found edges between some of the shapes of the flowers and foliage, and their shapes and the background. I then used the same dark tone for the bottom right-hand corner to strengthen the parameters of the picture plane. I flooded more Green Gold on some of the foliage and then painted around the negative spaces of the foliage to define the shapes and let them emerge from the background. This is quite a slow process as layering the washes works better when each layer dries, resulting in more fresh and vibrant colour. Although using a hairdryer is an option, I prefer to leave the surface to dry naturally when time is not an issue.

Stage 5

I worked my way to the left-hand side of the painting to carry out the same process and define more of the shapes. This is the stage for assessing shapes, making sure the composition is well-balanced and harmonious. Working in mixed media meant that at any time I could take away or add shapes where needed. I felt the echoing shapes of the flower heads created unity and the variation in their size brought the necessary variety to avoid the image becoming boring. My limited colour palette gave a harmonious feel to the colour scheme, punctuated with small dabs of purple and blue where the initial washes of inks had gone over the white of the paper. I look for these little gems and try to retain some of them for accents of colour.

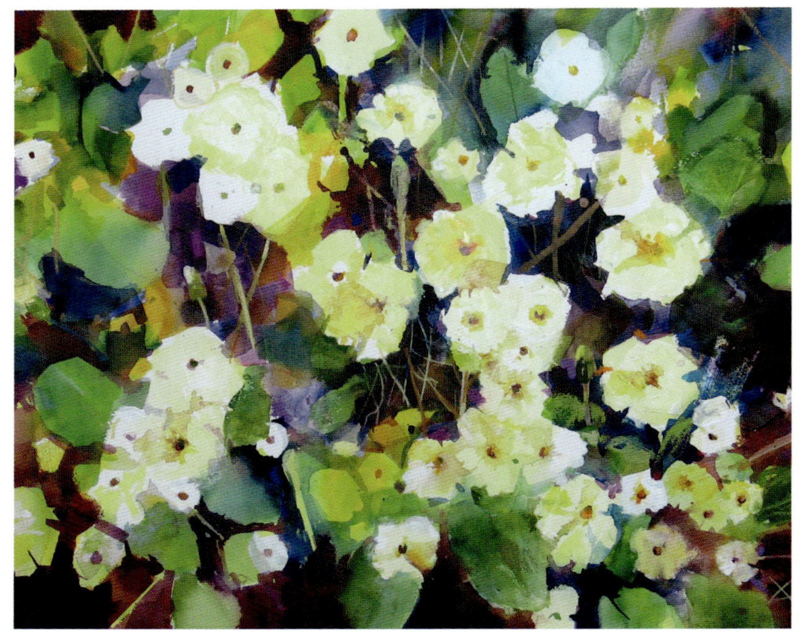

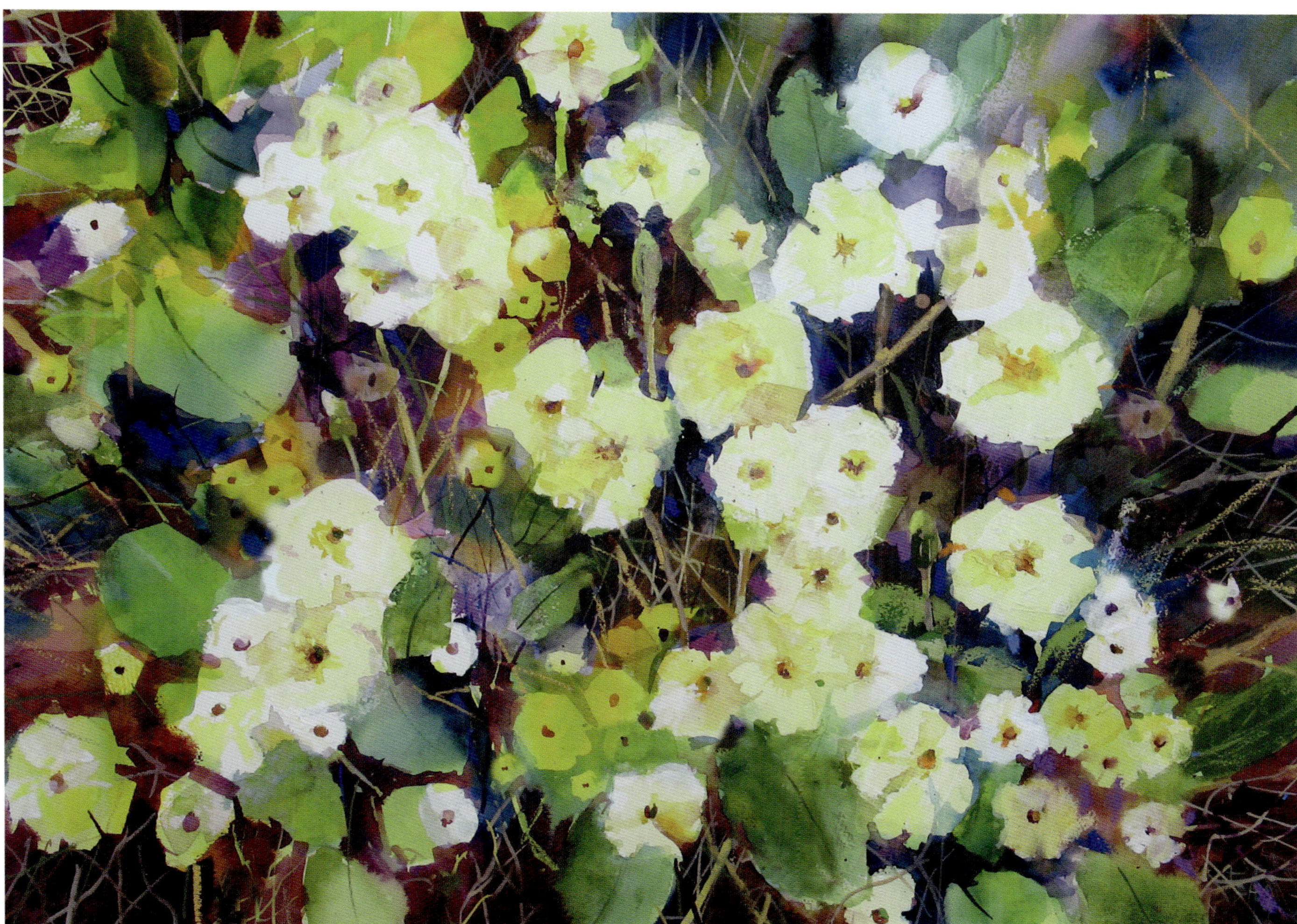

Stage 6

This is my favourite stage of consolidating all the shapes and putting on the finishing touches. I initially focused
on the pattern created by the flowers and turned some more of the shadowy shapes from the background into
distant flower heads to create more depth. These lovely self-sown wild primroses pop up in my garden every year
and what I find most attractive about them is the way they are often nestled among the bark and dried grasses
and branches from autumn and winter. I had created dark backdrops to paint these details and used some Raw
Sienna and Light Umber wax crayons, plus an Orange Yellow oil pastel, to add some of these in the background.
I also added some of the stems, taking care to avoid overdoing this – in fact at some point I took some away by
overpainting them as I felt they were too distracting. I then dabbed a few accents of colour with Brilliant Blue,
Ultramarine Blue and Light Purple oil pastels to create yet another path for the viewer to move around the
painting. My aim was to have a recognizable subject with some abstract passages incorporated, and when I stood
back I felt the painting delivered this intention. If time allows, I like to place a mount around a painting and look
at it with a fresh eye from time to time for a few days, seeing if there are any improvements to be made.

CHOOSING A FORMAT

As creatures of habit, we can easily become comfortable painting in a certain size and format. Sometimes this is dictated by the standard size of papers, canvases, boards or even frames we have collected over the years. However, the economic factor of fitting the painting within a ready-made standard size frame, though understandable, can potentially block the natural progress of the artwork. Let the creative process determine the size and configuration of your painting, rather than the materials you are working with. I have never conformed to painting to a certain size, and in the immersive process of art-making these issues are far from my mind.

Changing your routine is such a refreshing and transformative breakthrough for your art. When you become interested in a particular subject, try it out in a few different formats and see how far you can push it. You will find that some formats may prove to be much more suited to the subject and that a painting can be totally transformed from dull and boring to exciting and dynamic.

Square format

This is possibly one of the most visually pleasing of all the formats, making the most balanced design of all. The viewer is encouraged to move around the picture in a circular motion rather than the side-to-side of a landscape (rectangular) format. Simplicity and balance are the two major factors in the popularity of this modern format.

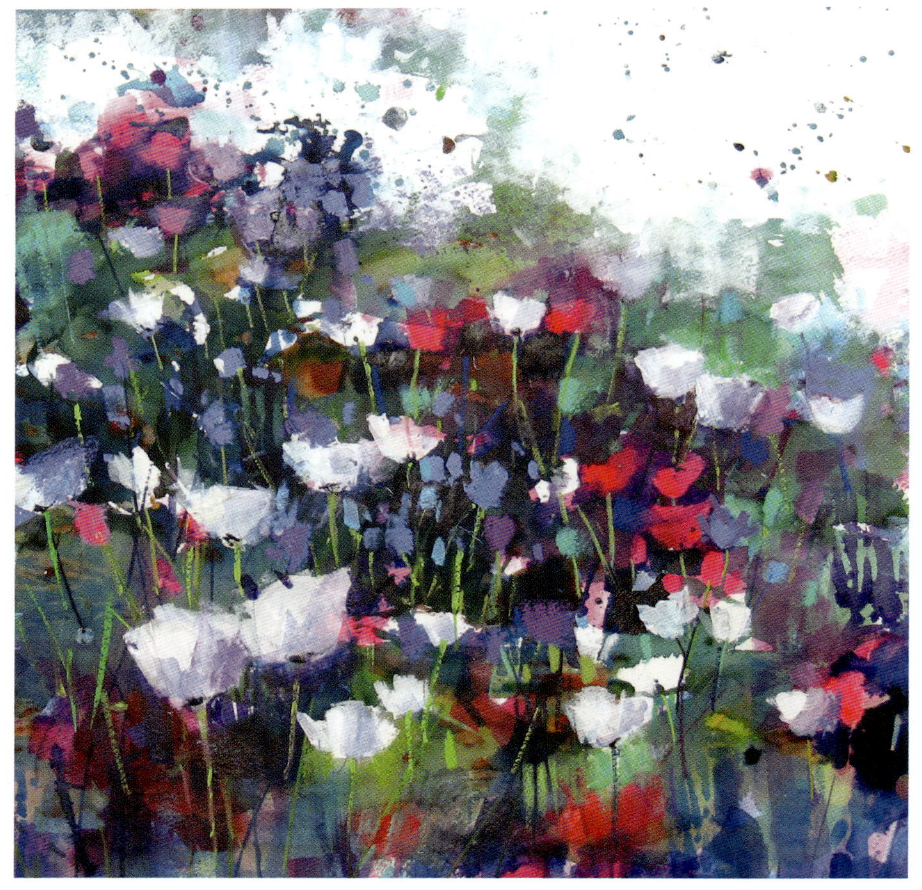

Meadow with White and Pink Poppies
46 × 46 cm (18 × 18 in)
Mixed media on watercolour paper
In this image I invite the viewer in with the one single white poppy at the very foreground and help them meander through the zigzag of white poppies as well as the underlying pattern of the pink ones.

Vertical long and narrow format

The long and narrow format looks elegant and graceful. It also engages the viewer in guessing where the subject ends on either side of this picture plane. Is there life beyond the narrow parameter of the image? It leaves you wanting more. Paintings of this format look great displayed on equally long and narrow spaces and give the illusion of height.

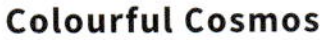

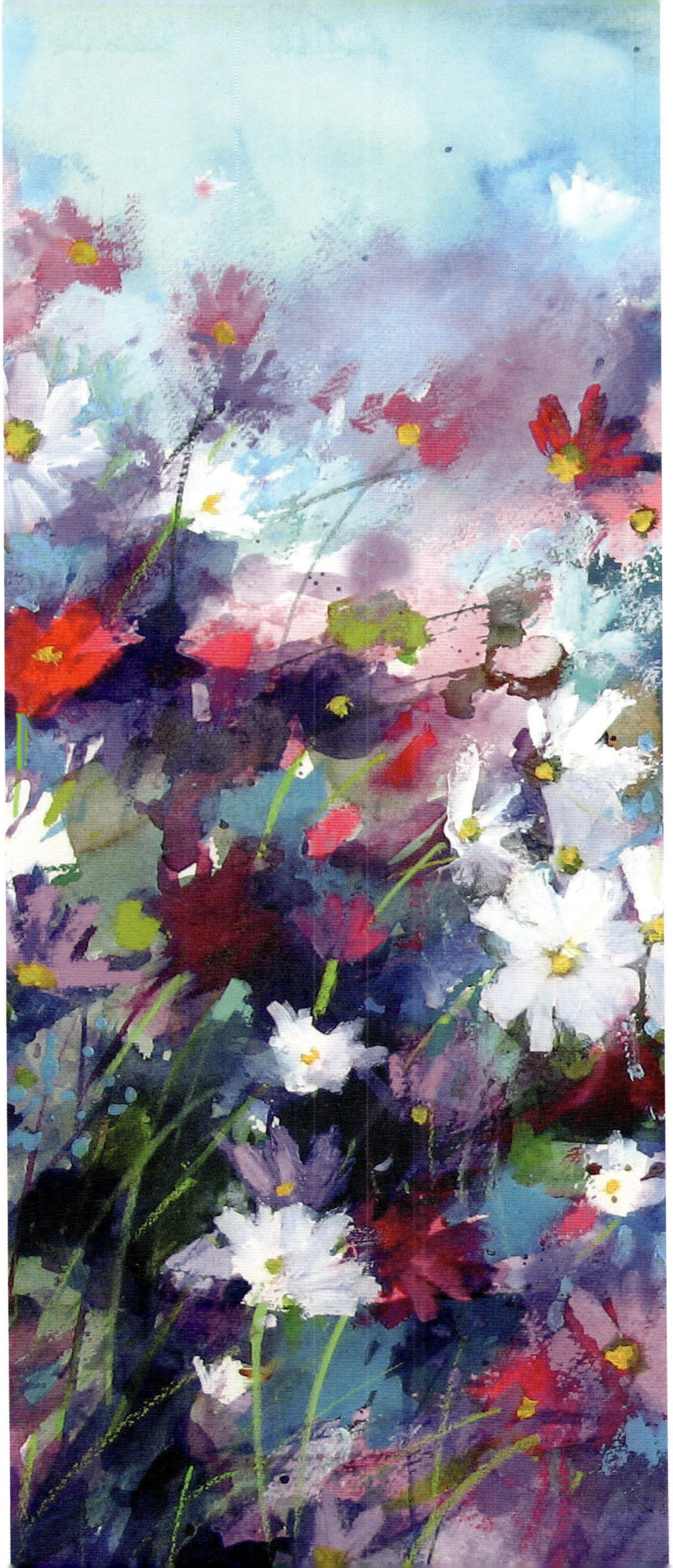

Colourful Cosmos
53 × 25 cm (21 × 10 in)
Ink, pencil, acrylic paint and oil pastel
on watercolour paper
In this painting I aimed to frame a section of a wide border of beautiful cosmos flowers blowing to the right in a summer breeze. I am sure the viewer can feel the continuity of the subject on either side of the narrow window. I find the height gives this format a rather elegant and graceful appearance.

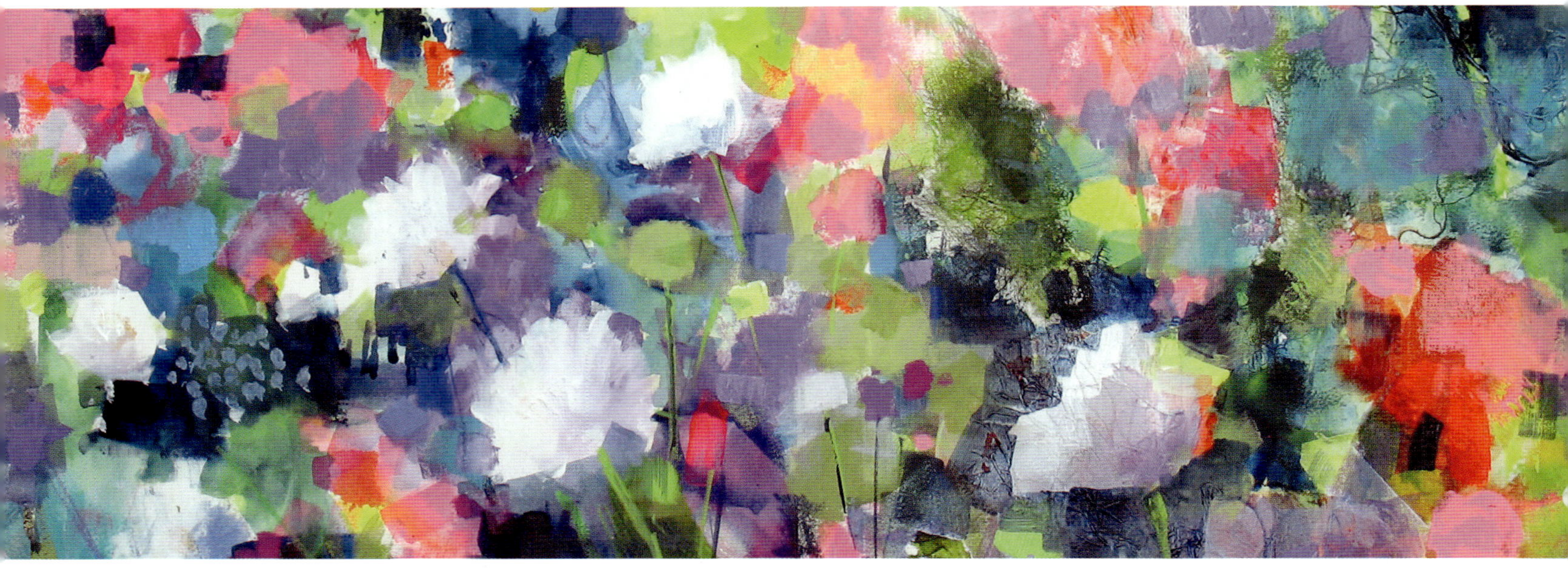

Panoramic format

This format is one of my personal favourites. It almost teases the viewer with the anticipation of imagining what more is above and below and covers a wider area of the subject than the usual landscape format. It engages the viewer in a different way from the more mainstream painting formats.

Rose Garden
23 × 58 cm (9 × 23 in)
Heavy body acrylics, paper collage and oil pastels on paper
For this format I always make sure I have a larger piece of paper so that when it is cropped some of the elements go beyond the confines of the picture plane rather than painting to the edge.

Circular

The curve of a circular image is the easiest for the human eye to navigate, as there is no transition from one edge to another. For this reason, circular formats are the most restful and sensual of all the formats. This way of producing images has been popular for many years. Large-format circular images or relief sculptures are known as tondos, a word derived from Italian *rotondo*, meaning round.

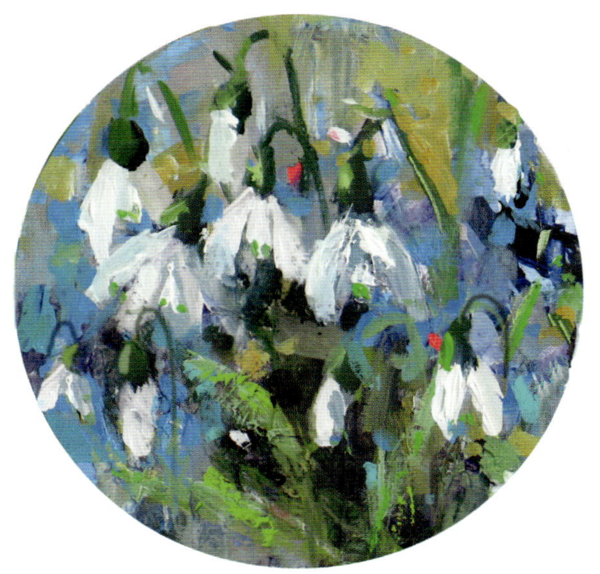

Snowdrops
There are many round canvases and panels available from art shops. I also have several round mounts for cropping circular sections from other formats.

Finding little gems through cropping

A failed large painting can be a very disheartening
experience and the thought of the wasted time and
materials is very discouraging indeed. However, before
you consign it to the graveyard of failed paintings
or gesso the surface, move a few smaller mounts of
various shapes and sizes around the painting to see if
you can find any hidden little gems. The composition
may not have had the impact you were hoping for in a
larger format, but you may be surprised to find smaller
paintings with perfectly sound compositions within the
failed larger work. Make cropping and editing a routine
part of your creative process to turn a disappointing
painting session into a happy one and your trash
to gold. What's more, these smaller paintings can
potentially generate ideas for future paintings.

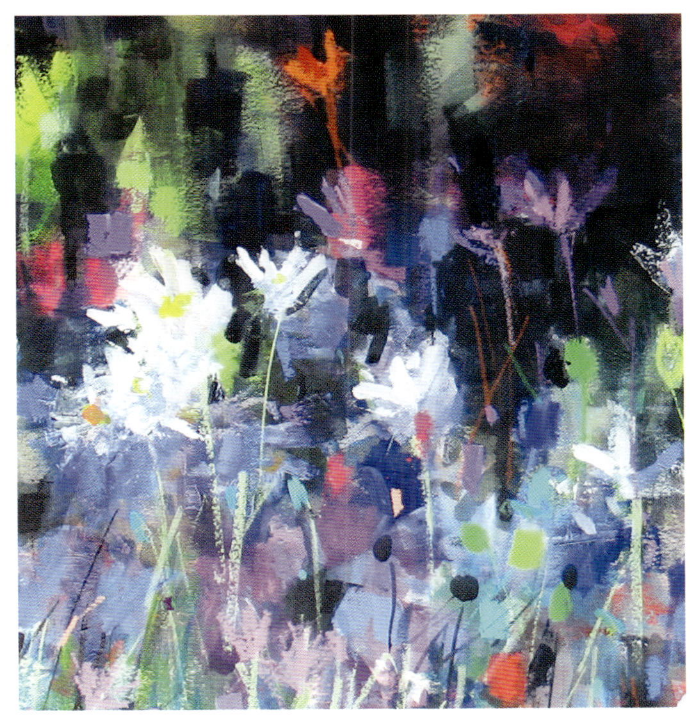

Rainbow flower border (cropped paintings 1 and 2)
I started a large painting of a lovely flower border
which I was really inspired by. I loved the tangled mass
of beautiful summer flowers against the dark of the
background boundary but by the time the painting
finished I was really disappointed with the result. Too
many similar shapes were vying for attention and
the evident lack of impact was quite dispiriting, but I
managed to get a number of smaller pieces that I liked
better and here are a couple of samples.

THE LIGHT ELEMENT

Alongside colour, light is one of the most captivating elements in a painting. In fact, without light there is no colour; it is the light and shadow that creates the forms as well as generating a sense of drama and an uplifting quality to an image. You can make the light as dramatic or as low-key and subtle as you wish, but without variation of light and shade the subject will appear flat and boring. We can often disregard the local colour of objects, but the colour value, or tone – the degree of lightness or darkness – plays a more important role, and the depth and underlying structure of the painting depends on it.

Light has the power to make the most mundane subjects spring to life, and choosing your light source will definitely have a great impact on the mood of the painting. A subject illuminated by artificial lighting has a very different feel to one lit by the radiant glow of sunlight. The direction of light also transforms the whole atmosphere of the painting – for example, a subject lit from the side is very different to one that is backlit. There is so much to explore and experiment with while introducing light to your paintings. This is another area where practice and experimentation will reward you with much more powerful images.

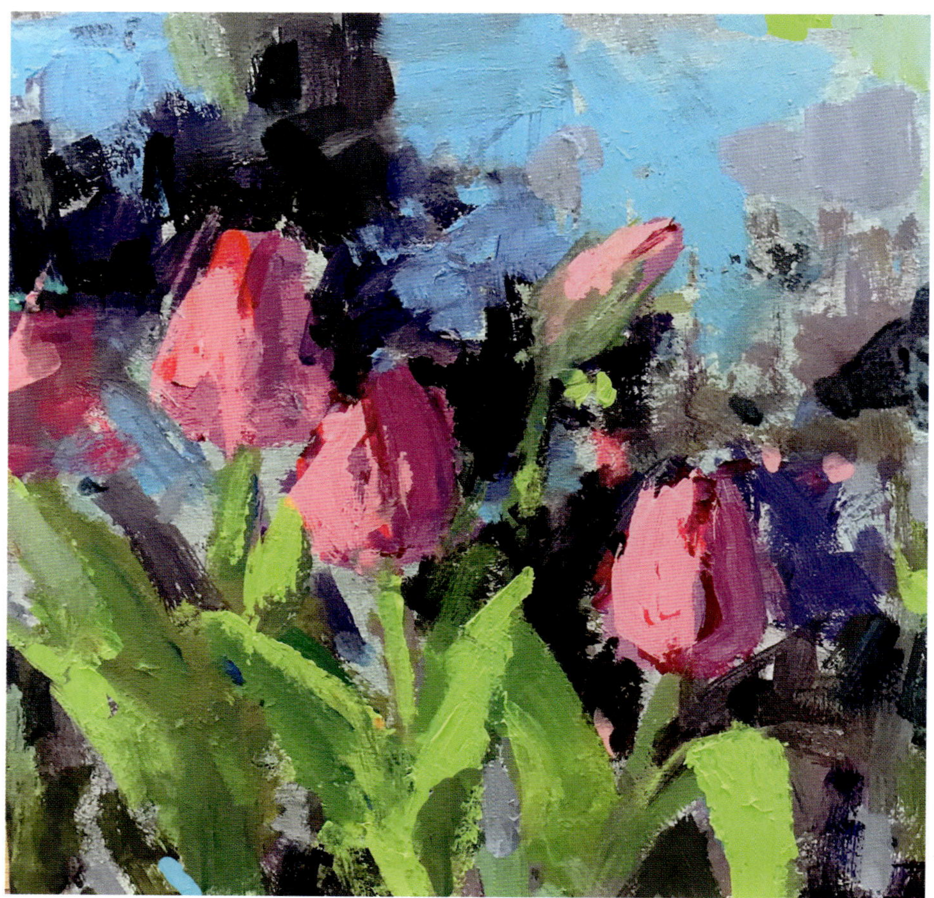

(Opposite page) **Pink Blooms in a White Jar**
21 × 23 cm (8¼ × 9 in)
Gesso, heavy body acrylics and oils on mount board
The contrast of the artificially lit side of the white jar against the dark background gives this painting more of a dramatic feel than the tulips on the opposite page.

(Left) **Sunlit Tulips**
15 × 15 cm (6 × 6 in)
Gesso, heavy body acrylics and oils on artist's wooden panel
This small study of dusty pink tulips would have been boring without the side lighting that has brought great energy to the image. The tulips are lit by sunlight, which has a totally different feel compared with the flower pot in *Pink Blooms in a White Jar* (opposite), which is illuminated by artificial light against the dark background.

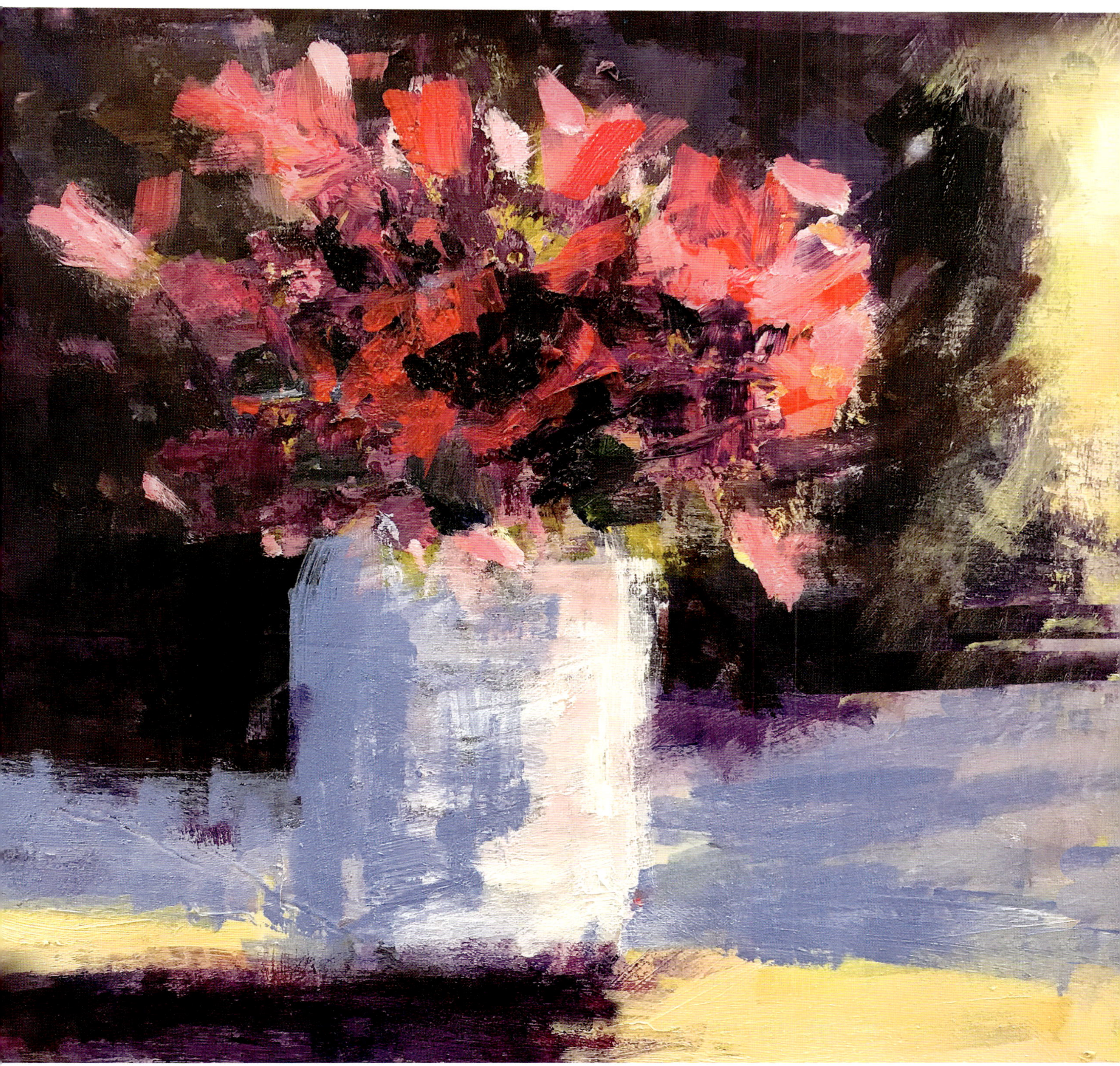

THE LANGUAGE OF COLOUR

Colour is by far the most evocative aspect of your painting and the first element that draws your viewer's attention. The flower painter is often faced with all the dazzling hues of nature and interpreting these in paint can be a challenging task. To create chromatic equilibrium, it is important to learn to harness your enthusiasm for colour and balance the vibrant hues with the more quiet and sophisticated colourful greys and neutrals. In this chapter we shall look at the attributes of colour and pigment characteristics as well as colour relationships to help you compose flower paintings that sing with great energy and vitality.

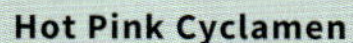

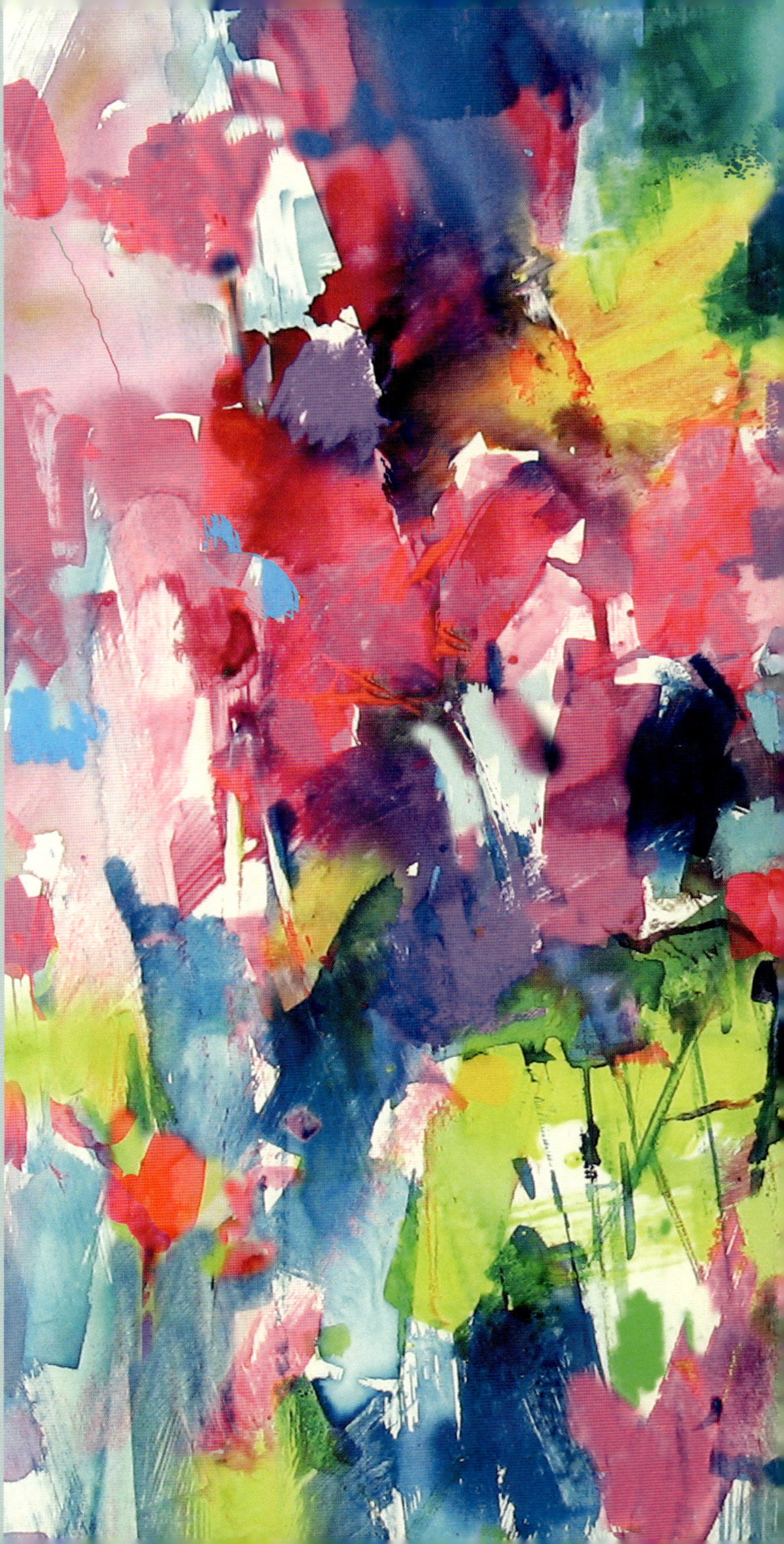

Hot Pink Cyclamen
50 × 68 cm (19½ × 27 in)
Mixed media on watercolour paper

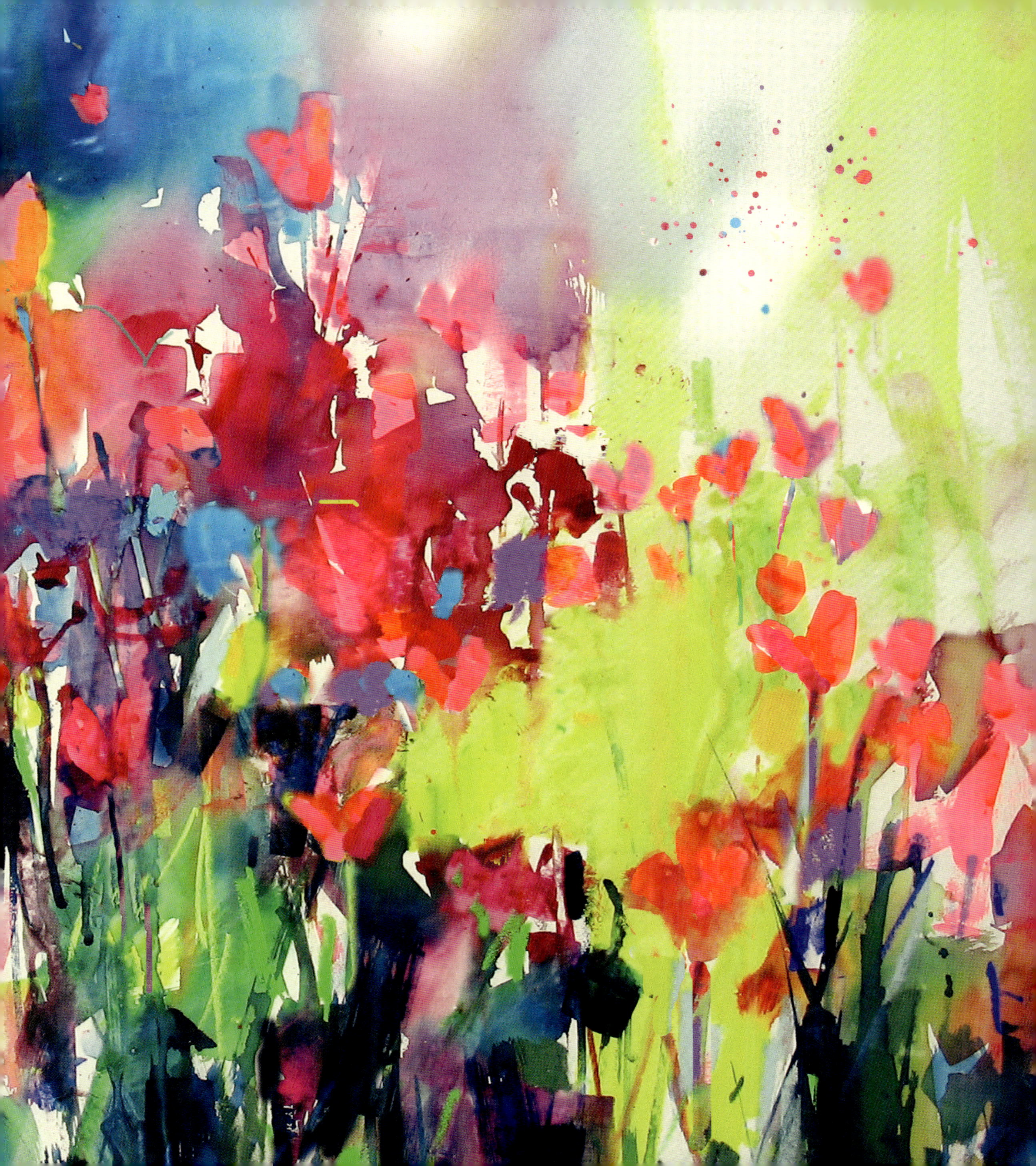

ATTRIBUTES OF COLOUR

Throughout the history of art, numerous visionary colourists have presented their theories about the vast and multi-dimensional subject of colour. Delving into this minefield of information is a daunting prospect for many beginners to painting.

Vivid colours with great clarity play a major part in a flower painting's composition and colour scheme. Understanding the three main attributes of colour, as well as colour temperature, pigment characteristics, transparency/opacity and the principles of dynamic colour schemes, will help you to take the guesswork out of both colour mixing and composing with colour and keep your chromatic frustrations at bay.

The three main attributes of colour are as follows:

Hue simply describes the name of the tint, shade or tone of a colour – for example lime is a hue of green, lemon is a hue of yellow and aqua is a hue of blue.

Lemon yellow

Lime green

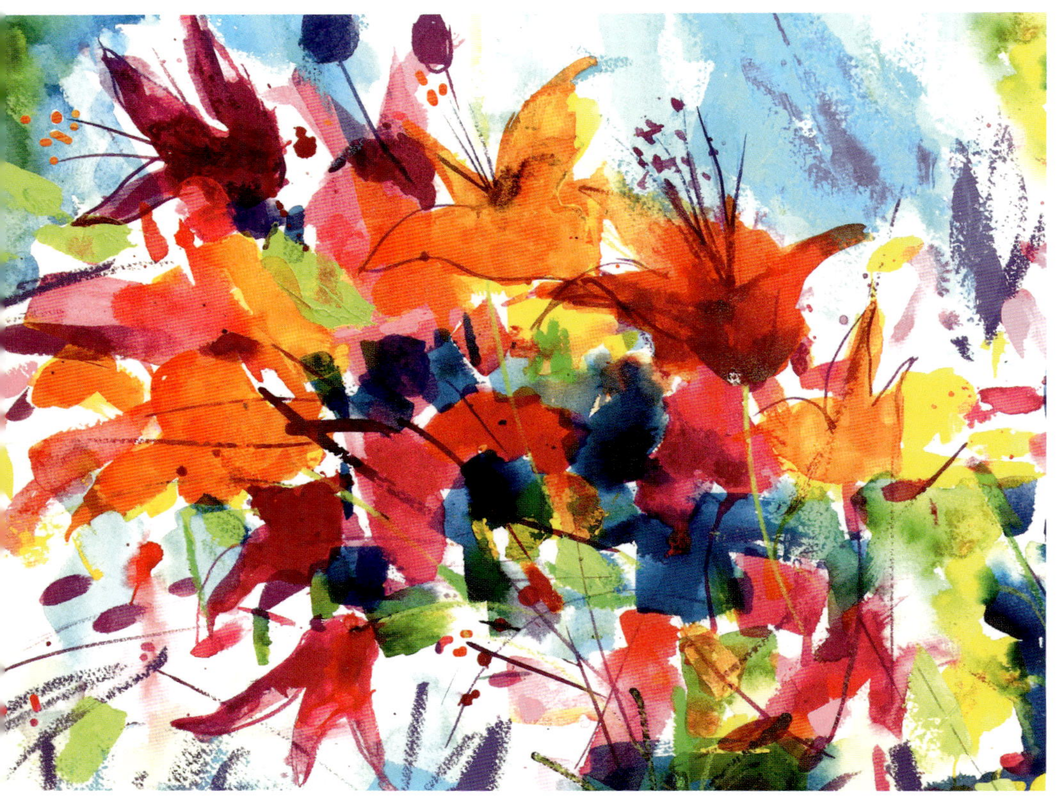

Abstract Lily Shapes
25 × 32 cm (10 × 12½ in)
Mixed media on watercolour paper
This spontaneous sketch of lilies shows hues of lemon yellow, cherry red, lime green and aqua blue as well as muted versions of green and magenta and darker values of red and blue.

Saturation or chroma is the measure of intensity or vividness of a colour – in other words, it describes how bright or dull a colour appears. For example, the colour red at its highest saturation appears a pure red. The chroma can be greyed down by adding a little of its opposite colour, green, or a touch of grey. With the addition of each dab of grey or green the colour becomes less saturated and more subdued until it becomes totally grey.

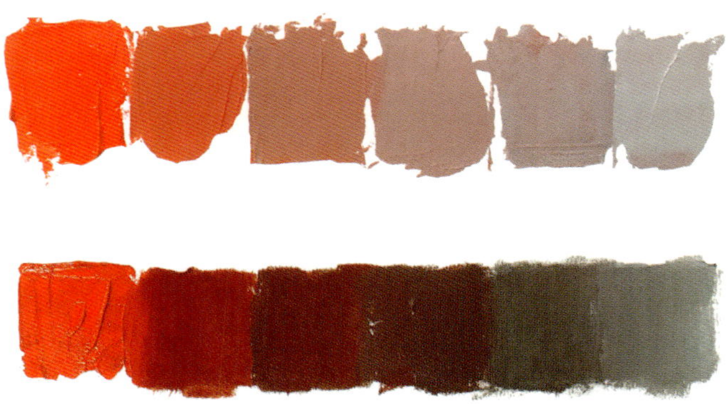

Desaturating the colour red
You can grey down a colour by adding a small amount of its opposite colour, in this case green, until the two colours totally neutralize each other (top), or by adding grey until the red becomes totally neutral (bottom).

Value, or **tone**, is the degree of lightness or darkness of a colour, and the most important attribute of colour that turns a shape into an apparently three-dimensional form. You can often ignore the local colour of an object, but if the tonal values are well considered the form will still read correctly.

This step grey scale shows the value scale from 0, the darkest, to 10, the lightest. This is the best way to assess the tonal value of your colours.

COLOUR TEMPERATURE

To create depth in a painting, it is vital to grasp the concept of colour temperature, since warm colours appear to advance while cooler ones recede. Yellow, orange and red – the colours of sun and fire – are regarded as warm, while green, blue and violet are cool. However, there are cool and warm versions within each part of the spectrum – for example, a cadmium red light biased towards orange is a warm red, whereas quinacridone magenta, which is biased towards violet, is a cool red.

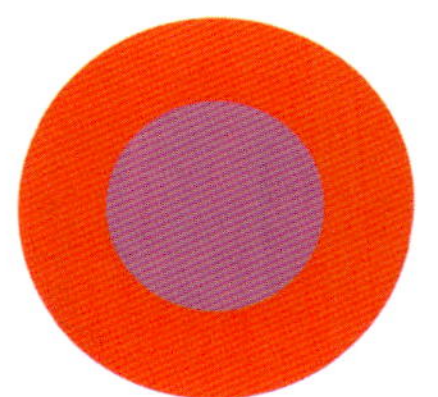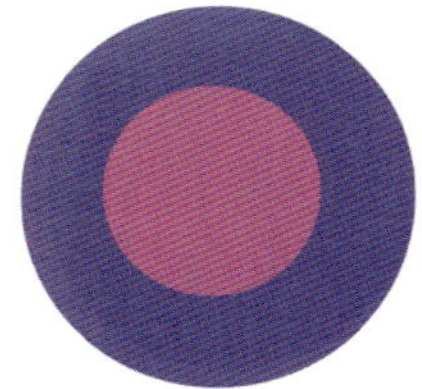

Warm and cool colour contrasts

All contrasts of colour are relative concepts and are rather meaningless in isolation – a colour that appears warm, when placed next to a warmer colour, will then look cool by comparison. Colours affect each other a great deal. Here the light magenta circle appears cool next to cadmium red light, whereas it looks warm placed on top of a cooler violet.

Reds from warm to cool

This example shows cadmium red light (the warmest) then the cooler cadmium red, crimson and the coolest red, quinacridone magenta.

Hampshire Summer Meadow (detail)

Mixed media on watercolour paper
The warmer tones of yellow, orange, orange red and lime green come forward while the cooler magenta and blues recede. You can add depth to your paintings by using the contrast of warm and cool colours.

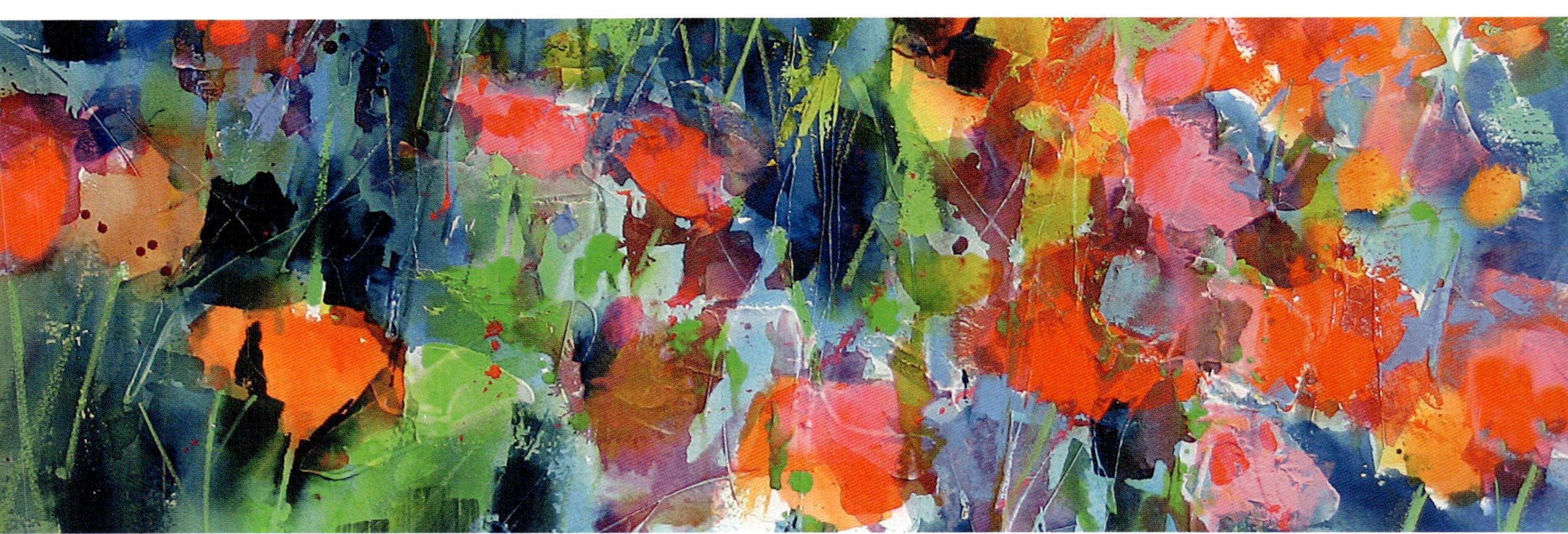

PIGMENT CHARACTERISTICS

Pigments are divided into two categories: modern organic and inorganic. Natural inorganic pigments are among the oldest and have been available since antiquity. Known as earth colours, they range from yellow to green, red and brown – examples are raw sienna, terre verte, red ochre and raw umber. These are obtained through grinding and washing of clay rich in iron oxide or grinding of stones. Despite their permanency, these colours can be inconsistent and today we are lucky to be able to enjoy the superior and stable synthetic versions of these colours such as yellow oxide and burnt sienna.

Another group are the synthetic inorganic pigments made through chemical manufacturing, such as cadmium and cobalt. In general this category's pigments are of low intensity and tinting strength and are mostly either highly opaque or semi-opaque.

Modern synthetic organic pigments are the high-performance wonder pigments that we are privileged to have at our disposal today. These are of high intensity with strong tinting ability and a great degree of transparency. They are produced through modern carbon chemistry under intense heat and pressure. You can mix colours with great clarity with these modern pigments that resemble stained glass. Examples of these colours are quinacridones and phthalocyanines.

I cannot emphasize too highly the importance of really getting to know the colours you wish to work with. Try out your different tubes of watercolour and acrylics and test the pigments for the degree of tinting strength, granulation (in watercolour), transparency and opacity. Make a chart to refer to until you feel confident about your colour choices. A limited palette that you know intimately is far better than having many tubes of colour you are not familiar with.

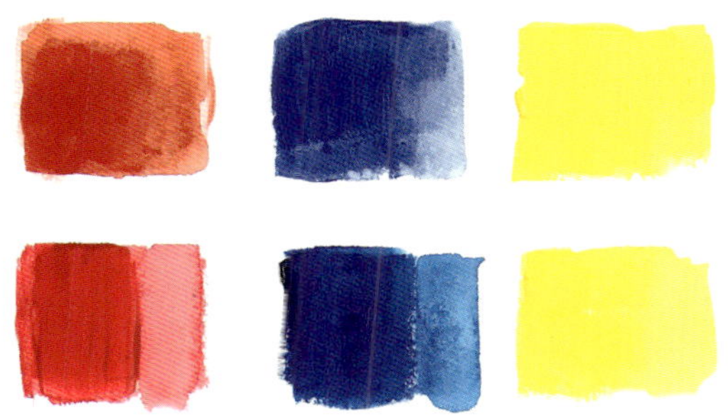

Examples of inorganic and organic primary colours

Top row from the left: Cadmium red, cobalt blue and cadmium yellow medium are examples of inorganic pigments.

Bottom row from the left: Quinacridone red, phthalo blue and Golden Benzimidazolone Yellow Medium are examples of modern synthetic organic pigments.

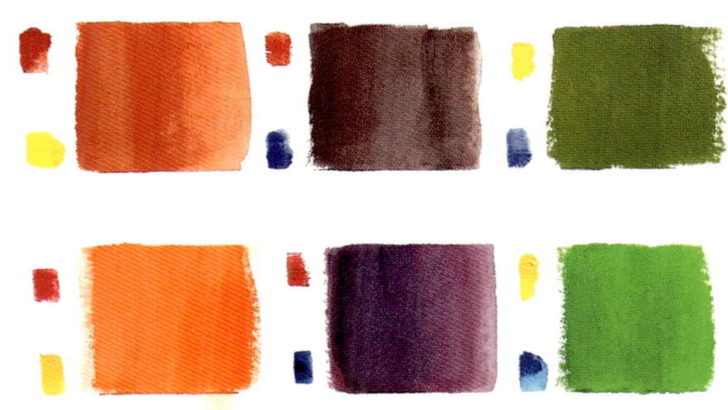

Examples of inorganic and organic secondary colours

The top row is of secondary colours made from inorganic pigments, which are much denser and less vibrant than the organic pigments. The orange is acceptable, the greens are often more natural, but the violet is very subdued and though it is a very useful dark colour, it does not suffice when a vibrant violet is required.

The secondary colours made from organic primary colours are more vibrant, with more clarity. Trying out your colours in this way helps you to make the right colour choices for your paintings.

A WELL-BALANCED BASIC PALETTE

We make numerous colour choices in our everyday life, from the clothes we wear to the colour of our cars, furniture or the paint on our walls. Using colour as a painting tool, however, throws a few confusing spanners into the works. The biggest issue is the huge range of colours available in every medium. In subtractive colour mixing, a well-balanced basic palette should consist of a warm and cool version of each primary colour plus titanium and zinc (optional) whites in oils and acrylics. With this set of colours you should be able to make an infinite number of secondary and tertiary colours, neutrals, darks and tints. Ideally, any other single pigment primary you add should be through an informed choice because of the specific qualities you may need in a certain pigment. The reason for adding ready-made versions of colours that you can mix yourself is for convenience, time-saving and consistency. In this chapter we are going to narrow down the reasons for the choices you need to make regardless of your personal preferences.

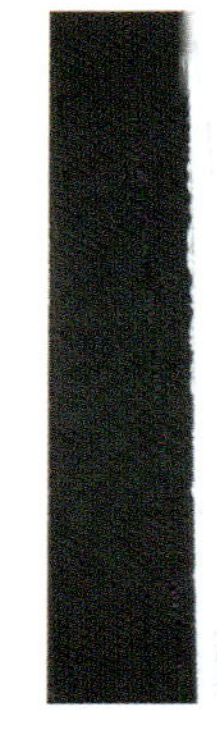

Suggested colours for a well-balanced basic palette
Golden Benzimidazolone Yellow Light (cool) – Golden Benzimidazolone Yellow Medium (warm) – cadmium red (warm) – quinacridone magenta (cool) – phthalo blue (cool) – ultramarine blue (warm) – titanium white (neutral). This palette is based on modern colour theory. You will find that individual artists have their own version of a palette that works for them. Once you are more familiar with pigment properties you will be able to assemble your own equivalents of warm and cool primary colours that work best with your style of painting.

Titanium white and zinc white
Titanium white (left) is an opaque white with the greatest covering power for when you need tints or whites to cover an area. Zinc white (right) is semi-transparent and makes beautifully translucent tints or can be used as white when you need to push an area back or just partially cover it. This diagram shows the difference of covering power between the two whites and their tints of magenta.

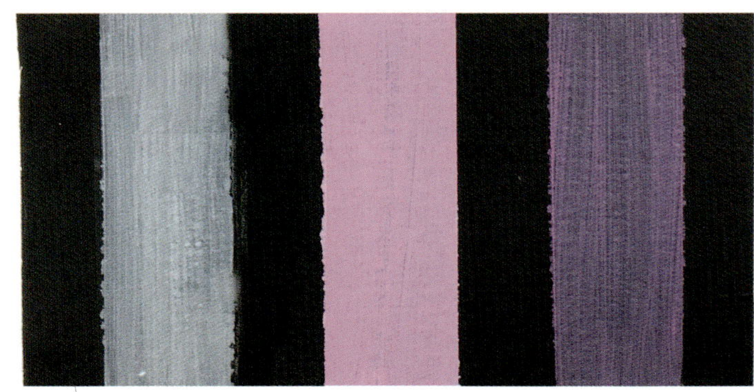

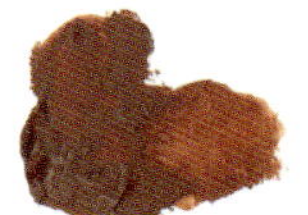 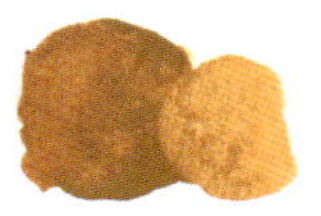 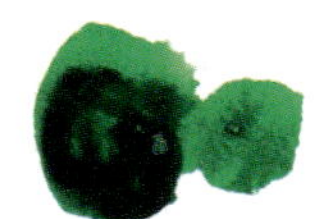

Additional colours 1
Although you can mix colours to resemble burnt sienna (left) and yellow ochre (centre), it is handy to have them for convenience. Phthalo green is also a very useful base green for mixing numerous beautiful greens.

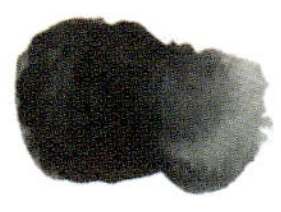 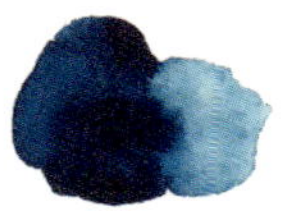   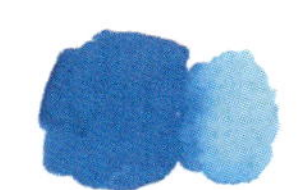

Additional colours 2
Left to right: Payne's grey, Prussian blue, dioxazine purple, buff titanium and manganese blue. These few colours are also very useful to have for convenient darks. Buff titanium is a softer and less harsh white, and manganese blue is a beautiful, cool light blue.

Opacity, transparency and translucency

Watercolours, oils, acrylics, inks and gouache all come in a range of transparent, translucent and opaque colours. It is important to recognize this quality of your paints to be able to mix the right pigments together for the colour you wish to achieve. Although you can find this information on your tube or jar of paint, it is much better if you spend some time to grasp it through doing a few simple exercises. The one here is the simplest way for you to test out your colours and find out for yourself which category they belong to. Try out a swatch of your chosen colour on a strip of black to find out if the colour is transparent, translucent or opaque – but remember that every opaque colour used thinly can become translucent and any transparent colour used in its mass tone straight out of the tube can appear to be opaque. While you can make a transparent colour opaque, you cannot make an opaque colour transparent – it may appear translucent but will never possess the qualities of a true transparent colour.

Semi-opaque colours, such as raw sienna, are less translucent than semi-transparent colours, such as Hooker's green, which basically means the latter allow more light through the paint layer.

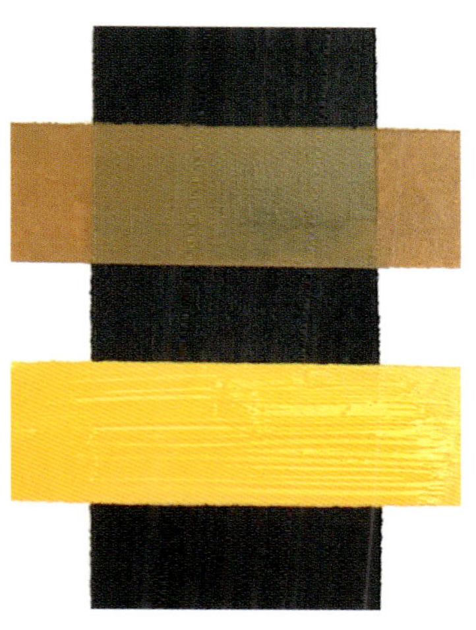

Semi-opaque raw sienna vs opaque cadmium yellow deep
The translucency of raw sienna still allows the black to show through, whereas the black is totally covered by the opaque cadmium yellow deep.

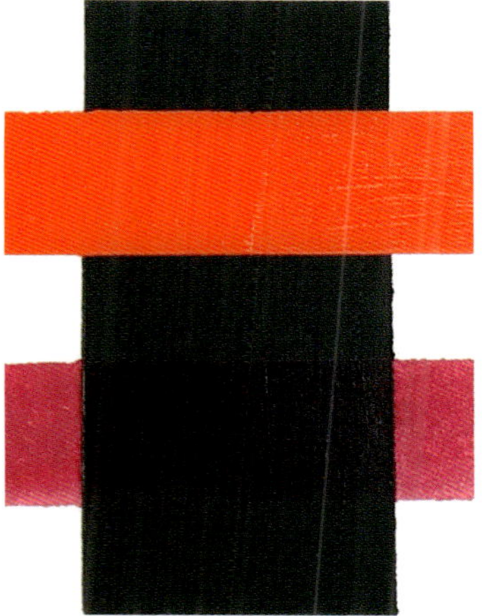

Opaque cadmium red light vs transparent quinacridone magenta
Cadmium red at the top is opaque so it can cover the strip of black; below, the black can be seen through the transparency of quinacridone magenta.

SHADES

By adding a small amount of black to a colour you create a shade. This is always darker than the pure colour. It is useful to remember that the amount of blue in black will turn yellow to green rather than darkening the colour; however, the result is a useful olive green. To darken yellow you need to add a little of its opposite colour, violet.

Using black always creates some controversy among artists – some will never touch it, while others won't paint without it. There is no reason why you shouldn't use black if the painting calls for it; every colour in the right amount and in the right place can be beautiful and useful, even black.

I often make my blacks by mixing complementary colours of orange-red and a dark transparent blue. This mixes a beautiful and lively near-black. But sometimes I need to use an actual black, and if I need the darkest, most neutral black, I use Golden's Carbon Black; for a warmer black I use Mars Black or even warmer Bone Black. You can tell the difference in the temperature of black by mixing it with white. Payne's grey is another go-to useful dark for me when I need more blue content in my dark value.

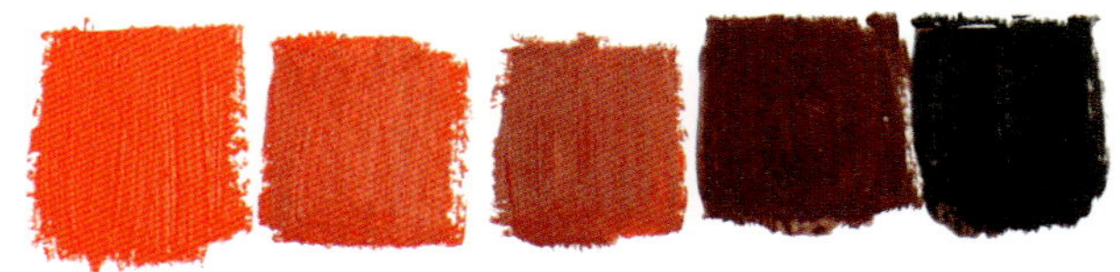

Shades of red by adding small amounts of black.

Tint of quinacridone magenta with titanium white.

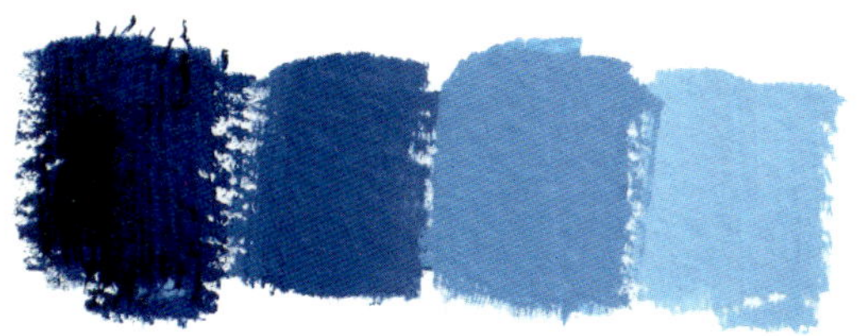

Tint of phthalocyanine blue with titanium white.

TINTS

A tint is a mix of any colour with white. In watercolours, the white of the paper and dilution of the paint is often used to create lighter values. Using oils and acrylics provides the artist with an infinite number of beautiful tints to work with. Tints are soft and often more sophisticated than pure colours. It takes a while for watercolourists to get used to the idea of tints and their incredibly beautiful and useful chromatic contribution to a painting. Tints are particularly effective for painting flowers with softer hues.

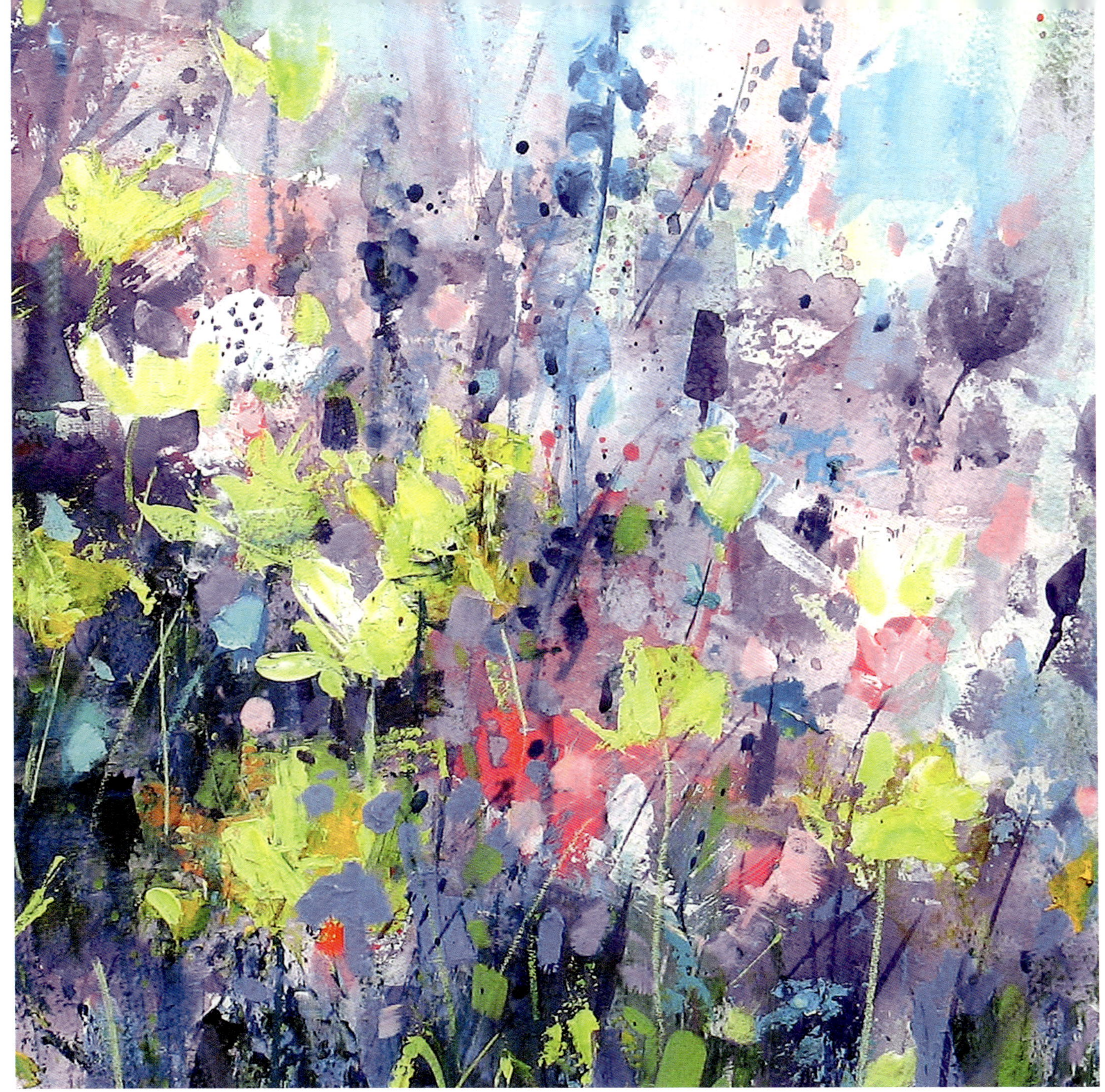

Wild Flower Medley

38 × 33 cm (15 × 13 in)

Mixed media on watercolour paper

In this painting, I really enjoyed using the softer tints of yellow, magenta, green, violet and blue, plus shades of violet and blue. I also toned down some of the magentas, violets and blues to create some chromatic greys. The result is a tranquil and harmonious overall colour scheme despite having the complementary colours within. The more muted overall effect allows the small accents of Opera Rose to shine.

COLOUR HARMONY

The expressive qualities of colour makes it an incredibly powerful element in your flower painting. Fundamentally, it is not just your choice of colours but the all-important relationship between the colours that sets the mood and atmosphere of your painting. The visual contrasts that exist between colour combinations are the key to achieving not only chromatic balance and harmony but the excitement in your painting. It is crucial to understand the relative concept of colours, which is to say how the nature of a colour changes depending on other colours it is placed next to. Any changes in tonality of one hue may mean reconsidering the other colours related to it to retain your overall colour balance.

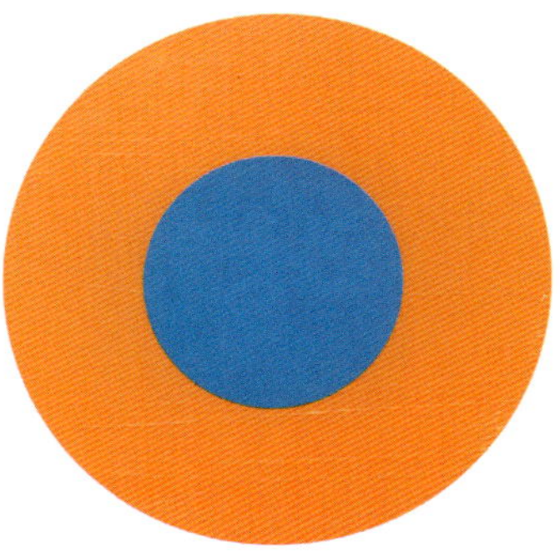

Orange and blue complementary colours
These two colours make a stunning contrast. The ratio of one colour to the other can determine the mood of the painting, from energized to more sedate.

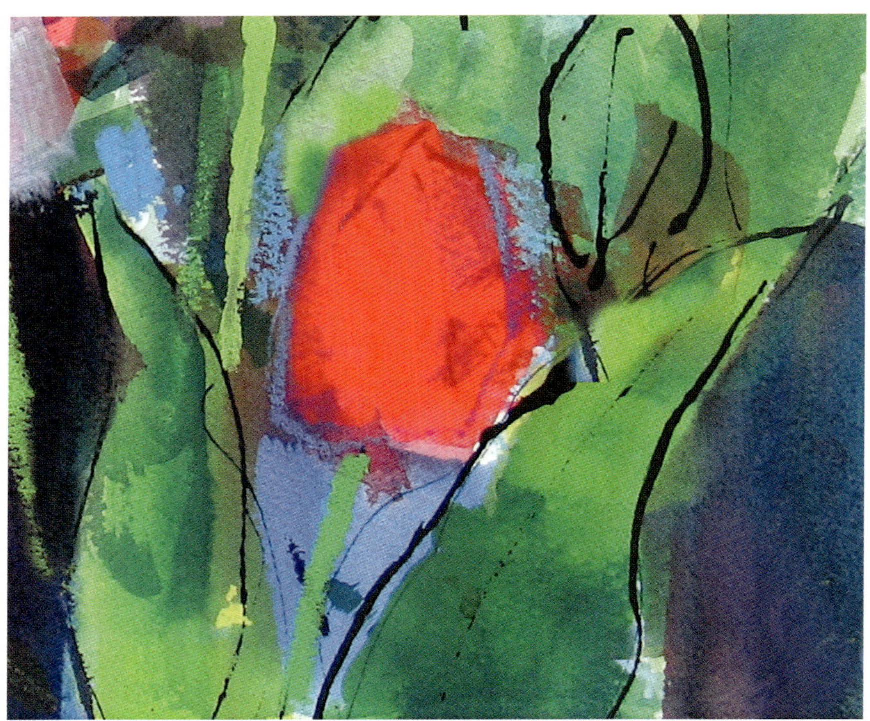

The Red Tulip
10 × 9 cm (4 × 3½ in)
Mixed media on watercolour paper
Red and green can create a striking combination, and here pure red is placed next to a very vibrant green. A touch of red was added to make the bright green darker and more natural for parts of the foliage. The dark grey background allows the brighter hues to show off beautifully.

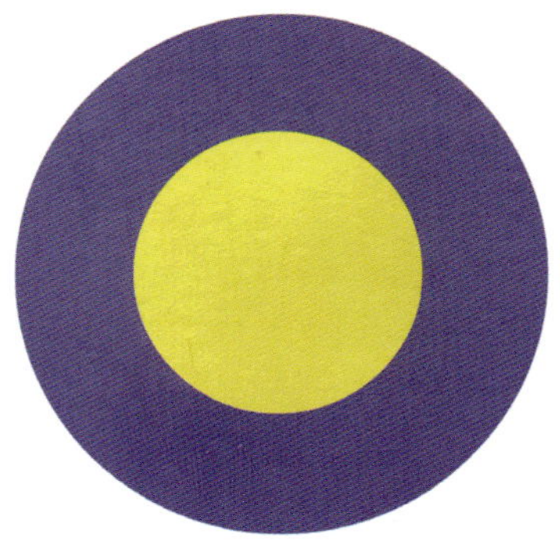

Violet and yellow complementary colours
I approach this combination cautiously in order to avoid a garish result. Gauging the tone of each colour and the proportions are very important to get the balance right.

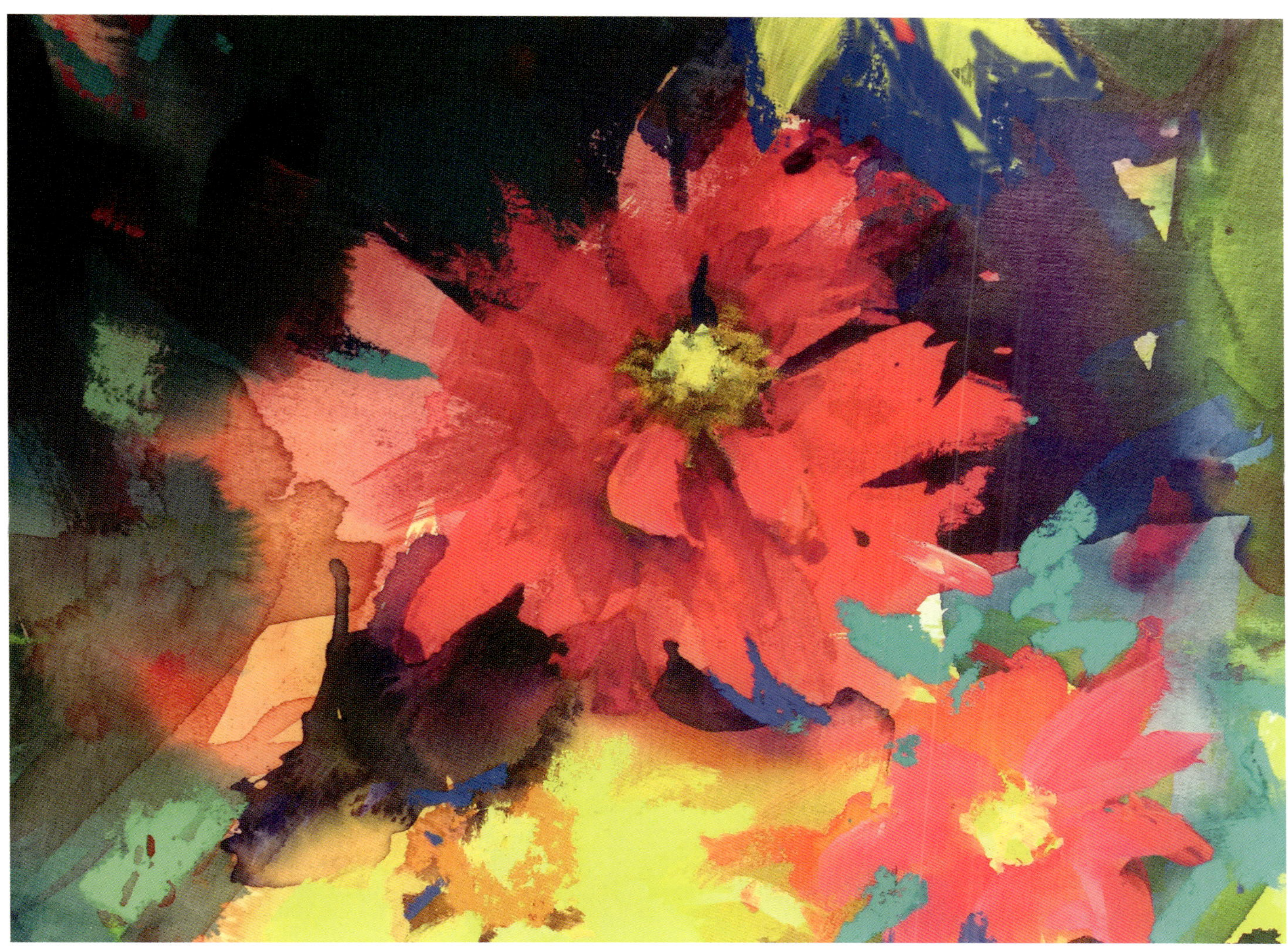

COMPLEMENTARY COLOURS

Red and green, orange and blue, and violet and yellow are known as complementary colours. These colours are situated opposite one another on the colour wheel. The relationship between them plays a crucial role both in colour mixing and creating colour schemes that not only have great coherence but sing with vitality. Darkening a colour by adding a small amount of its complementary colour to it is another important function, and as you increase the amount the colour becomes more and more desaturated until it reaches neutral. For two complementary colours to totally neutralize one another they need to be absolutely opposite one another on the colour wheel; most of the time artists work with near-complementary colours to make beautiful and very useful colourful or chromatic greys.

Colourful Dahlias
20 × 17 cm (8 × 6¾ in)
Mixed media on
watercolour paper
The stunning contrast of
teal with quinacridone red
brings a great buzz and
energy to this image. Little
dabs of royal blue also work
well against yellow.

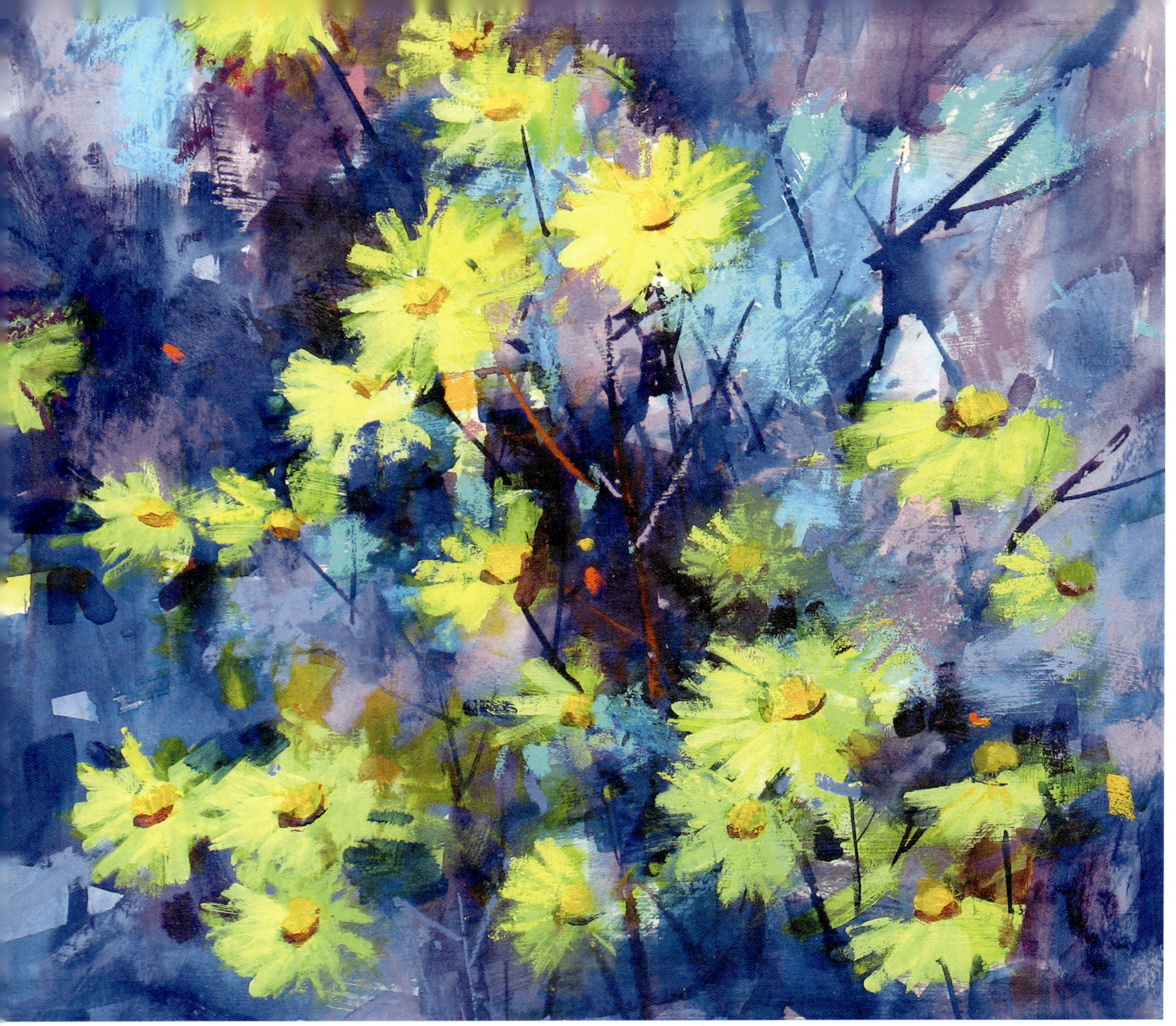

Yellow Daisies Against the Blue Sky

38 × 35 cm (15 × 13¾ in)

Soft pastels and acrylic inks on mount board primed with Golden pastel ground

Yellow and blue are visual complements. This means they look great together but do not have the function of complementary colours – for example, you cannot darken yellow by adding blue to it. In this painting I have used nuances of violet, which is the complementary of yellow. This complementary colour scheme is a much more soothing contrast to the red and green of the two previous pages.

HARMONIOUS ANALOGOUS COLOURS

Analogous colours are the neighbouring colours on the colour wheel with one primary colour in common, such as green, yellow green and yellow, or blue, violet and magenta. There is a much smoother transition of one colour to another in analogous colour schemes, so they promote a feeling of tranquility. This colour scheme suits moody and atmospheric subjects as the colours reflect the same light waves and are easier on the eye. These rather pleasing combinations happen frequently in nature and I often bring in more than three neighbouring colours in my flower paintings – sometimes up to five – and then add the opposite of the most dominant colour as an accent to bring more excitement and energy. The painting still has a more sedate colour scheme but remains interesting.

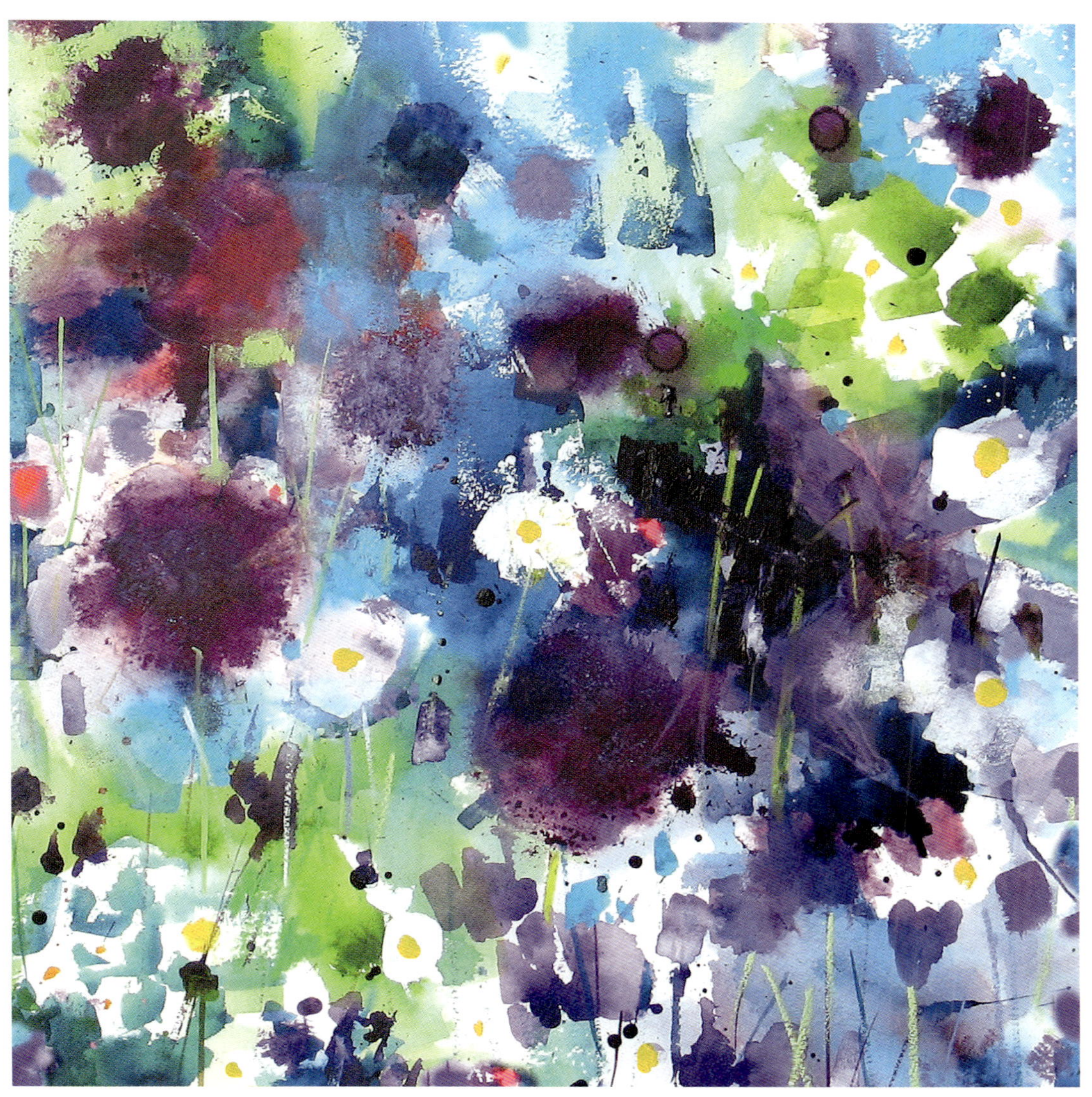

Alliums and Feverfew (detail)
Mixed media on watercolour paper
Here, green, blue green, blue and violet make a lovely and calming colour scheme. I have brought in small accents of yellow in the centre of the daisies, which is a complement both to blue and violet. Adding the warm yellow-green avoids the colour scheme becoming too monotonous.

COLOUR VALUES

Value, or tone, is the degree of lightness or darkness of each colour and the most important attribute of colour. It is the value of a colour that turns a flat shape into a form and creates depth and structure in a painting. Ironically, it is the most difficult attribute of colour to grasp. Paintings that appear flat and lifeless despite having a sound composition and handling of media are almost certainly lacking in value contrasts. Value is a relative concept and the contrasts can be drastically exaggerated or subtle and understated. The lack of value pattern in either form will lead to a lacklustre and flat image.

There are a number of steps you can take to help you recognize the value pattern of your subject. The first step is learning not to concentrate too much on the local colour of the elements of your subject, but instead to focus on how light or dark the colour appears within the subject. Look at your subject, whether from life or photographic reference, through half-closed eyes, as this should eliminate the details and help you to focus on the tonal patterns. If you are not painting from life, turn your source material into a black and white copy to help you concentrate on the tonal pattern. Allow for a degree of colour shift towards a lighter value in watercolour and slightly darker in acrylics as the white polymer dries clear. Turn the painting upside down and sideways to evaluate the tonal pattern; create a nine-step value scale for every colour you work with. All these steps will become instinctive with practice, so paint and sketch in monochromes frequently to make assessing the tonal values second nature.

Dancing Snowdrops

Sometimes when I am not quite happy with the value pattern of my painting halfway through I take a photograph and desaturate the colours to assess the progress of my painting and the value pattern, as shown in this black and white image of snowdrops.

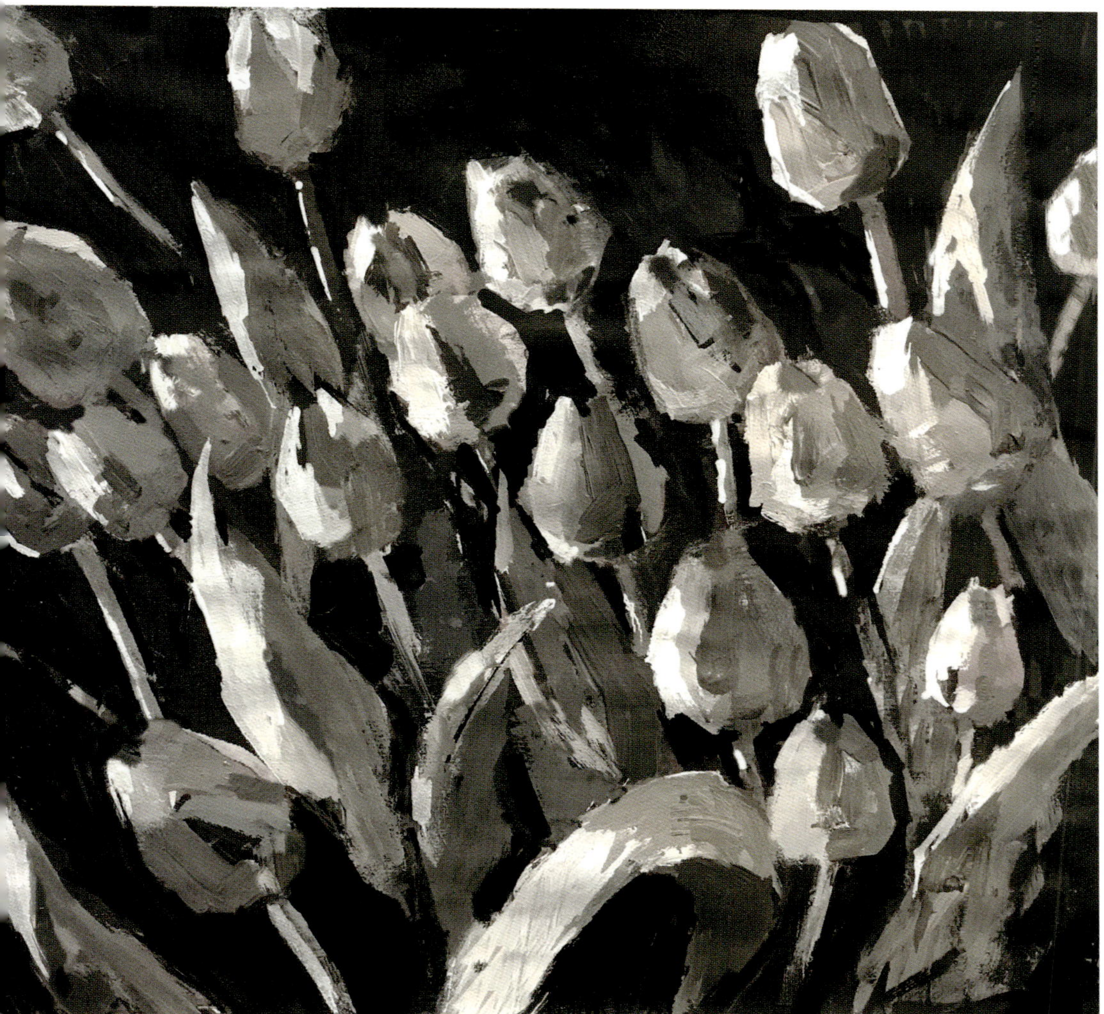

MONOCHROMATIC PAINTINGS

Make painting monochromes part of your art practice, for in the absence of numerous colours, you can get to grips with the importance of value rather than the local colours of your subject matter. It also teaches you the value of a limited palette and how to harness your inclination towards putting too many colours in one painting. I often use sepia, a transparent clear dark such as Payne's grey or a dark blue such as Prussian. These colours break down easily from a very dark value into mid-tones and lights. You can use the white of the canvas or paper for your lights or apply either zinc white or titanium white. Alternatively, you can use one colour that you have mixed, for example a dark purple made from phthalo, Prussian blue or ultramarine blue with quinacridone magenta. This practice can be done in any wet or dry medium.

COLOUR MIXING

Working with colour is at the heart of painting flowers. Practising your colour mixing can go a long way towards your becoming confident with this vital step in composing your painting with beautiful and harmonious colour schemes. The exercises here will help you to mix a wide range of vibrant, slightly muted and muted secondary colours, chromatic greys, tints, greens and darks, and understand the logic behind them.

Mixing secondary colours

Using the basic palette of warm and cool primary colours, mix a range of vibrant, slightly muted and muted secondary colours. I have given the bias of each primary colour to make it easier for you.

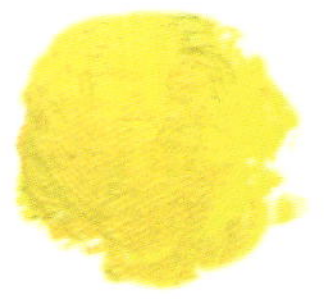

Warm yellow (orange bias)

Cool yellow (green bias)

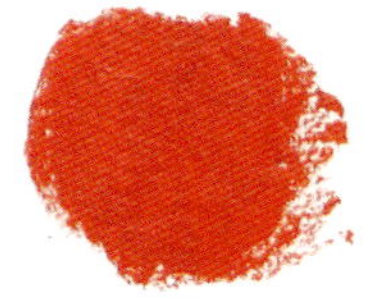

Warm red (orange bias)

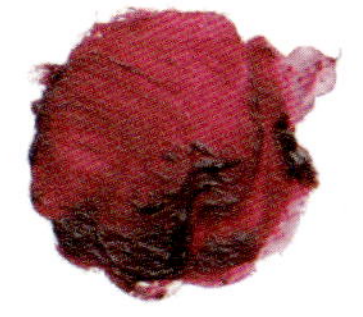

Cool red (violet bias)

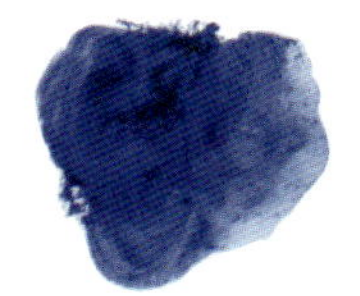

Warm blue (violet bias)

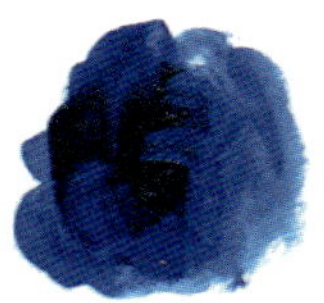

Cool blue (green bias)

Vibrant mixes

To make vibrant secondary colours you need to pick the two colours that are both biased towards the secondary colour you wish to mix.

Now use the other sets of two primary colours to mix vibrant violet and vibrant orange.

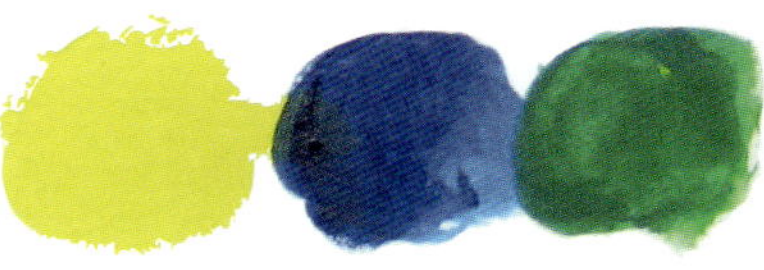

Cool yellow + cool blue = vibrant green

Slightly muted mixes

To make slightly muted versions of secondary colours, choose one colour that is biased towards your secondary colour and one that is not.

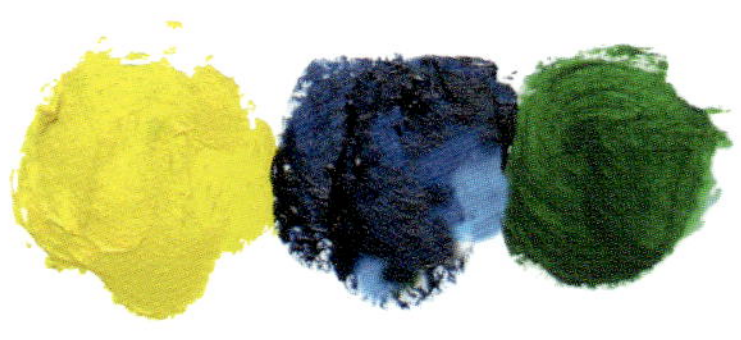

Cool yellow + warm ultramarine blue = slightly muted green

Muted mixes

To mix totally muted versions of secondary colours, choose the two primary colours that are not biased towards the secondary colour you wish to mix.

Now use the other two sets to mix further swatches of muted secondary colours.

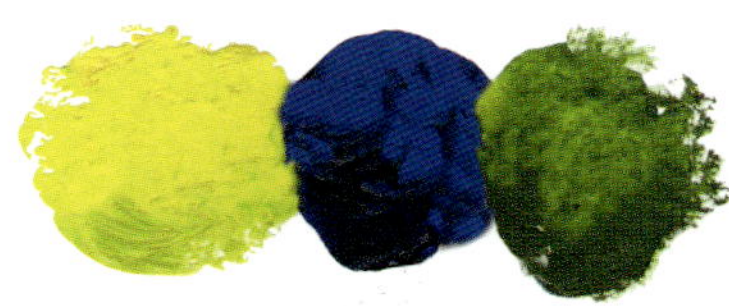

Warm yellow + warm ultramarine blue = muted green which is much closer to the colours in nature

Mixing chromatic greys

Mixing two complementary colours results in a near-black, brown or neutral grey. To become totally neutral the colours need to be exactly opposite one another, therefore most of the time we are creating colourful greys that are extremely useful in most paintings. These quiet and understated colours bring balance to a painting made up of vibrant colours and allow the more vivid hues to shine. For this exercise use sets of complementary colours, mix them together using different ratios plus white, and make a chart to refer to.

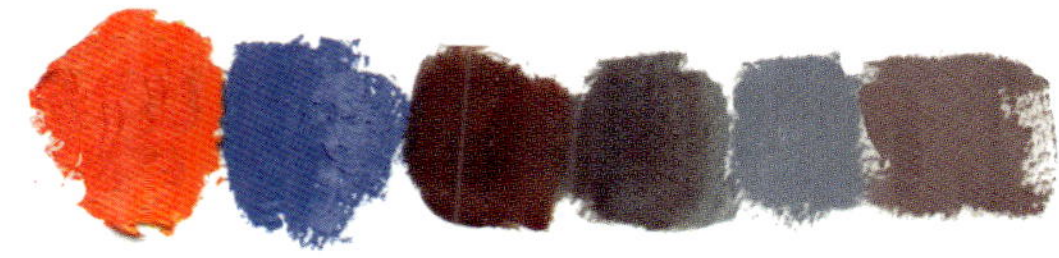

In this example I have used cadmium orange and manganese blue hue. These two colours mix wonderful browns and greys and great neutral tints when mixed with titanium white.

Mixing tints

This exercise is particularly useful for watercolour painters who are new to oils and acrylics. Mixes of every colour with white will give you beautifully soft and gentle versions of colours to work with. These tints are especially useful for the flower painter in order to replicate the subtle colours of nature.

From left to right: Tint of ultramarine blue; tint of dioxazine purple; tint of cadmium red light; tint of quinacridone magenta.

Mixing greens

Reaching for a tube of ready-made green without modifying it or changing the range of values is a classic mistake made by many beginners. This usually results in floral or landscape paintings lacking in natural greens with a correct range of tonal values and earning the colour green a reputation as a problematic colour. However, ready-made tubes of green can be useful either in small accents or as a base to mix a variety of more natural greens. In this exercise, take any tube of green you have and modify the colour by adding a small amount of various reds to tone it down, then add different yellows and blues to mix an infinite number of beautiful greens from darkest to lightest values and tints with the addition of white. Also use your tubes of blues and yellows, including earth yellow, to mix numerous useful greens. This exercise should help you to never shy away from using the colour green.

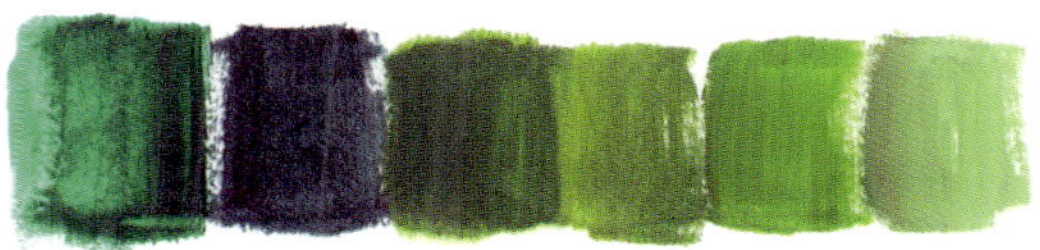

Modifying phthalo green: by adding a touch of quinacridone magenta, then mixing with a green-biased cool yellow such as lemon yellow, you can mix a range of natural greens. A whole range of tints with titanium white can also be very useful.

Mixing darks

Dark values add depth and structure to a painting, but reaching for black is not always the answer. Use sets of complementary colours to mix a variety of darks from lively near-blacks to rich browns. Each set gives you different, equally useful hues to work with.

Burnt sienna is an orange red and makes a lively black when mixed with its opposite colour, ultramarine blue. Adding more blue makes a darker value and conversely adding more burnt sienna makes the mixture lighter towards a lovely rich brown. You can repeat the exercise with sets of complementary colours and see the wide range of useful dark hues that you can incorporate in future paintings.

THE IMPACT OF UNDERPAINTING

I believe that underpainting creates extra vital depth and if chosen and handled thoughtfully can add the elusive wow factor that we all strive for in our art-making. An underpainting as your first layer can address several important issues that can contribute to making a stronger image, including the ability to set the mood for your painting from the outset. A high-key colour, such as a yellow hue, as the first layer generates a warm and sunny atmosphere, as opposed to the soothing and tranquil feel of a cool blue or grey. Choosing a colour that is complementary to the most dominant hue in your painting will create great buzz and energy if you allow snippets of the underpainting to show through the subsequent layers. This could be a brilliant blue for an orange bloom, a bright lime green for red flower heads or vice versa. These fragments of colour echoing through the top layer unify the whole image and create a pleasing rhythm and movement through the painting at the same time.

Orange Day Lilies on Blue

51 × 28 cm (20 × 11 in)

Heavy body acrylics, gesso, coarse and extra-coarse pumice gel, aquarelle pencils and oil pastels on mount board

Here I used a mix of phthalo blue with white as the underpainting. The orange day lilies are complementary to the blue and bring vibrancy and excitement to the image. The underpainting both unifies and creates a great contrast to make an uplifting impact.

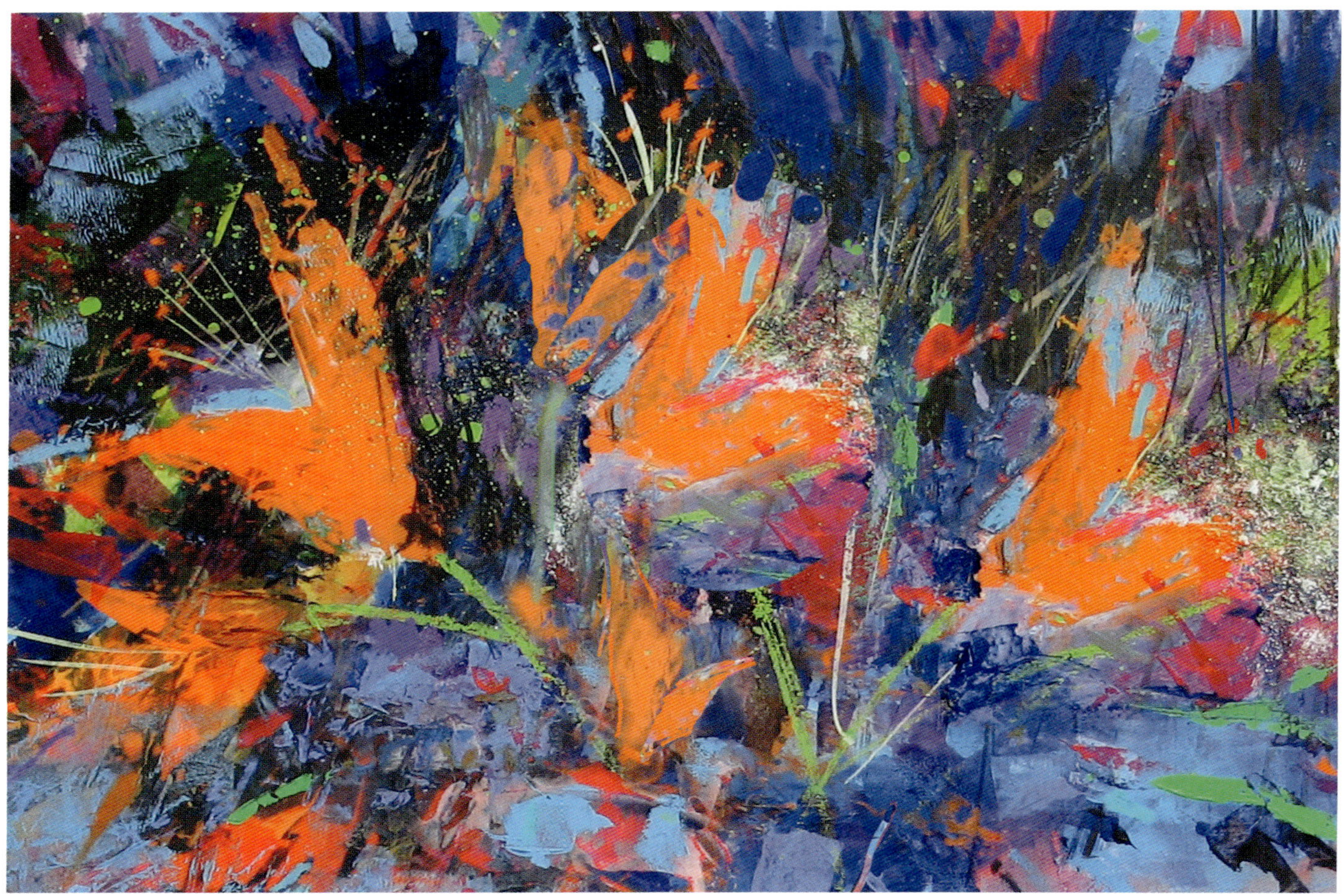

An alternative way to tackle the underpainting is the traditional method of the old masters called grisaille. Here you set the tonal values by blocking them in with the darks, mid-tones and lights and build the subject on this framework. You can achieve this by choosing a clear transparent dark colour. My personal preference for blocking in the initial underpainting is a permanent paint such as acrylic or acrylic ink – I avoid charcoal as this can compromise the vibrancy of my colours even after fixing, but it does work for some artists.

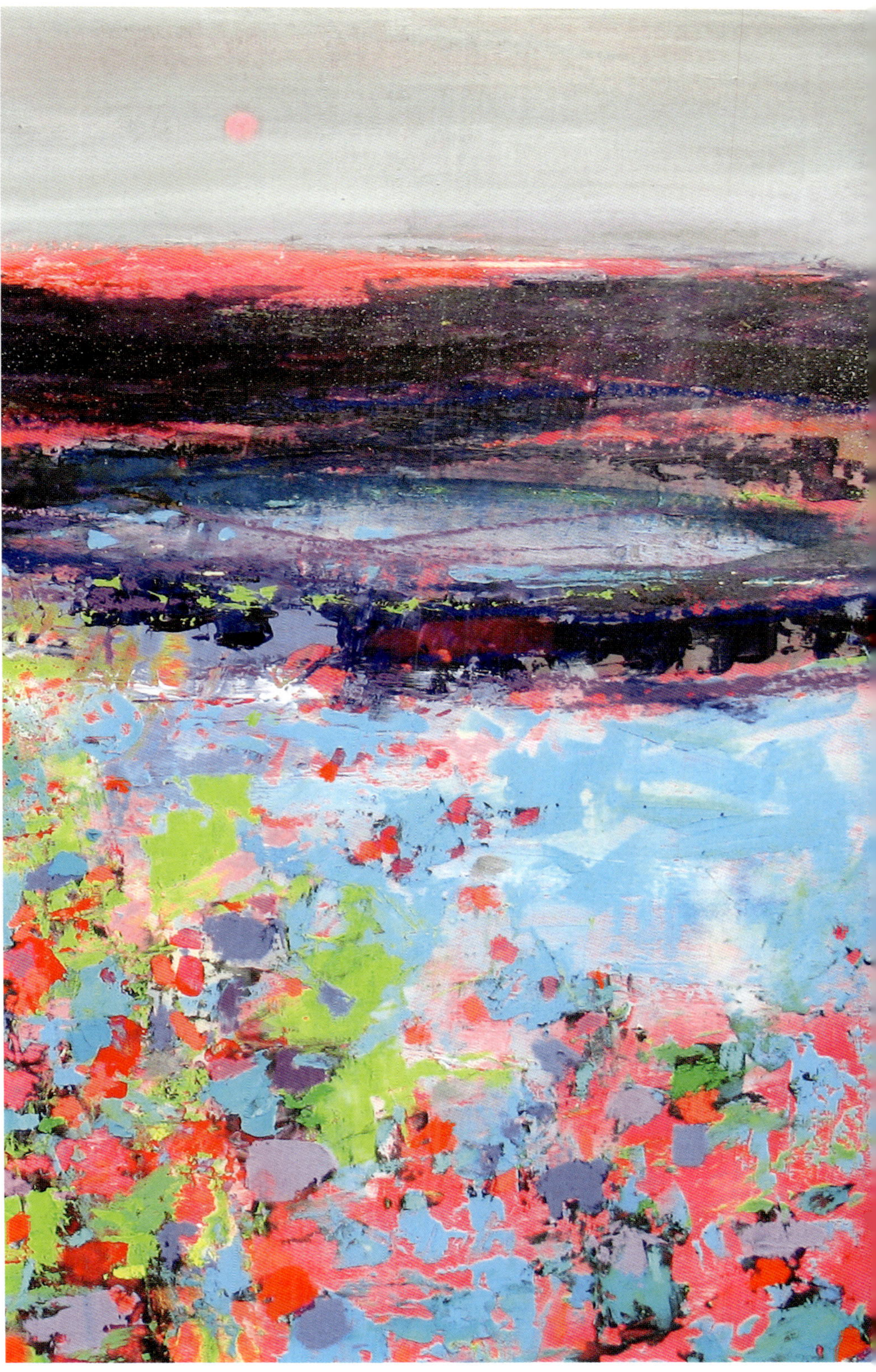

Summer Poppy Field

51 × 24 cm (20 × 9½ in)

High Flow inks, soft pastels, oil pastels and spray paint on mount board

The entire underpainting of this artwork is done with a mix of magenta with titanium white. The fragments of pink are coming through the many top layers of blues and purples, allowing some of the underpainting to be read as abstracted flower heads. The underpainting acts as a perfect unifying factor for the whole painting.

CHINESE LANTERNS

The colour scheme of a floral subject is partly dictated by the colour of the flowers and foliage. However, it is the background colours that can make or break an impressionist-style floral painting; they should complement rather than fight the colour of the flowers. The vivid orange pods of the Chinese lantern look great against the light green foliage and I aimed to bring some shades of purple to create a secondary triad of green, orange and violet – a pleasing combination that many landscape gardeners take advantage of when designing the colour scheme for their flower borders. In this painting I have added extra visual impact by incorporating some turquoise blue in the background, which is a complement to the stunning orange pods.

Materials

Golden Fluid colours
Indian Yellow Hue
Pyrrole Orange
Benzimidazolone Yellow Light

Golden High Flow colours
Ultramarine Blue
Quinacridone Magenta
Green Gold

Pastels and crayons
Turquoise oil pastel
Light Green wax crayon

Support
200lb Saunders Waterford watercolour paper, NOT surface, 55 × 30 cm (21½ × 12 in)

Stage 1

The first stage for me is always a very simple drawing outlining some of the main shapes of the composition. I prefer to lay down as many washes of my brightest colours over the white of the paper as I can to get the benefit of clean and vivid colours. The outlines are therefore necessary to remind me where to lay the washes of vibrant colours for my flower heads.

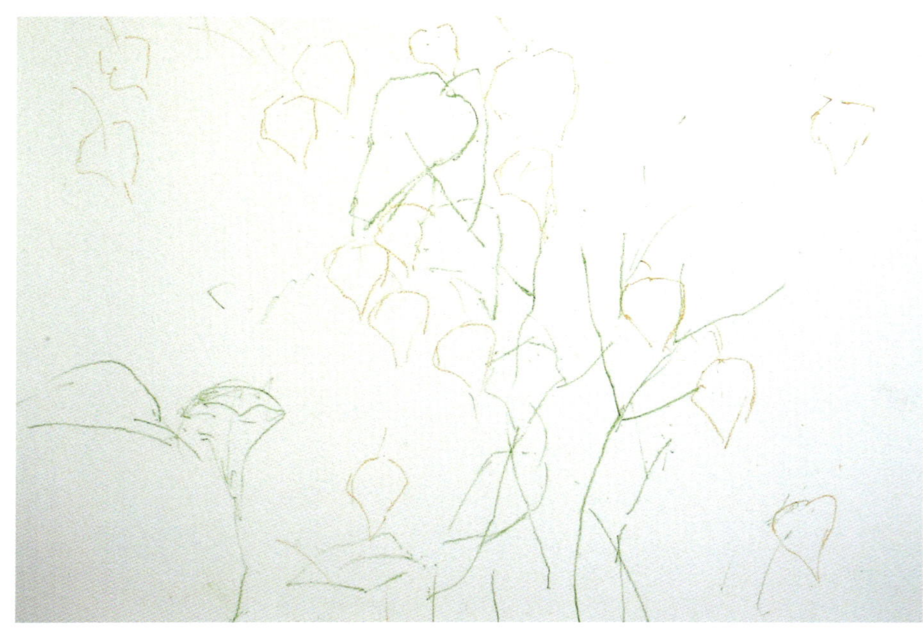

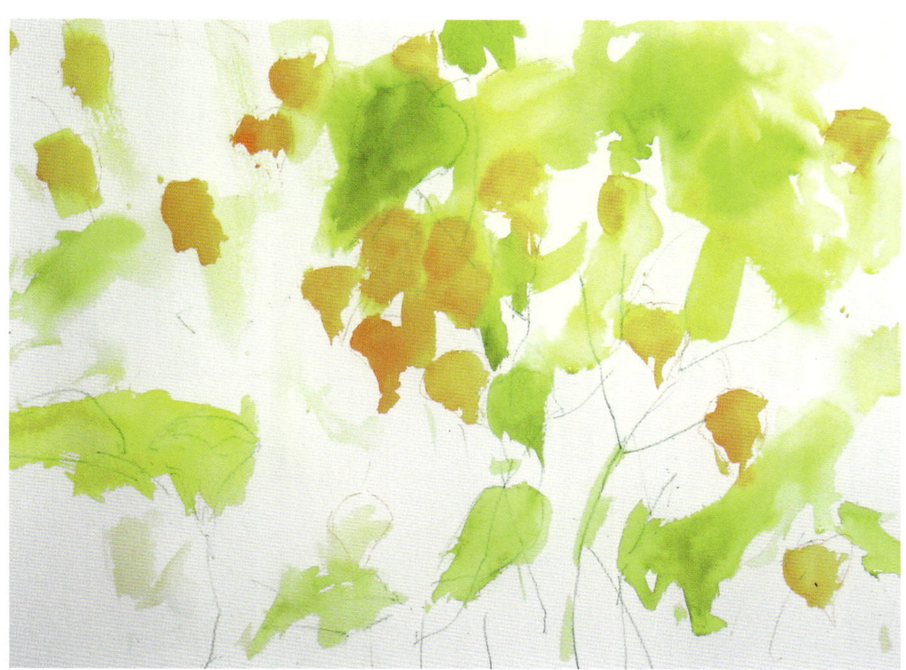

Stage 2

I enjoy this stage as I can be quite free with the washes and have nothing to lose – I can't wait for the colours to start mingling in a random way and giving me some wonderful shapes to work with. If I am using inks and fluids then I keep things fairly wet and workable to avoid making too many hard lines at this stage. I started with a loose wash of Benzimidazolone Yellow Light followed by Indian Yellow Hue Fluid colours over the pods. I then flooded the foliage with Green Gold High Flow colour, a wonderful golden yellow green which is the perfect shade for the foliage of this beautiful and unusual flower.

Stage 3

This is the stage where I like to introduce washes of the supporting colours such as Ultramarine Blue and Quinacridone Magenta in varying degrees to start bringing the background into the equation. I strengthened the colour of the pods with more washes of Pyrrole Orange to give them their local colour at this point. I don't worry about the colours being rather messy and untidy as I know that these shapes will be consolidated by the end of the painting.

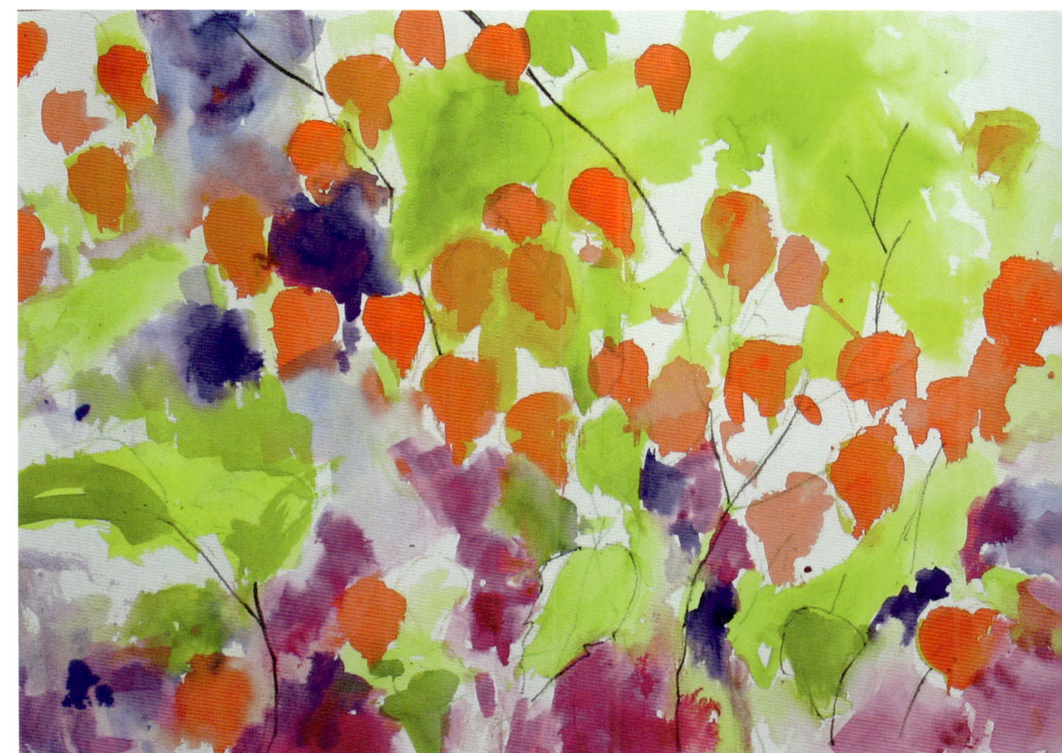

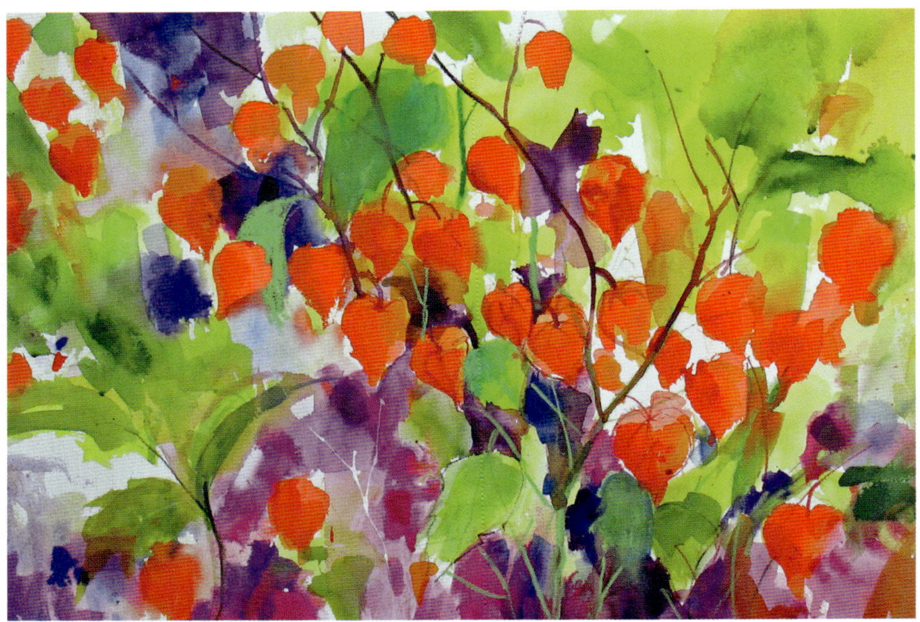

Stage 4

I initially reapplied the colour on the orange pods with yet another strong wash of orange over them, then I let the surface dry before moving onto applying the darker tones in the background by laying down strong washes of dark violet (a mix of Quinacridone Magenta and Ultramarine Blue). Then I used the green wax crayon to bring in the stems – I love their chaotic formation and how they bring in the linear marks to encourage the eye to move around the picture and focus on various shapes. I then applied stronger colour on the leaves and gave some of them a more defined form while keeping others loose and less defined.

Stage 5

I strengthened the colours of both the flower heads and the foliage and made them slightly darker. Then I introduced some dark values, using Ultramarine Blue and Quinacridone Magenta, to create an underlying dark pattern to move the eye around the painting. I added more linear marks for the same purpose and used a mixture of dark violet and yellow to bring in a mass of darker stems. I added some markings on the pods, then made a few dabs and dashes with my turquoise crayon as a complementary colour to the orange pods to finish the painting.

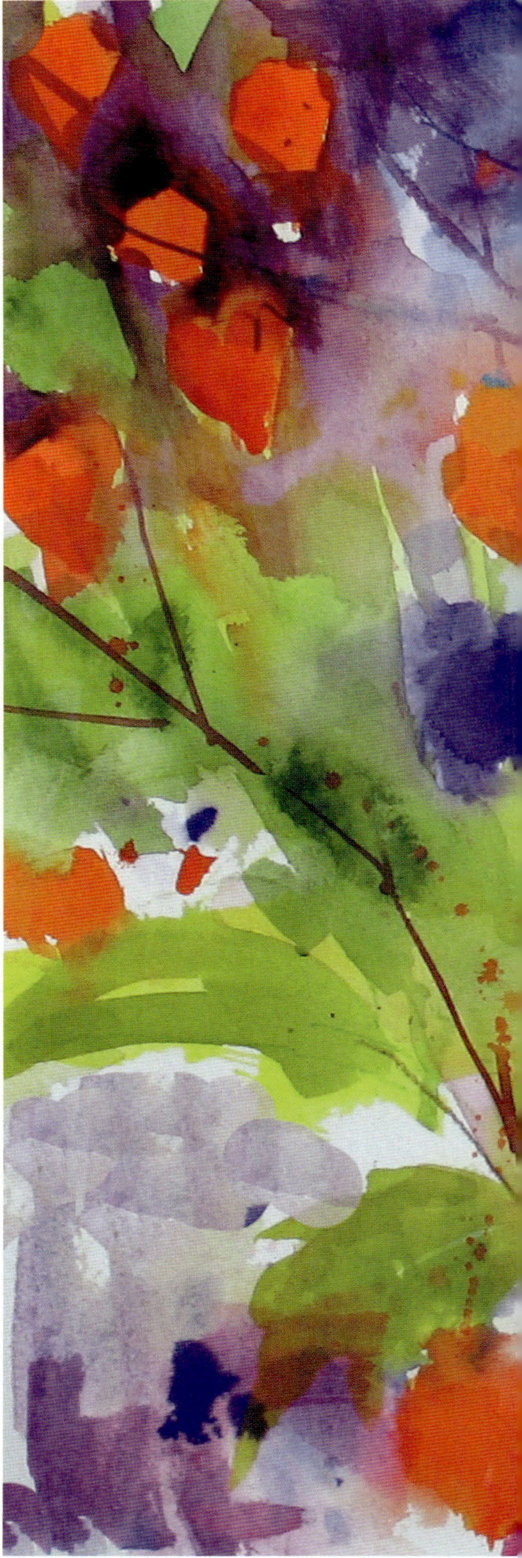

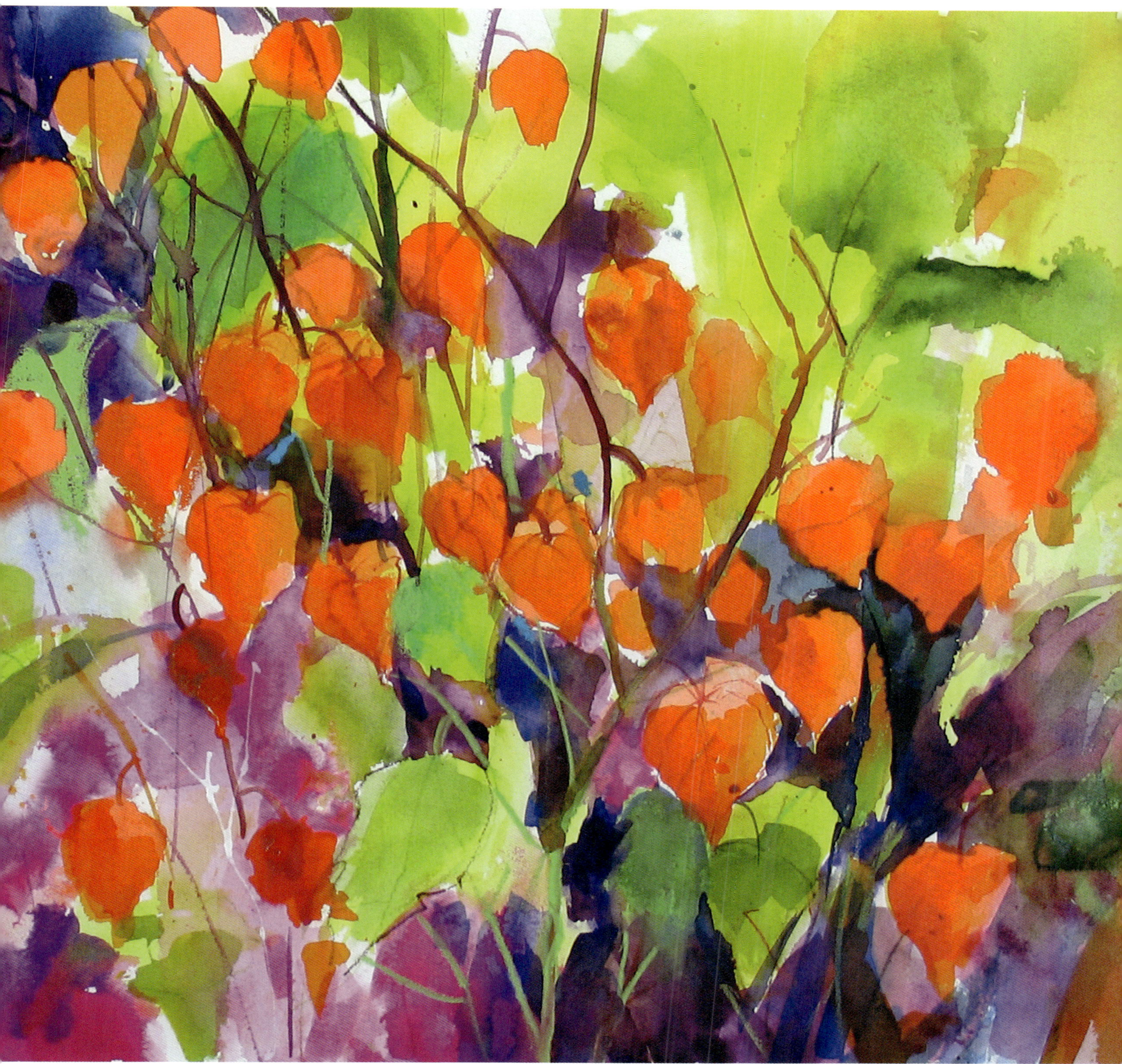

SEDUCTIVE SURFACES

As one of the main elements of design, the surface quality makes a significant contribution to the visual impact of a painting. The wide variety of mediums and supports, plus a whole range of gels, pastes and collage materials, presents endless opportunities to the mixed media artist to push the creative boundaries. This chapter will guide you through a few ways of using these materials to transform a mundane painting into one that is exciting and extraordinary.

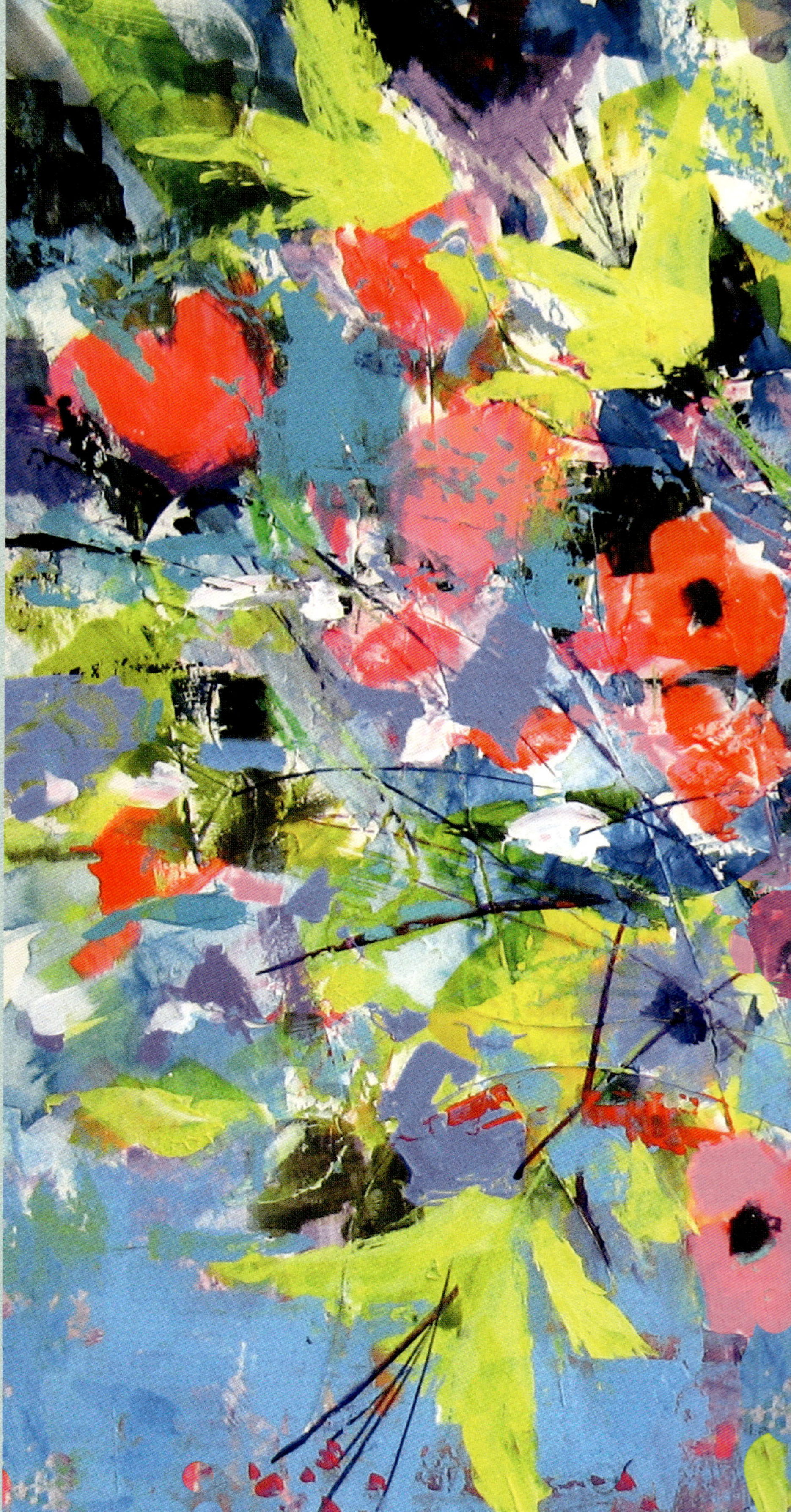

Yellow Lilies and Anemones
72 × 56 cm (28½ × 22 in)
Mixed media on mount board

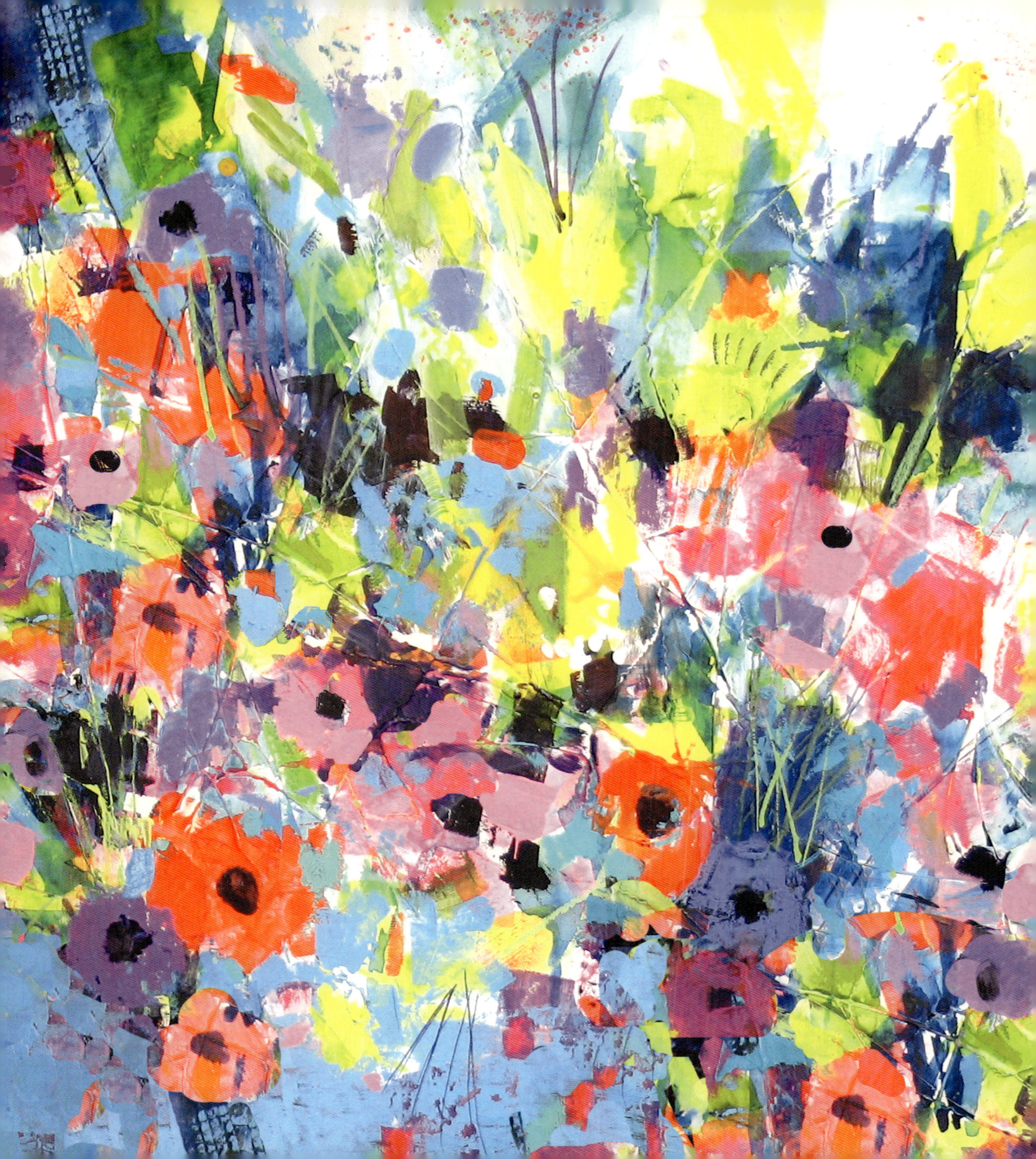

EXPERIMENTS WITH GESSO

Gesso is laid on surfaces to prime them for painting with oils and acrylics, creating a barrier between the paint and the support. Today, an acrylic-based product is mainly used. While it is a must when painting with oils, gesso is only an option for acrylics, but you will find that certain supports such as canvas and wood become much more receptive and less wasteful to paint on when primed. Gesso is intended only for priming – while it contains titanium oxide it is not a substitute for Titanium White paint as it doesn't have the same consistency and has a chalky, matte finish. While I do use gesso sometimes in top layers it is usually for eliminating unwanted passages and making them ready to be painted over.

Gesso varies a great deal in viscosity, quality, sheen and texture (smooth or gritty) from brand to brand. It is available in white, black, clear and some pastel shades. You can easily make your own coloured gesso by adding a few drops of ink or acrylic paint. Gesso can be so much more than just a primer and with some imagination you can use it to create lively and exciting textures prior to painting. Experiment by adding the gesso with a piece of card and scratching into it, adding collage, or making an imprint on it.

(Opposite page) **Scottish Thistle on Black**
33 × 38 cm (13 × 15 in)
Black gesso, acrylic paint and soft pastels on mount board
I love the matte sheen of Golden's black gesso. Here it creates the ideal background to show off the bright purple of the thistles and the silvery grey-green of the foliage. The dramatic darkness of the background creates such a different mood compared to the softer transition of hues on white gesso.

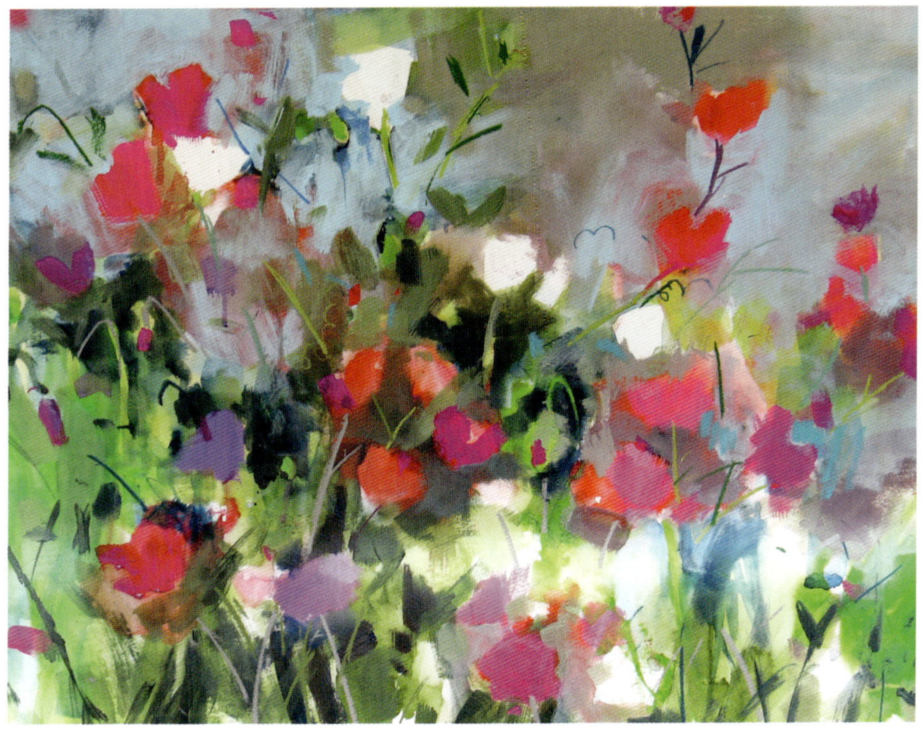

(Left) **Sweet Peas at Lynstead House**
41 × 51 cm (16 × 20 in)
Acrylic paint and soft pastel on paper
I used heavy body colours with a few dabs of brilliant pink soft pastels on watercolour paper primed with white gesso for this painting. The colours of the flowers really sang against the pale blue wall behind and the greenery of the foliage created a great foil for the vibrant colours of the flowers. By comparison with the image on the opposite page, painting these vivid colours on white has created a softer feel than the dramatic contrast on black gesso.

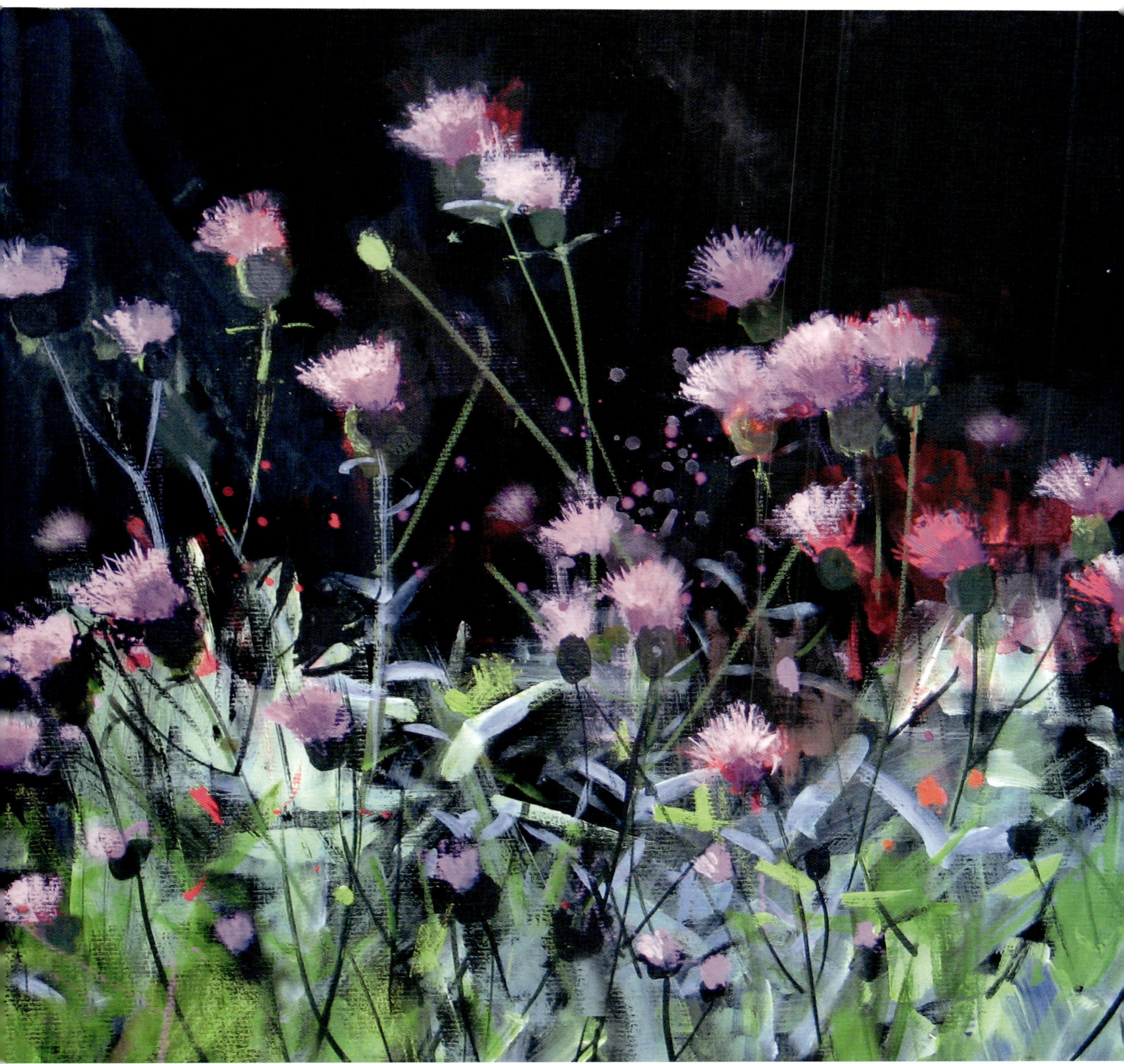

PASTEL GROUND

Golden's pastel ground is an acrylic-based primer that contains sand (silica) and creates the perfect gritty surface for dry media such as pastels and all types of crayons. To get the best results, dilute the pastel ground with 20–40 per cent water and apply a few thin layers with a brush or roller for a smooth surface. For a rougher surface, use a household or bristle brush and mix layers of thick and thin applications to get some great textures to come through layers of pastels and acrylics. As the surface can accept wet mediums as well, it makes an ideal primer for any mixed media combination with wet and dry materials.

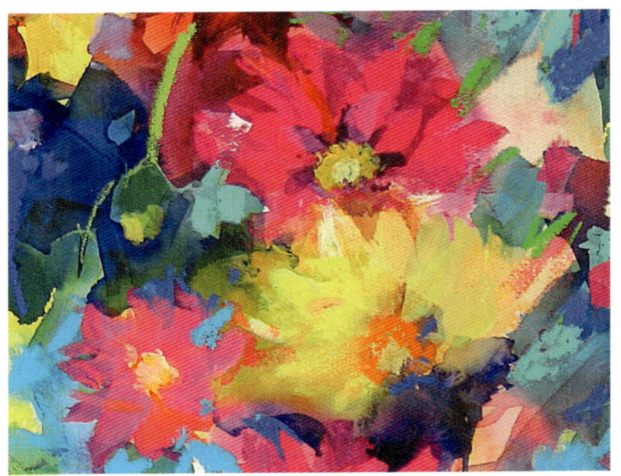

Colourful Dahlias (detail)
In this close-up you can see the textures created by pastels over the pastel ground application. Priming the surface in this way means you can apply many layers of pastels and create great depth in your painting.

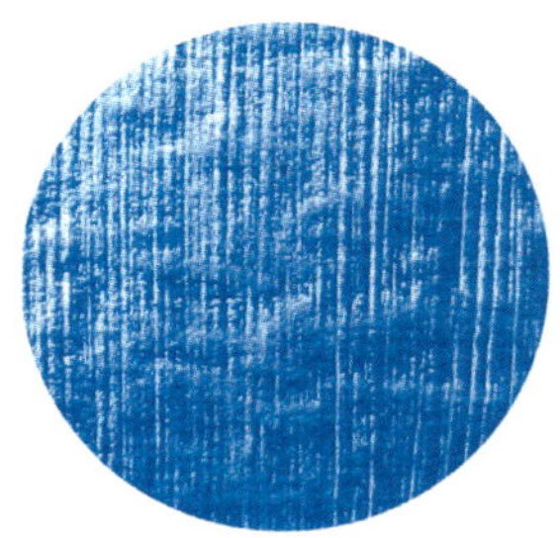

Examples of matte and gloss mediums.

ACRYLIC MEDIUMS

Acrylic gloss and matte mediums give you the option to change the sheen of the acrylic colours and extend the paints either by mixing them with the paint or adding them as a final layer. The mediums can also be used to stick down collage or as a primer to seal your support instead of gesso. When I use either of them to dilute my paints, I wash my brushes in plain water between applications and dry them before dipping into the medium and paint. Mediums can be applied to a painting where matte and glossy finishes of the pigment need unifying. The deep shine of the gloss medium deepens and brings out the colours and enhances certain subjects, while matte medium gives the acrylic a much nicer matte finish. Although applying the medium as a final layer offers some protection it is not as effective as varnish and cannot be removed to reveal the clean colours underneath. It is, however, very effective as an isolation coat before varnishing your painting.

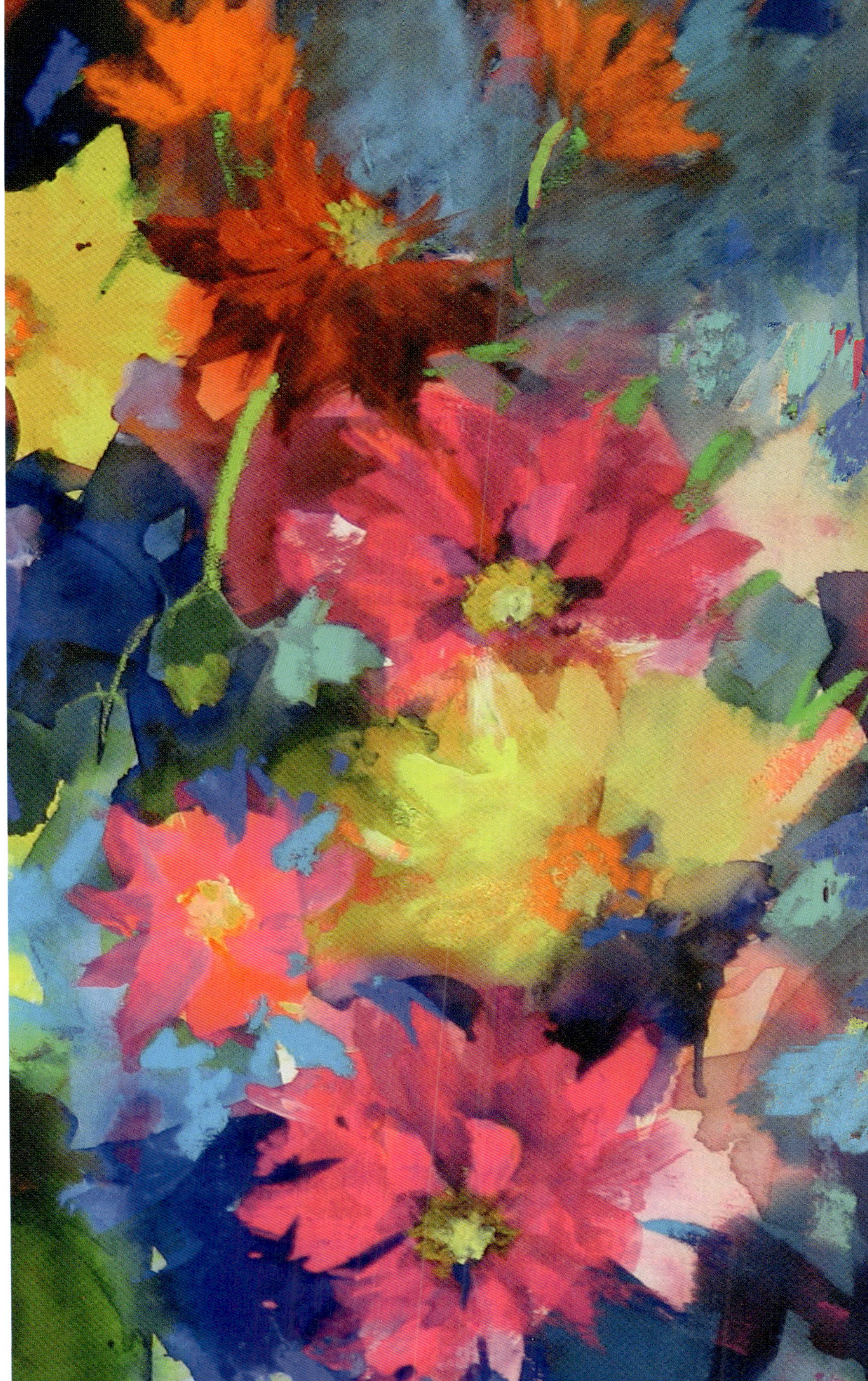

Colourful Dahlias

37 × 22 cm (14½ × 8½ in)

Acrylic ink and pastel on mount board
I applied very thin layers of pastel
ground to my mount board, letting
each layer dry before applying the
next. I then flooded the surface with
acrylic inks in yellow, magenta, red and
blue and let the colours mingle. Once
the surface dried I used soft pastels
to shape the flower heads. Since this
surface takes water-based media,
I could go back with the inks many
times to cut the edges of the dahlias in
the negative areas to shape the flowers
and give them more definition. I love
this process as it is a proper mix of
leaving some shapes to chance while
having the control of defining where
necessary. I am not afraid of flooding
the surface with inks if I feel the shapes
are getting too tidy and contrived –
taking some risks hopefully leads to
richer surfaces and more spontaneity.

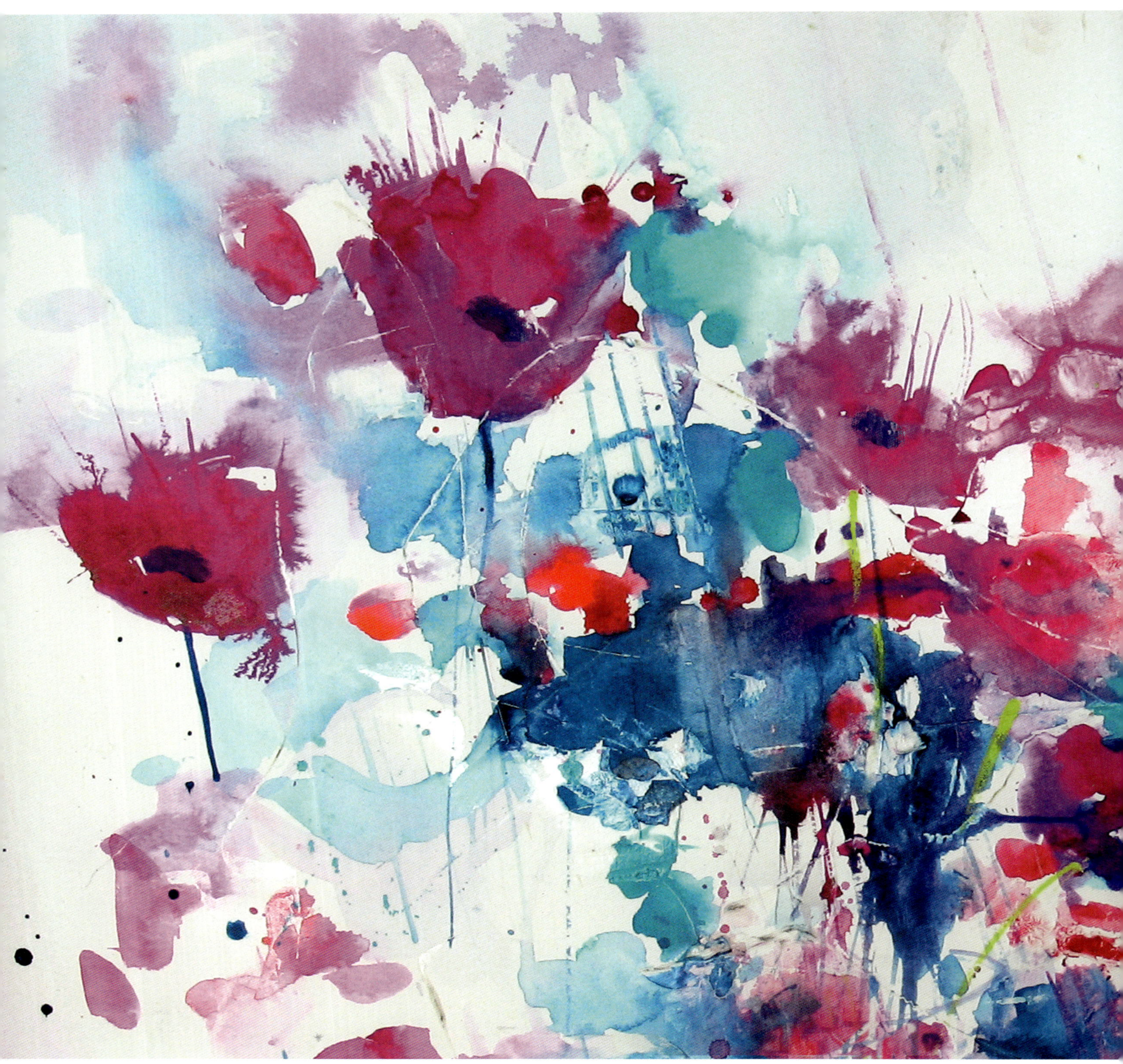

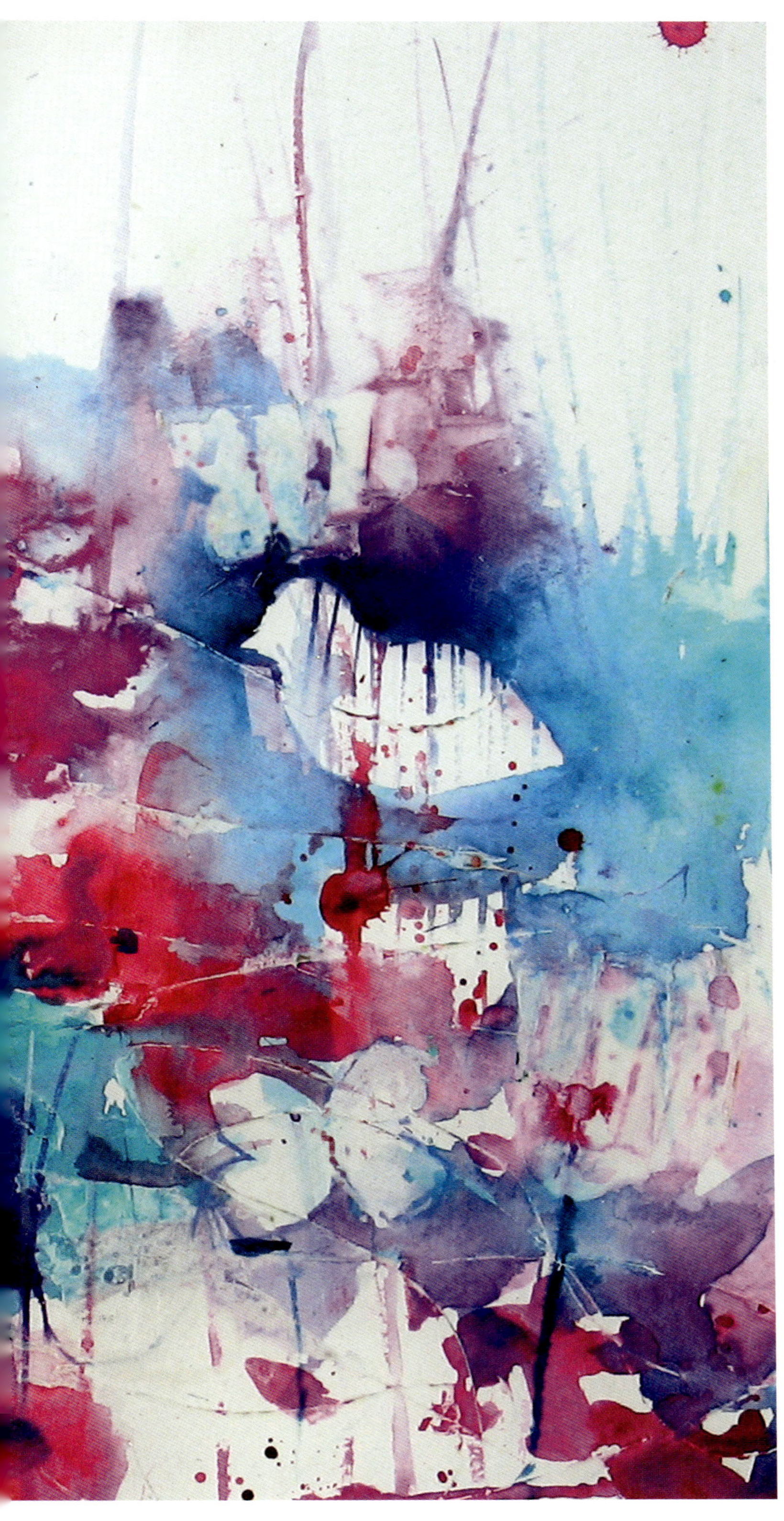

WATERCOLOUR GROUND

Going beyond the traditional methods of painting in watercolours makes this unpredictable and challenging medium even more exciting. For this painting I prepared the board with two coats of gesso, then once that was dry, I applied two thin layers of watercolour ground, a primer similar to gesso in appearance that creates a beautifully receptive and absorbent surface for water-based mediums. This can be done on any grade of paper, canvas and wooden artist's panel with different effects. I then drizzled random drips of clear tar gel to create more abstract shapes. I let the surface dry completely before applying washes of Quinacridone Magenta, Quinacridone Red and Opera Rose. I followed these with washes of Teal and Phthalo Blue.

I then looked at the washes to see what shapes I could make more recognizable, in this case a few flower heads. Working on this surface allowed me to lift some colour to create shapes of birds and butterflies. This kind of painting is quite open-ended as you can continue to play by adding and lifting colour and really enjoy the organic progress rather than the more predictable process of traditional watercolours. Unwanted areas can be eliminated using the watercolour ground and more watercolour can be applied once the surface has dried, keeping your colours fresh and vibrant. Going with the natural flow of the painting is both therapeutic and energizing, especially if you let go of striving for a masterpiece. If the end result is good then it is the cherry on the cake.

Pink Poppies, Birds and Butterflies
43 × 67 cm (17 × 26½ in)
Watercolour on board

ACRYLIC GEL MEDIUMS

You can think of gel mediums as paint without the added pigments that determine the price of your artist's grade paints. Gel mediums are made of 100 per cent polymer and are an economical way of creating impasto paintings, building up highly textured grounds, or simply extending your paints to make them go slightly further. Golden offer a variety of different grades, such as soft gel, regular gel, heavy and extra heavy gel, as well as high solid gel which contains more acrylic solids for a denser consistency. You can even choose your preferred sheen from matte, gloss and semi-gloss to give you great scope for making highly individual pieces.

I find the gels elevate the versatility of acrylics to yet another level. Those with added aggregates, such as pumice gel or glass bead gel, will help you to emulate various textures whether man-made or found in nature. You can make your textural effects prior to painting or mix the gels with the paint to add body or extend the paint; you can also prime your surface with any of the gels or add a layer of gel over the top of the painting. Like all acrylic products, they have adhesive quality and can be used for sticking down collage. Their archival quality doesn't compromise the longevity of your artwork, unlike the possibility of damage from the impurity of natural materials, such as sand and grit from the landscape. They are resistant to chemicals, UV rays and water. Gels are only white when wet; gloss gels dry transparent and matte gels dry translucent, so there is little interference with colour values.

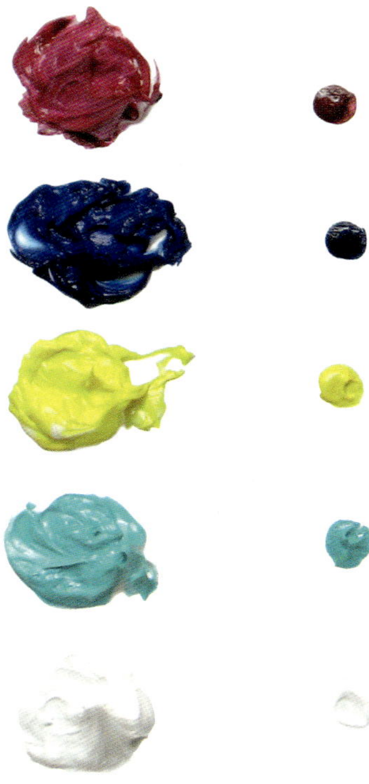

Extending paint with gel medium

This image shows how you can volumize your heavy body or Fluid colours by adding gel medium. You can even choose the sheen and viscosity by using different gels – for example, for a runnier consistency, try a small amount of Fluid colours with soft gel.

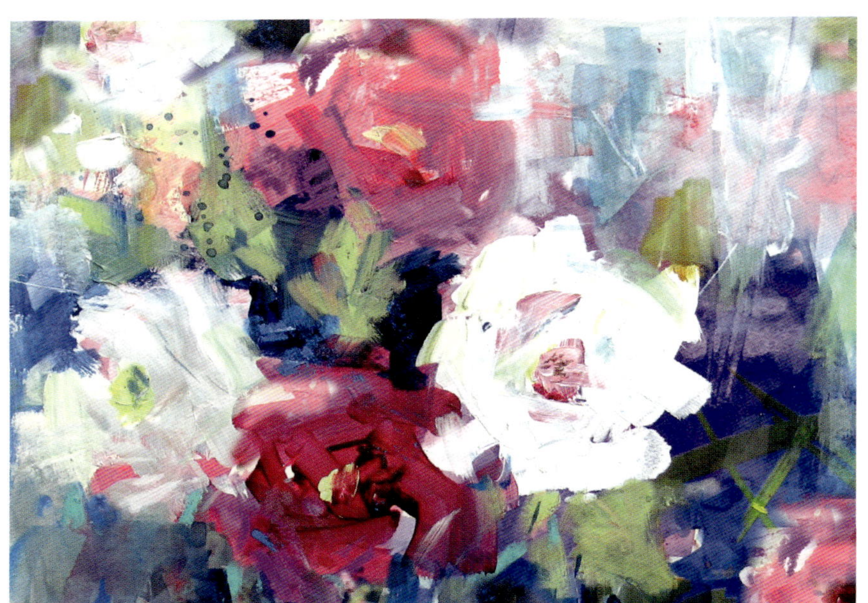

Pink and White Roses
26 × 17 cm (10¼ × 6¾ in)
Acrylic paint on watercolour paper
I mixed a very small amount of heavy body Quinacridone Magenta, Phthalo Blue, Benzimidazolone Yellow Light and Titanium White with regular gel medium to make the paints go further. This is a very economical way of using top quality paints. If I had felt that I had diluted the colours too much, then a glaze of the same colour at the end, when the paint had dried, would have given me the desired value.

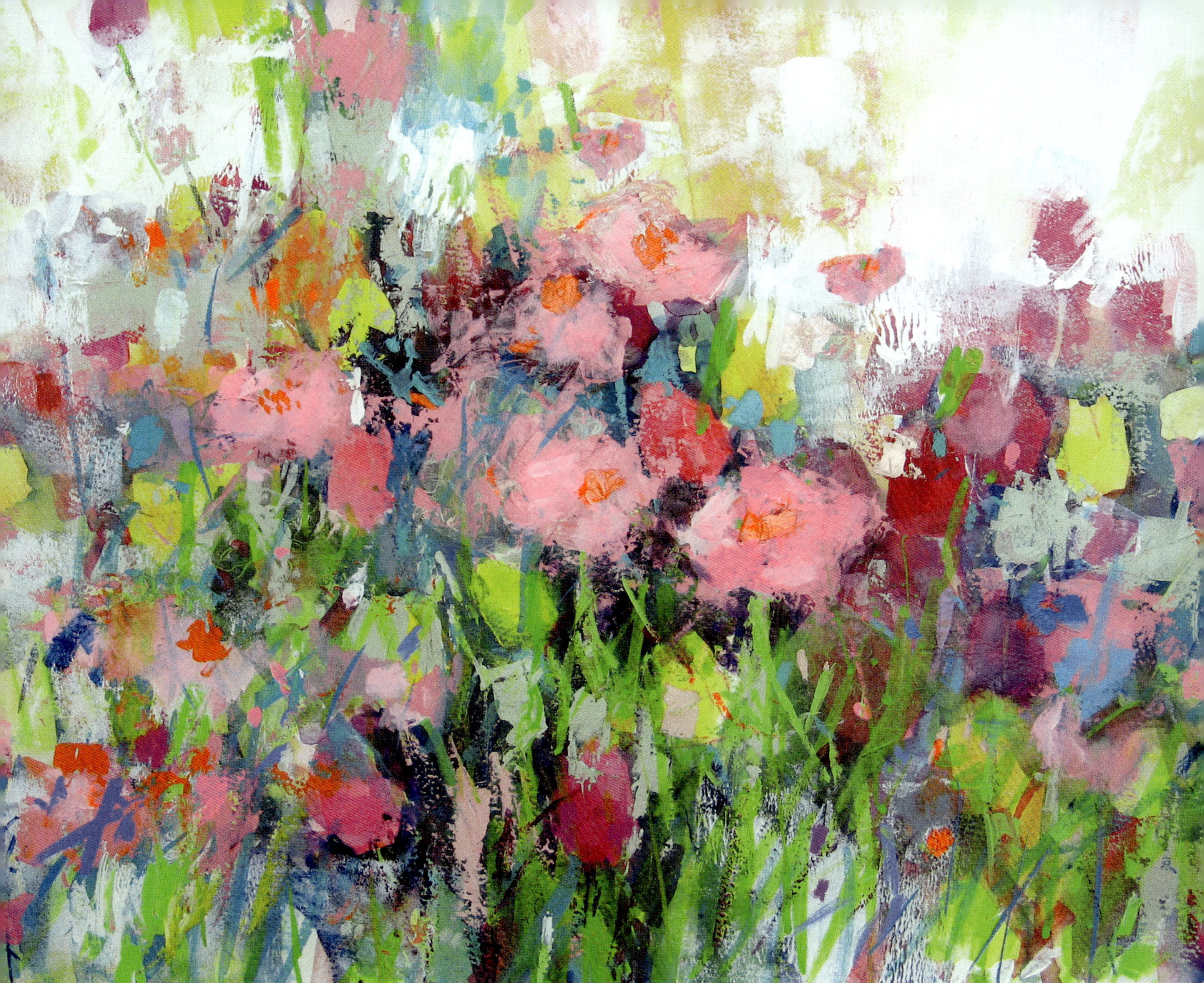

Dusty Pink Roses and Yellow Tulips

47 × 55 cm (18½ × 21½ in)

Acrylic paint on watercolour paper

For this painting, I used heavy body acrylics. Once the water evaporates from acrylic paint, it can lose up to 40 per cent viscosity; adding gel medium is a simple way of retaining the heavier consistency of the paint. Here I added some heavy gel matte medium to most of my paint mixtures to create a more impasto style of painting. However, I left some mixtures without gel so that there is some recession where the paint is thinner in consistency. I feel this creates an interesting visual tension between the two consistencies of paint.

PUMICE GELS

The pumice gel family are among my frequently used gels. There are three distinct levels of texture so you can choose the perfect one for your needs. All dry to a matte finish and are quite absorbent, so washes of colour sink into them. Like all other Golden gels they can be mixed with your paint or used as a ground to be painted over. Unlike other gels, however, pumice gel dries to a clay-like, greyish finish due to its pumice content; other gels dry either transparent and glossy or matte and translucent.

Fine pumice gel

As the name implies, this creates a fine, gritty and slightly greyish surface similar to pastel ground. It makes a great tooth for all dry painting mediums, but its absorbency means that it can also accept wet washes of ink or watercolour. I switch between this and pastel ground for priming the surface for my pastels and dry mediums. It is also a great primer for acrylic. I sometimes mix the Open acrylics with fine pumice gel to give the paints a slightly firmer consistency.

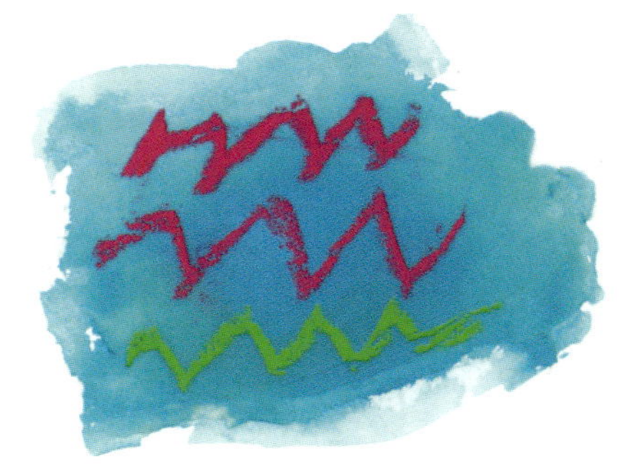

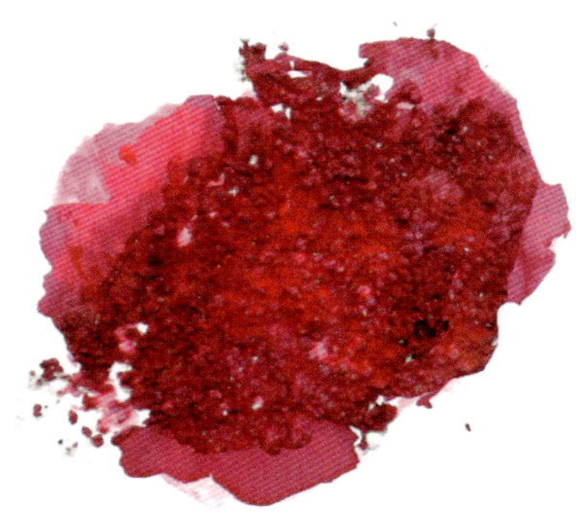

Coarse pumice gel

This has slightly larger pieces of pumice in the gel, and works well for enhancing your backgrounds or simply suggesting the texture of some flowers, such as hogweed or gypsophila.

Extra coarse pumice gel

As the name suggests, this has much larger pieces of pumice and is ideal for suggesting the texture of the centre of some flowers, such as echinacea or sunflower. It can be used wherever it may create a pleasing effect.

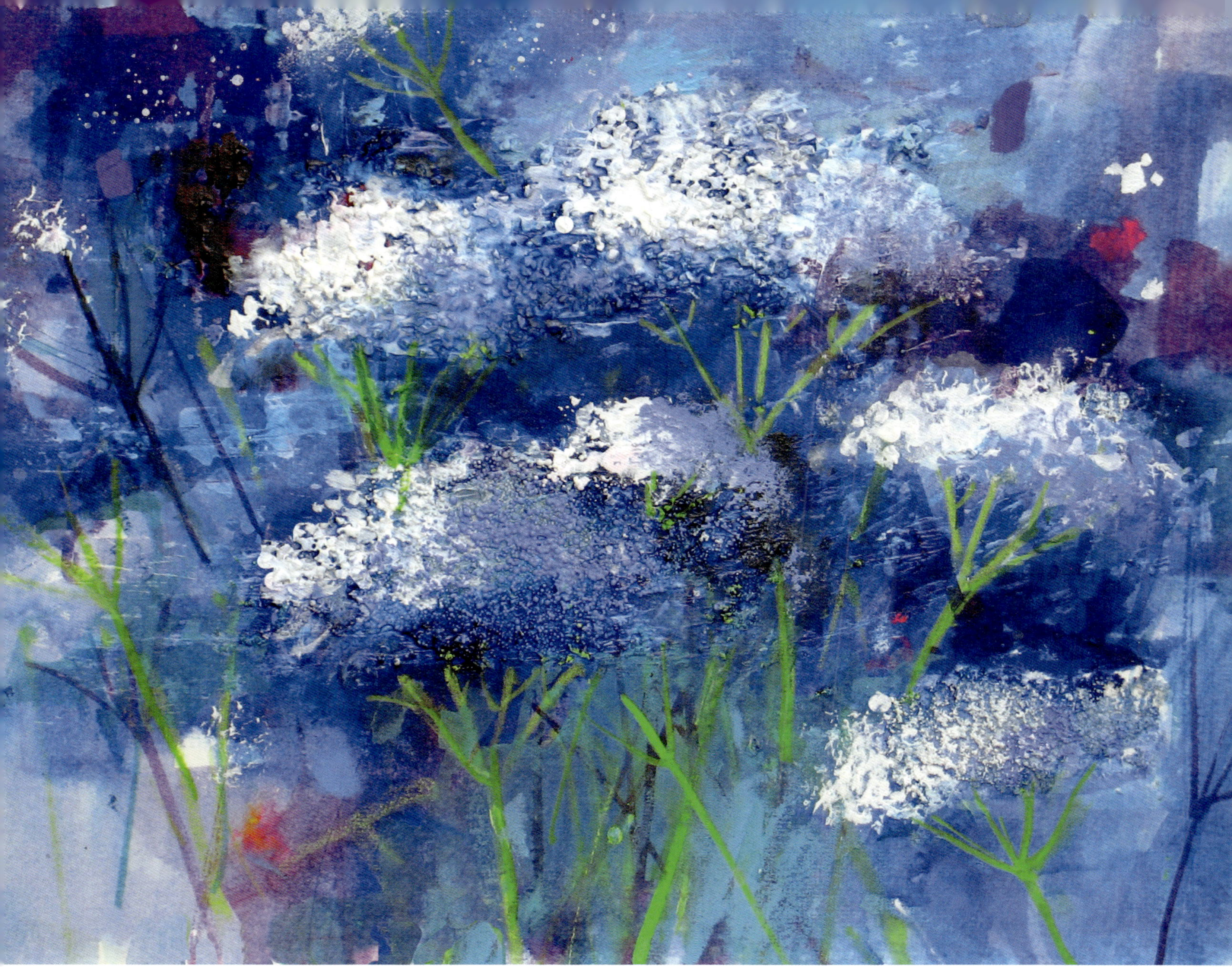

Hogweed

21 × 15 cm (8¼ × 6 in)

Acrylic ink and paint and wax crayon on mount board

I had great fun with this piece. I primed the surface with fine pumice gel to create tooth for my smooth mount board, then roughly placed the flower heads and applied both coarse and extra coarse pumice gel to the flower heads to suggest the texture of the flowers. I left the gels to dry, then applied washes of Phthalo Blue High Flow, Quinacridone Magenta and Teal. I then applied Titanium White heavy body paint to the lit side of the flower heads, leaving the blue side as shadow colour. Once the surface was dry, I used a light green wax crayon to add the stems. I think the tactile texture of the flower heads adds so much more to the expressive quality of the painting than creating this by means of brush marks alone.

CLEAR GRANULAR GEL

This gel resembles extra coarse pumice gel but is made with
granular acrylic solids. Unlike the grey, absorbent finish of pumice
gel, its translucent surface glistens through washes of colour. The
clarity of this gel doesn't alter the colour when mixed with paint. It
is another favourite gel that I frequently use in my floral paintings.

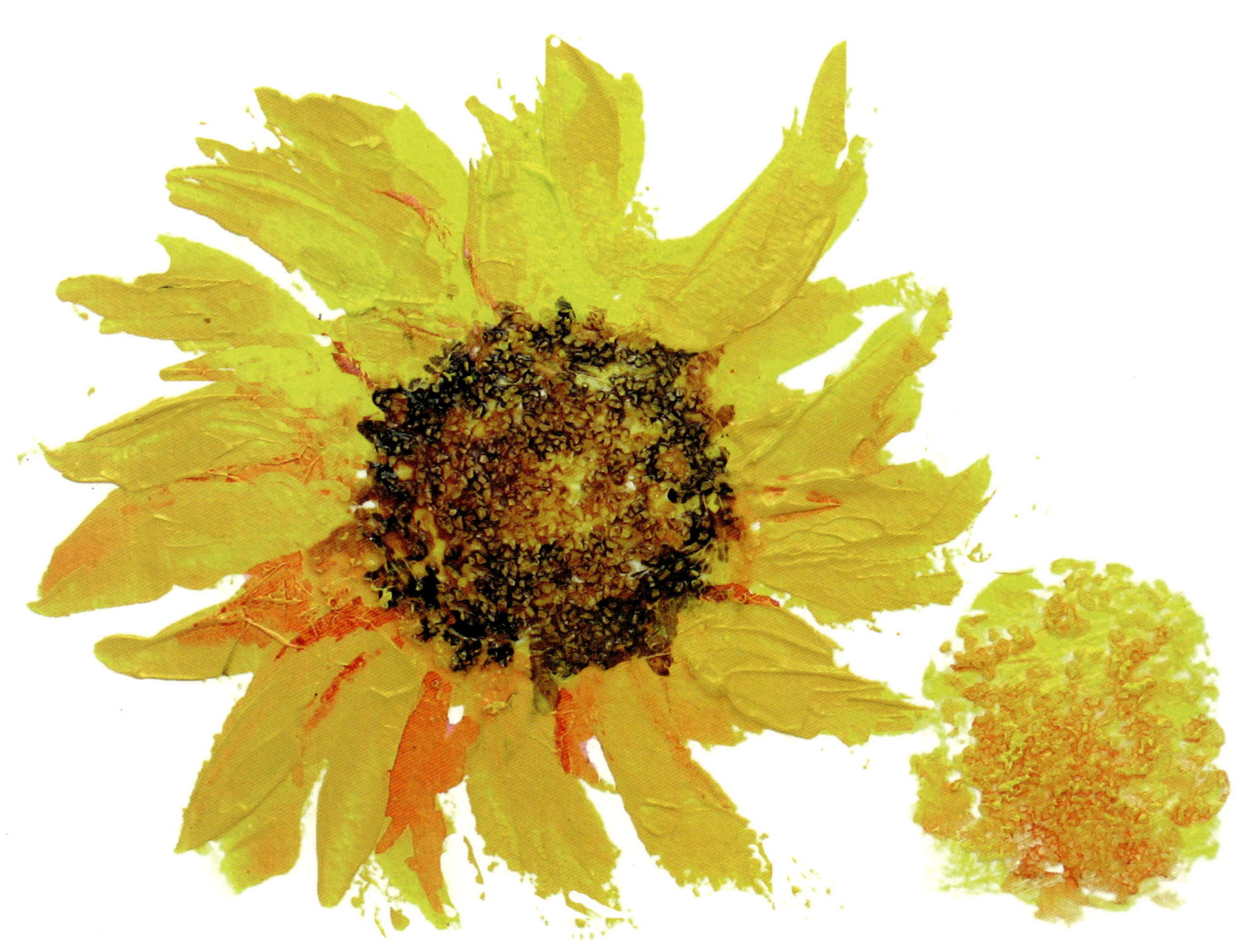

Sunflower

21 × 15 cm (8¼ × 6 in)

Acrylic paint and ink on watercolour paper

The coarse texture of clear granular gel makes it perfect for suggesting the bumpy surface of the centre of
sunflowers. I applied a wash of Transparent Red Iron Oxide High Flow and Sepia ink to build up the colours
in the centre of the flower head. The gels make the task of creating this kind of texture so much easier.

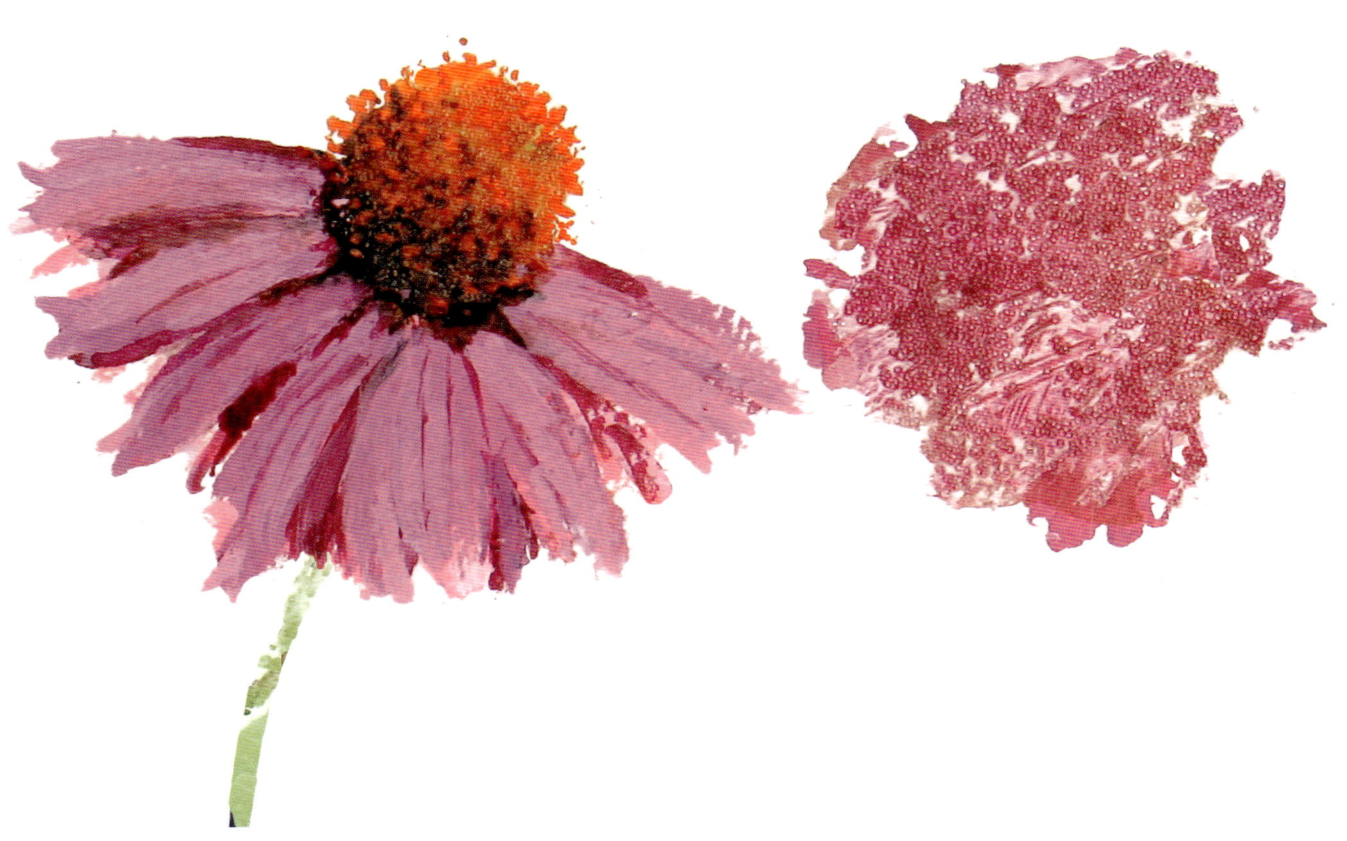

GLASS BEAD GEL

This gel contains tiny round balls of glass and dries to a beautifully clear, luminous and shiny surface – the perfect gel for enhancing floral paintings. Scraped over light areas, it creates a wonderful shimmering effect. It works really well with transparent washes of watercolour or ink and can create some fabulous effects with Golden's Iridescent and Interference colours (see pages 108–109).

Pink Echinacea

21 × 15 cm (8¼ × 6 in)

Acrylic paint and ink on watercolour paper
Glass bead gel with small, shiny balls of glass is the ideal gel for suggesting the texture of the centre of flowers such as daisies or echinacea. In this painting I applied washes of Flame Orange FW ink to the centre. Once those had dried I painted the base of the centre with Sepia ink and then added Sepia in between some of the orange texture to give the centre some substance. To enhance the centre even further I applied a small amount of Pyrrole Orange to the end of some of the glass balls. I think this is a very effective way of implying the flamboyant centre of echinacea flowers.

CLEAR TAR GEL

This gel has a runny consistency and a long rheology, which means it can be drizzled a bit like honey. The best way to apply it is with a palette knife. In time you will learn to gain some control of the stringy patterns that run off your knife, but part of the charm of this gel is its unpredictable nature and the random way it lands on your support, creating unique linear formations. The gel has a self-levelling quality, so if you pour it straight out of a jar onto a plastic sheet and let it dry, you can create some interesting acrylic skins for collage. Tar gel dries to a clear glossy finish, so it will resist a transparent colour wash over it with some lovely passages in the painting. You can add a few drops of ink or Fluid colours to the tar gel for some colourful applications, but try not to overload it or it will lose the stringy quality.

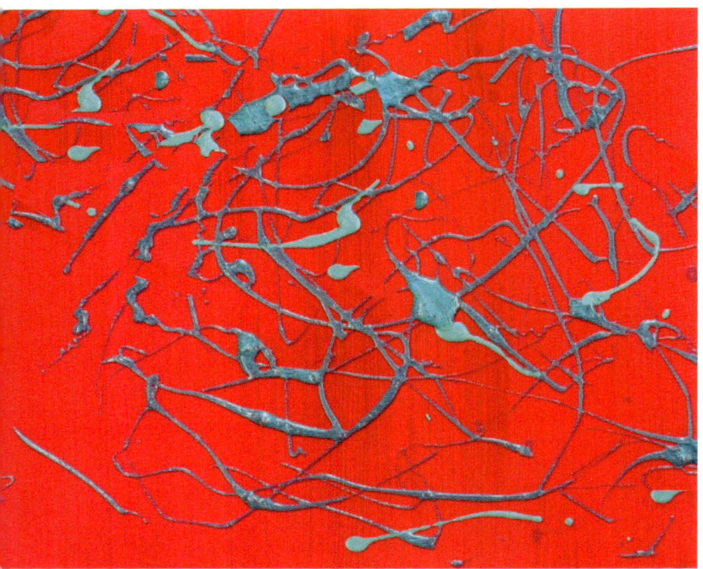

Coloured tar gel drizzle

In this sample I added a couple of drops of Teal ink to my tar gel and drizzled it over a Cadmium Red Light background. The two colours dazzle next to one another.

Clear tar gel patterns

Here I used clear tar gel without colour and let it dry before applying simple washes of Magenta and Teal. You can see the gel resists the washes and makes the most wonderful random patterns. With some imagination, you can use this funky gel to make some interesting passages in your paintings.

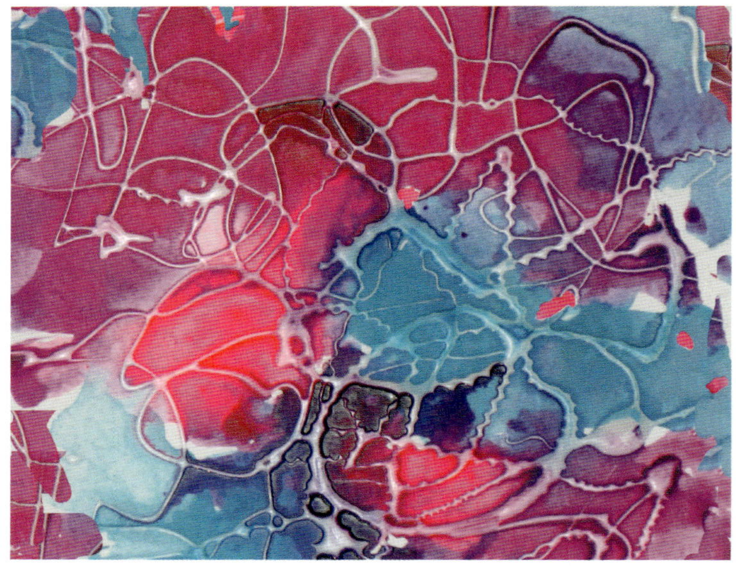

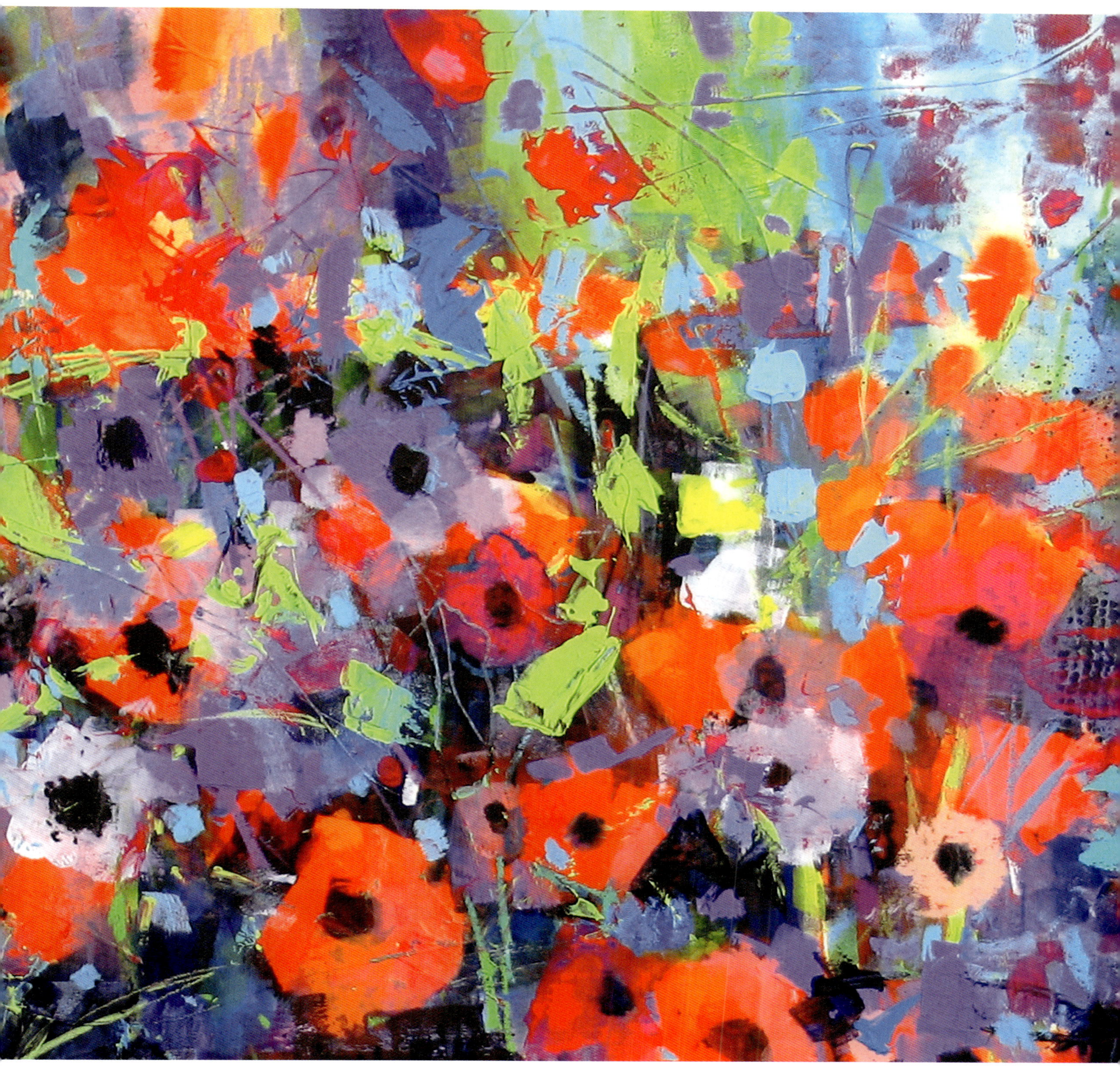

ACRYLIC PASTES

When I need to make an opaque and absorbent texture I use Golden pastes rather than the gels. Washes of ink and watercolour sink into the absorbent surface of the pastes while they tend to run off the lustrous surface of the gloss, semi-gloss and matte gels. The pastes contain marble dust, clay, or other similar fillers, which means they dry to a hard, absorbent, opaque and off-white surface. They can all be mixed with paint or made into a particular texture before painting and used as a ground to be painted on. You can either choose to create a textured ground or use them to smooth out a textured surface by filling in the grooves. Examples of these pastes include a variety of molding pastes, fiber paste and crackle paste, each with their own unique and useful formulation for a broad range of creative applications. In my own art practice the gels and pastes are indispensable and I make use of them in a way that is unique to my individual needs and process.

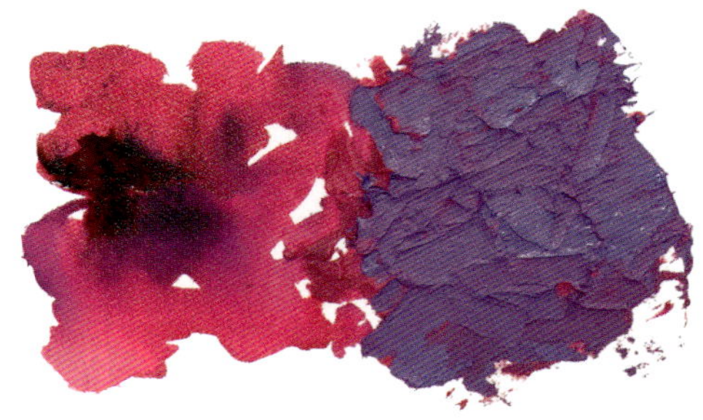

This sample shows a wash of colour on a base of light molding paste on the left and heavy body paint mixed with the paste on the right.

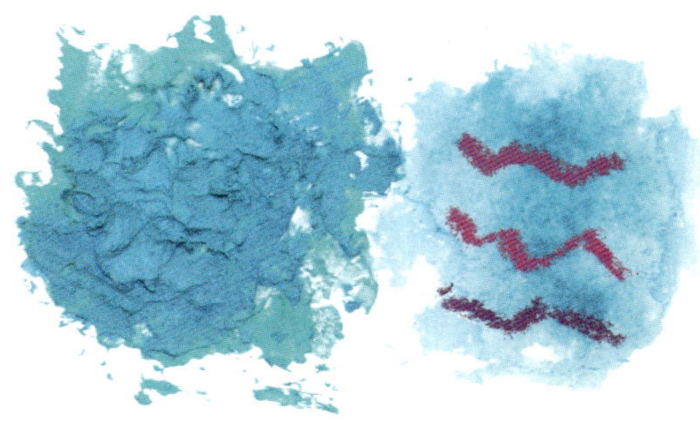

The sample shows the paste mixed with a few drops of Fluid colour and a thin base of coarse molding paste on the right, which makes a great base for applying dry mediums as well as wet washes of colour.

Molding paste

This has the same consistency and flexibility as heavy gel (see pages 90–91) but dries white. It makes a lovely surface to paint on and I particularly like it for the extra time it allows for me to lift colour, especially when working with Open and quick-drying acrylics. Note that all molding pastes will change the colour into a lighter tone when mixed with the paint.

Light molding paste

If you need an opaque, light and absorbent surface that is receptive to both watercolour and ink washes, as well as heavier paint and dry media such as pastels, then light molding paste is a good choice. The light weight of this paste is great for heavily textured large canvases as it doesn't make the artwork too heavy and bulky.

Coarse molding paste

This paste creates a fine, sandpaper-like surface that is receptive to both wet washes and dry mediums. It dries to a warm off-white colour and can remain translucent if applied up to 3mm (1/8in) thickness. I love mixing it with paint when I need thicker viscosity and brush marks that hold the peak. The sheen is matte to satin.

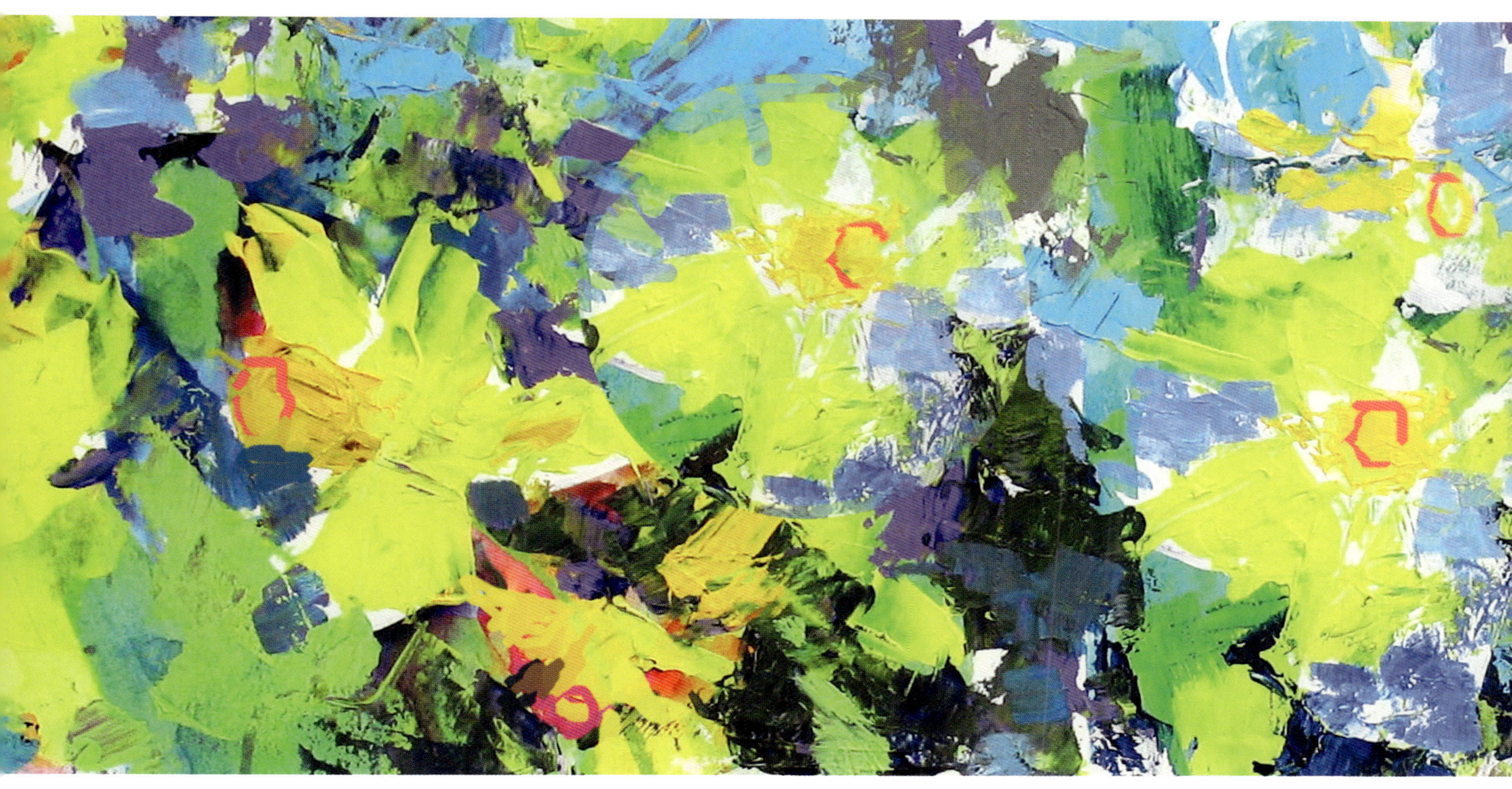

Hard molding paste

A paste that can be sanded down to create an ultra-smooth, glass-like finish, or manipulated into a heavily textured surface, this dries into an extremely durable hard and opaque surface. You can carve into this gel, embed objects for extra texture or make imprints with stencils. Like all other gels and pastes it can be mixed with the paint to create a heavier viscosity.

Daffodils
20 × 36 cm (8 × 14 in)
Acrylic paint on watercolour paper
For this painting I created a heavily textured ground with hard molding paste and almost sculpted the flower heads. I also added some molding paste to the paint. The result is an impasto style of painting without using copious amounts of expensive paint. I love the sculptural quality that adding these pastes gives the paint. When added to Open acrylics they cut down the drying time, and also reduce the creaminess of the paints, giving them a more buttery texture.

FIBER PASTE

Golden's Fiber Paste is yet another unique paste. It contains mineral fibres and can turn a piece of card into a superbly receptive surface for ink and watercolour washes. The surface resembles that of handmade watercolour paper. You have a choice of making a fine surface by applying the paste with a wet palette knife and skimming over the top for a thin, even layer, or applying it more thickly and roughly. It can also be applied randomly to texturize canvas or paper, or even mixed with your paint. To make pieces of collage, you can spread a layer of fiber paste on a plastic sheet using a spatula, peel off the fiber-paste 'skin' once it has dried, then paint it to create your own unique collage material.

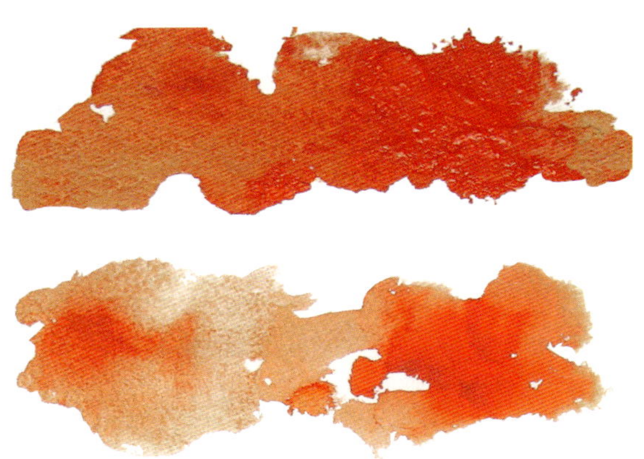

Fiber paste sample

In the top sample, I used the paste quite thickly, straight from the pot, with a palette knife. The result is similar to Rough surface handmade watercolour paper. In the lower sample, I applied the paste with a wet spatula and dragged it to make a thin layer. This creates a smoother surface to work on.

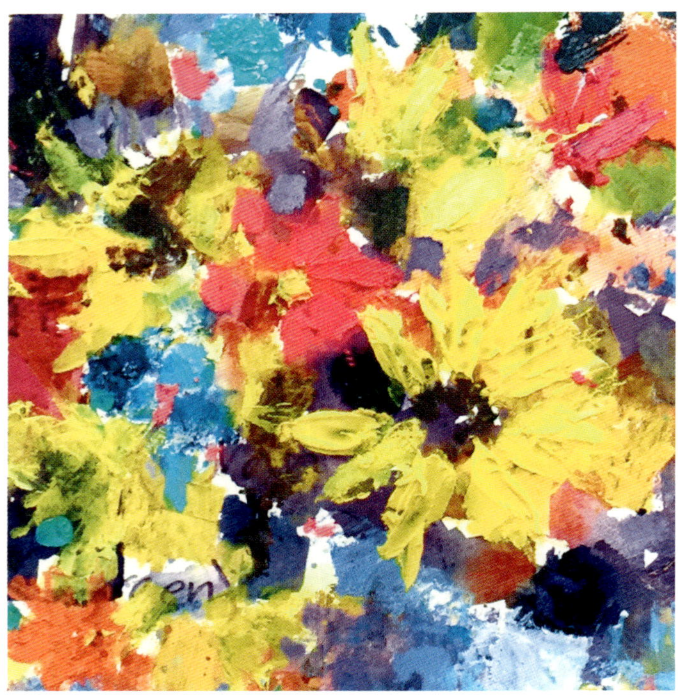

Summer Bouquet (detail)

This corner of the painting shows the texture that the fiber paste has given the smooth hot-pressed paper. You can even turn smooth card into a lovely receptive surface for water-based mediums with this wonderful paste. This image was taken halfway through the painting and further layers were added after this stage.

(Opposite page) **Summer Bouquet**
56 × 34 cm (22 × 13½ in)
Acrylic paint on paper
I prepared my base with thick and thin applications of fiber paste and then added light molding paste to my yellows, coarse molding paste to the purples and molding paste to the magenta. In close-up the difference in the type of texture applied to the flowers and the base gives this semi-abstract painting an energized feeling.

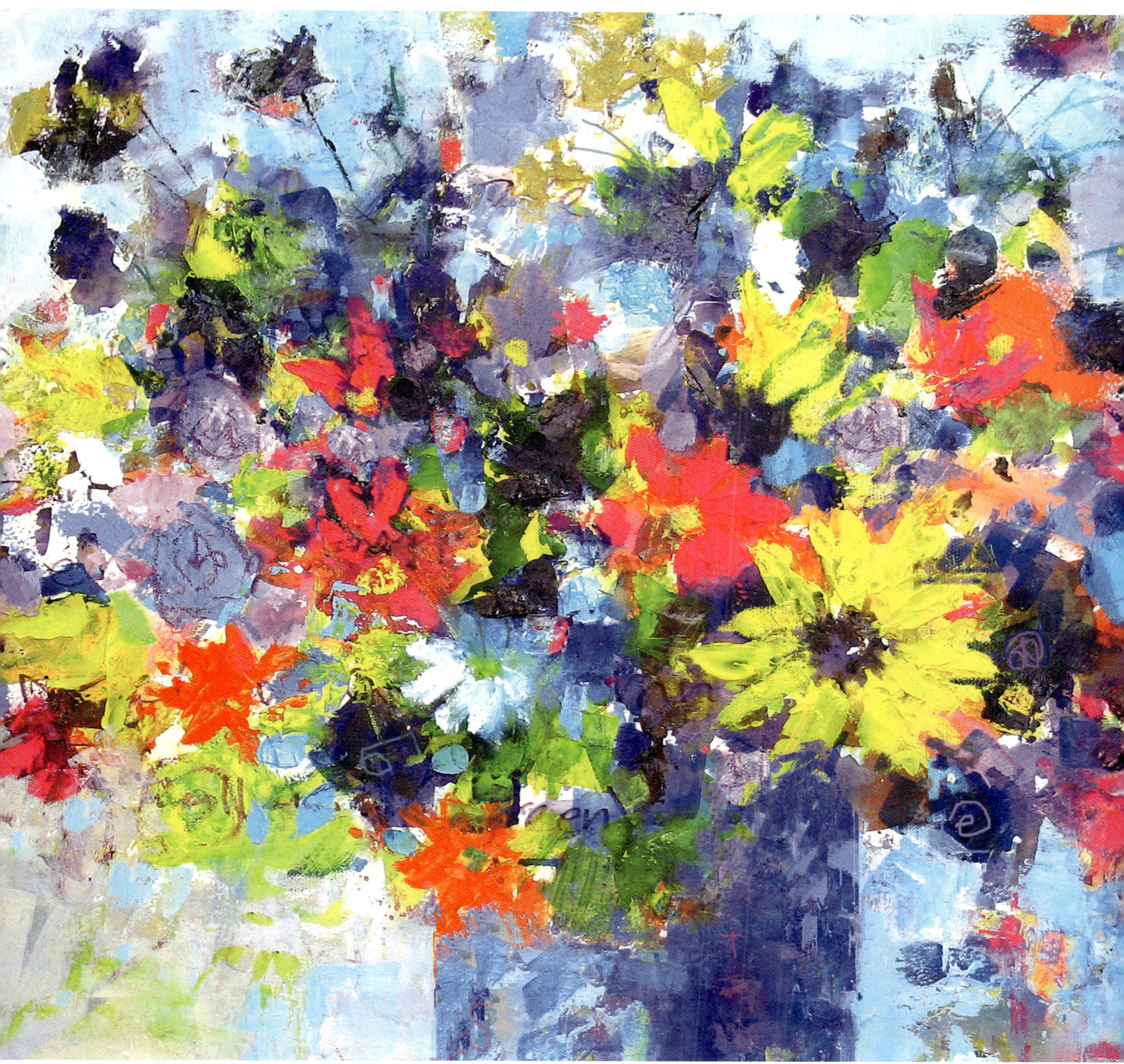

CRACKLE PASTE

Another unusual and quirky gel from the Golden texture-making repertoire, crackle paste is white in colour and has a light, fluffy consistency. As it dries it creates the most wonderful mosaic-like patterns. You need to be patient when using it as it needs to dry to develop the crackles. I have a lot of fun with it but find that it can be rather unpredictable in my hands; the shape and size of the crackles depends on the thickness of the application as well as environmental factors such as temperature, humidity and air flow. Crackle paste can be painted over with washes of colour or even individually painted to resemble mosaic. With some imagination you can use this gel to represent a certain texture or to make abstract areas within the background of your floral paintings.

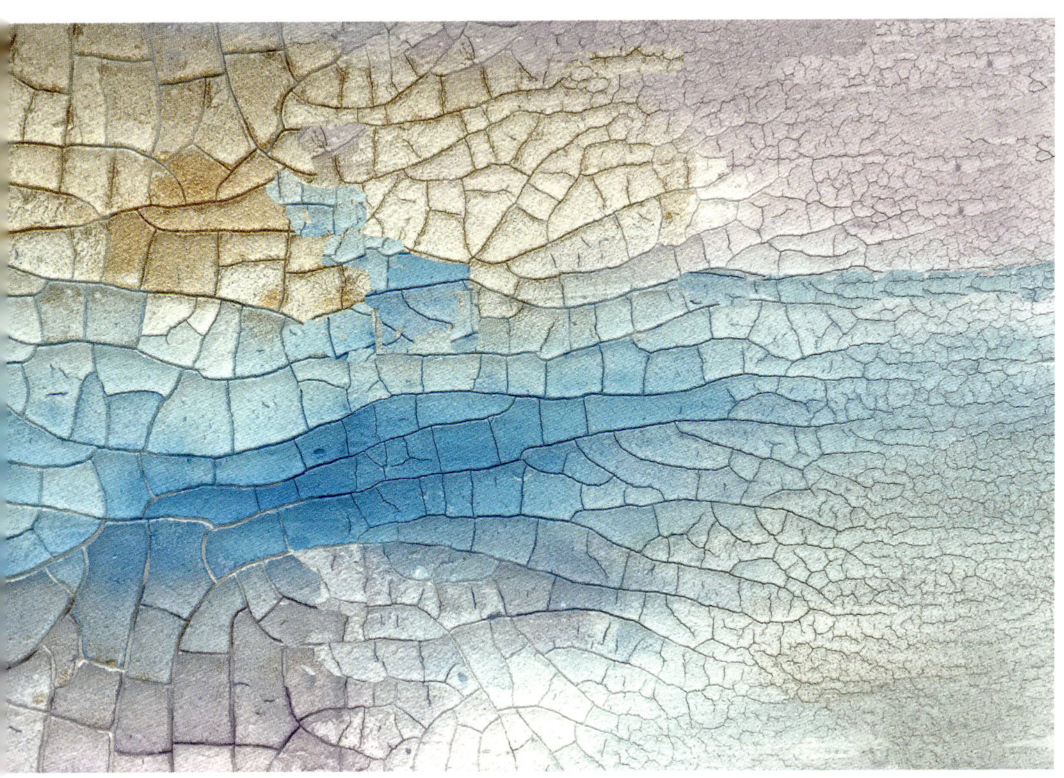

Sample of crackle paste

I was very pleased by how this small sample of crackle paste turned out, showing the wonderful random patterns that can be achieved with it. The thicker gel on the left-hand side has created larger shapes as opposed to the tiny patterns on the right where the gel has been merely scraped over the surface.

(Opposite page) **Gypsophila Bunch in Crazed Porcelain Jug**

46 × 37 cm (18 × 14½ in)

Acrylic paint and ink on mount board
Crackle paste provided the perfect texture for painting my crazed porcelain pot in this still life of a bunch of gypsophila. I used a piece of mount board as I find that crackle paste responds well to a rigid surface, making lovely patterns. I then applied a wash of Nickle Azo Gold High Flow ink as a first layer mostly over the pot and a small amount over the area of the flowers. This was followed by washes of Phthalo Blue and Dioxazine Purple High Flow inks to stain the board and parts of the pot before going in with heavy body Phthalo Blue, Dioxazine Purple and Titanium White to paint the mass of flowers. I added some gel to the heavy body paint to extend and thicken the paint, which meant I could then use the sgraffito technique to scratch out a few of the stems. I painted some of the stems with Light Green acrylic ink and used Titanium White heavy body paint for the light-filled flower heads.

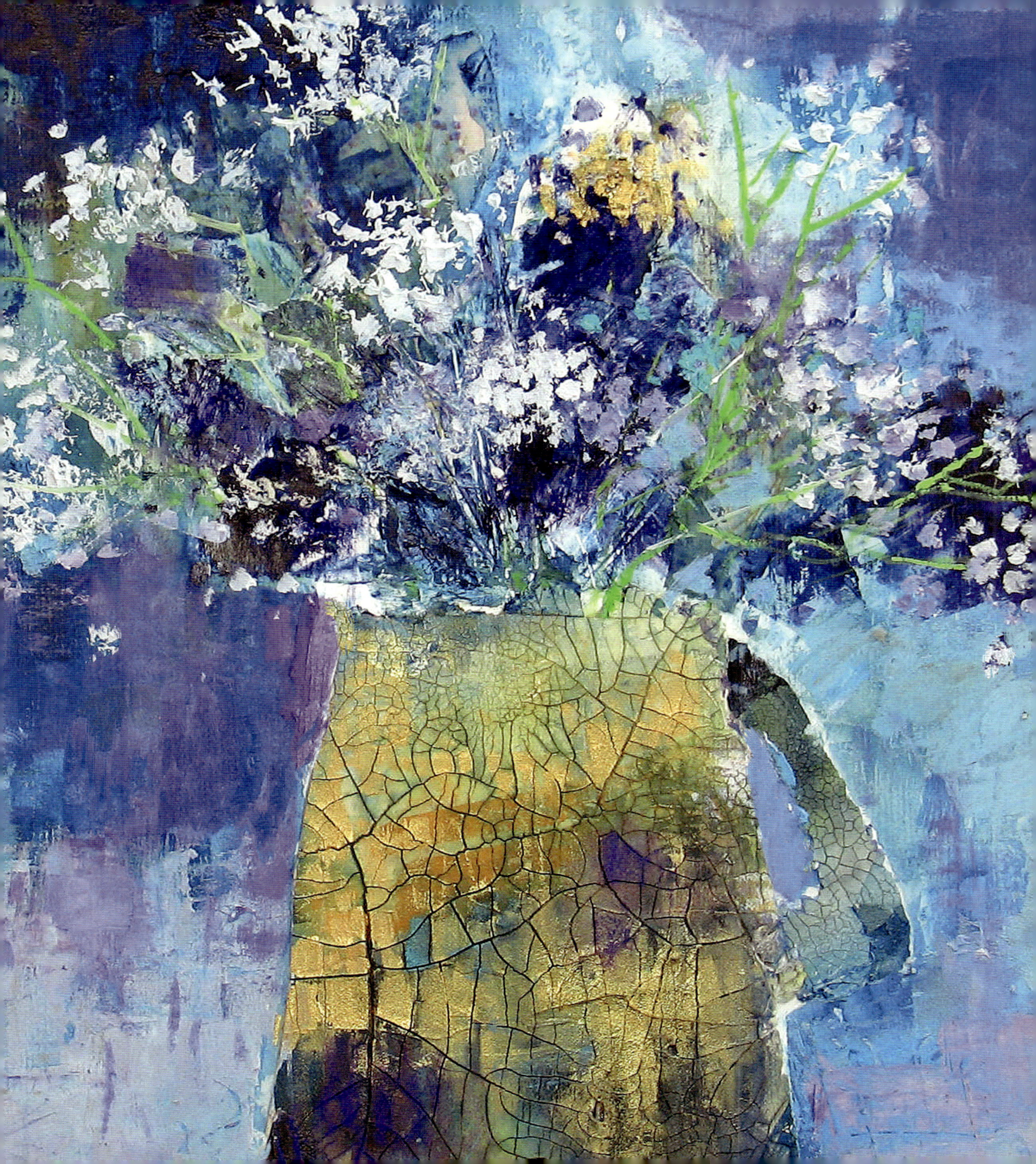

COLLAGE

Including collage in your painting is another creative way of introducing a tactile quality. In fact, a work can be made purely from collage where even the tonal values are applied by cutting small printed text and coloured passages from magazines, for example. In the context of this book, however, collage is added to create another layer of texture which would be more difficult or even impossible to achieve with paint and texture materials. Adding collage in the early stages of a painting is a great ice-breaker, eliminating the white of the support which some artists find rather daunting. My own favourite process is the interaction of collage material with inks and other water-based mediums. This stage often produces some unpredictable and intriguing passages that can be manipulated, either to imply a recognizable element of the subject, or create some abstract passages within the background to connect the shapes. Collage can be added at any stage of a painting and you should follow what works for you. However, while you can always add, be warned that taking away an unwanted piece of collage can be quite difficult or even impossible and can compromise an otherwise successful image.

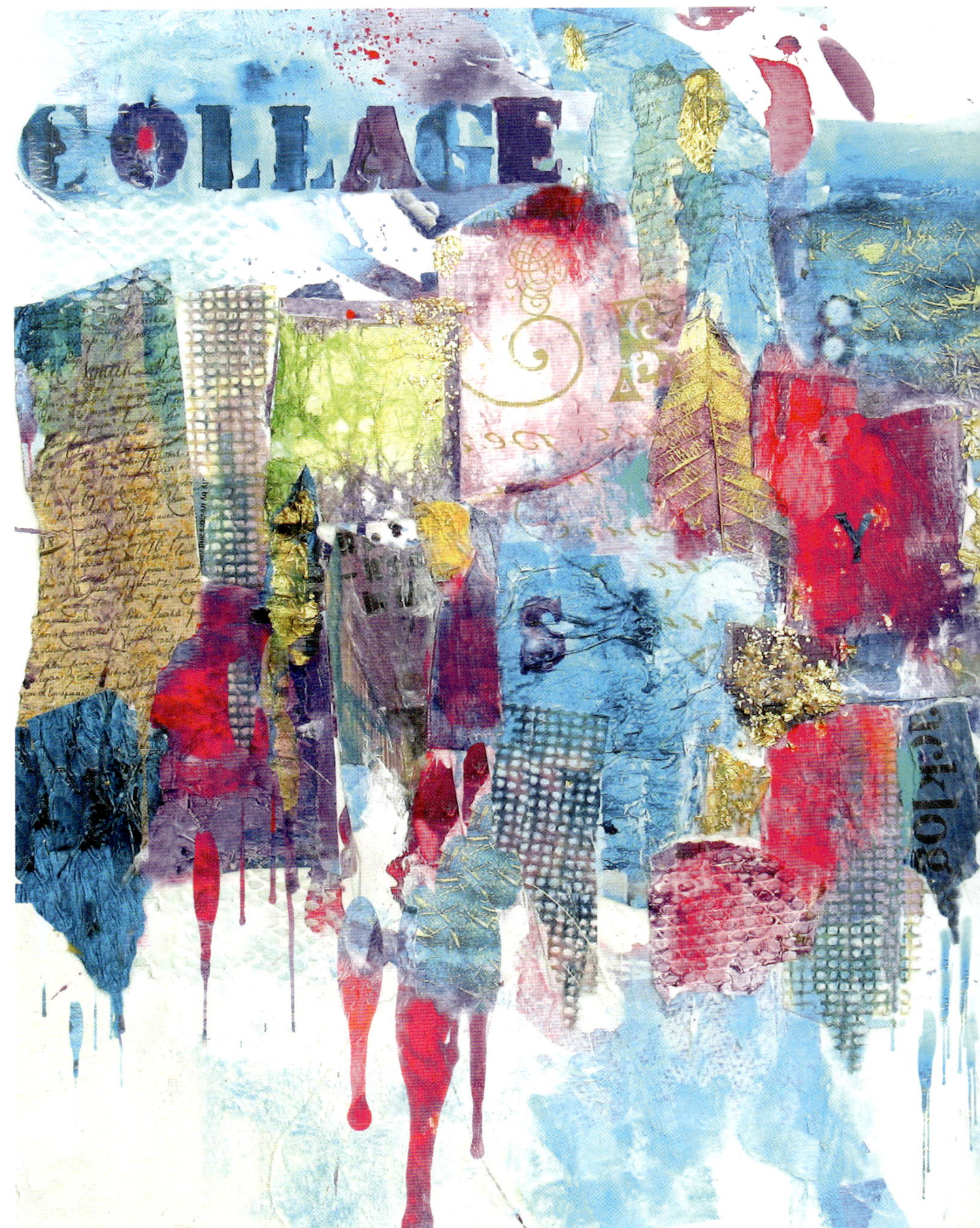

A selection of collage materials.

Collage materials

Found objects and materials, exotic handmade papers, printed texts and even humble newsprint and tissue paper can all be used as collage; tissue papers are often coloured with natural dyes and will fade in time, but I always make sure that all tissue paper is covered with artist's grade lightfast inks, and later on varnished for extra protection. It is very satisfying to give something as wasteful as junk mail a new and creative lease of life by including it in your painting. This is another opportunity to express your individuality by the materials you choose or the way you apply them; you should aim for a good balance between collage pieces and paint in much the same way as you decide on your other elements of design. Whatever you do, be selective, for collage can be an incredibly effective addition when it is in the right place and a total eyesore in the wrong area of the painting. Unfortunately, the unpleasant shapes in our paintings often get the most attention, so choose carefully and remember it is easier to add than to eliminate.

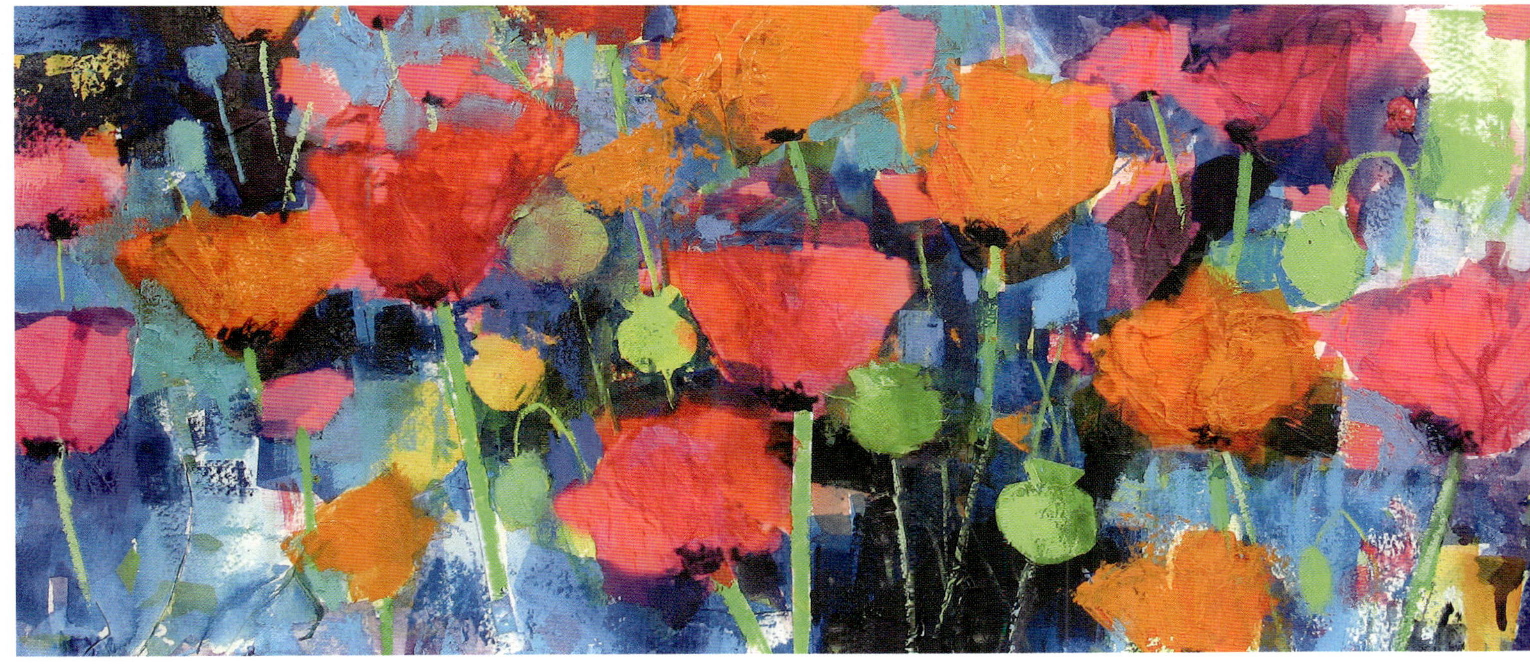

Poppy Fusion
54 × 28 cm (21¼ × 11 in)
Acrylic paint, pastel and collage on paper
I used a variety of coloured tissue papers to create my composition, followed by washes of inks to reinforce the colours. Once the inks dried I stood back to assess the shapes and then manipulated them to create my composition using heavy body paint and oil and soft pastels. Extra collage can be added at any time to add texture, change, enhance or even eliminate a part of the painting.

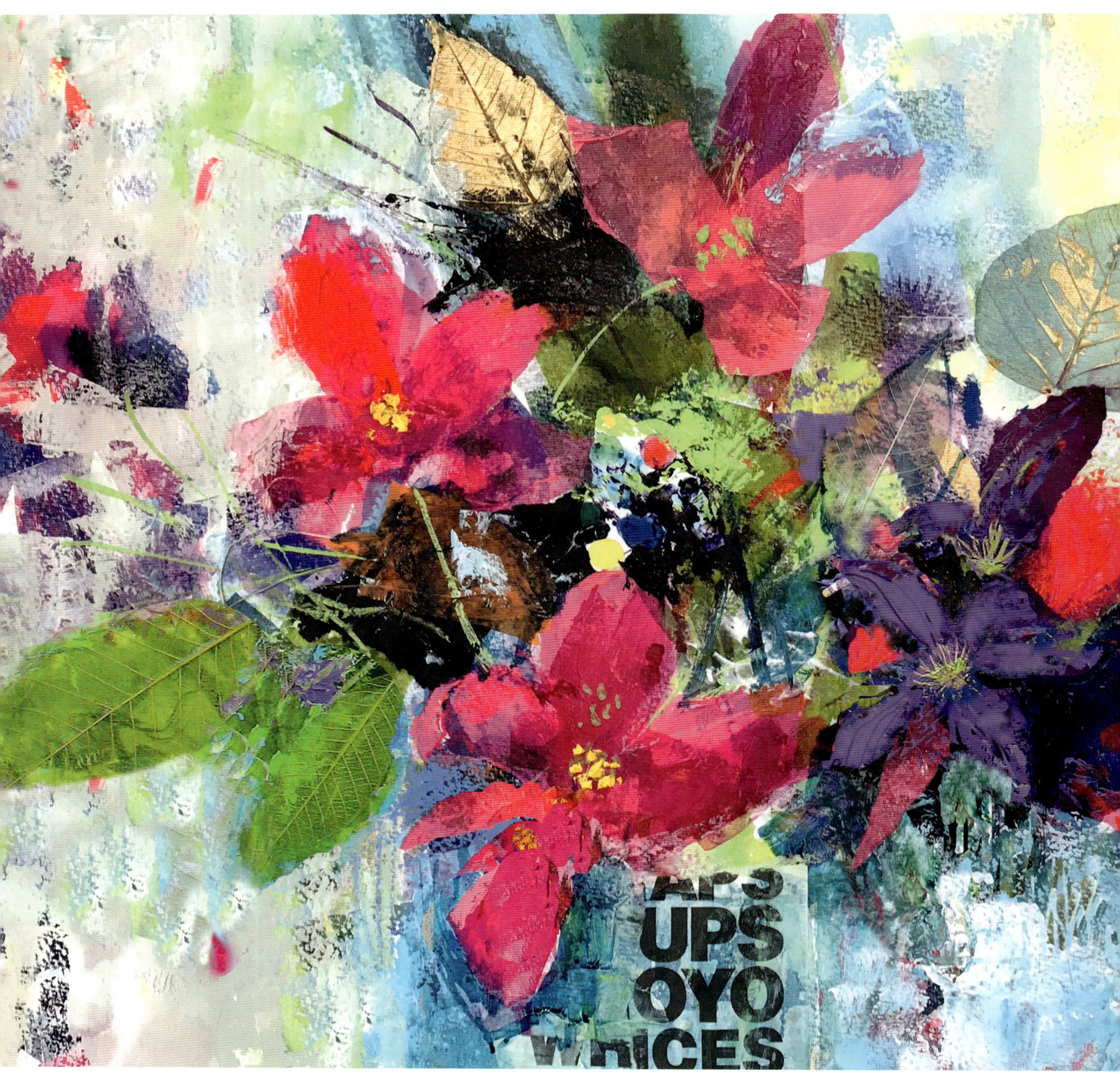
UPS
OYO
WhICES

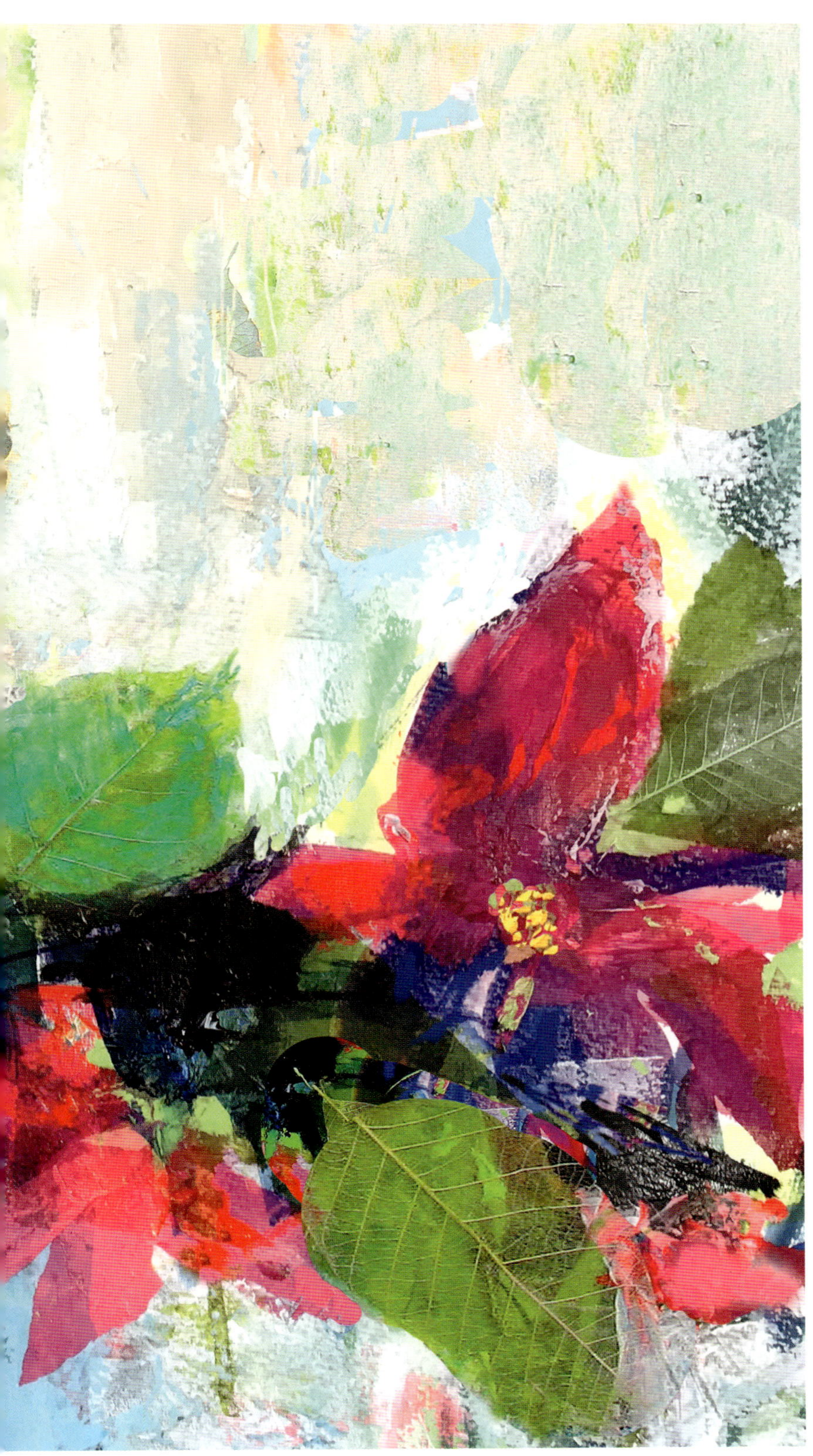

Pink and Purple Blooms

68 × 41 cm (26¾ × 16 in)

Ink and collage on paper

I started this painting initially with random washes of Quinacridone Magenta, Dioxazine Purple, and Green Gold High Flow inks to eliminate the white of the paper and establish some colour. I then added pink tissue to texturize the pink blooms and used the same process for the purple flowers. I placed black tissue paper in the negative spaces to create depth of tone and then added some delicate green hand made paper around the flowers to start creating some of the foliage. I also added some skeleton leaves. I love the shapes of letters, so I chose some printed text to cover the vase, which brings in another element. I then started to shape the flowers by going into their negative spaces while trying to keep some elements of abstraction as well. I added more skeleton leaves as the painting progressed as I felt they could contribute something. I let a painting such as this build up over a few days, allowing the layers to dry in stages if I am not in a rush to finish it. This way I can really see the nuances of colour appear as the paint dries and interacts with the collage. I even take some photographs in between and look at the painting on the screen to assess progress.

INTERFERENCE AND IRIDESCENT COLOURS

Golden's Interference colours have the unique ability to flip between their actual colour and its complement. This effect is more pronounced when the colour is used over a very dark surface and more subtle over white or light supports.

Iridescent colours such as Gold, Silver, Copper, Bronze, Stainless Steel and Mica Flakes can add an extra bit of magic and sparkle. These unusual colours can be used on their own or mixed with other colours to produce a beautiful range of hues. I tend to include them in more abstract pieces and love their shimmering effects and their power to invigorate an otherwise potentially dull painting.

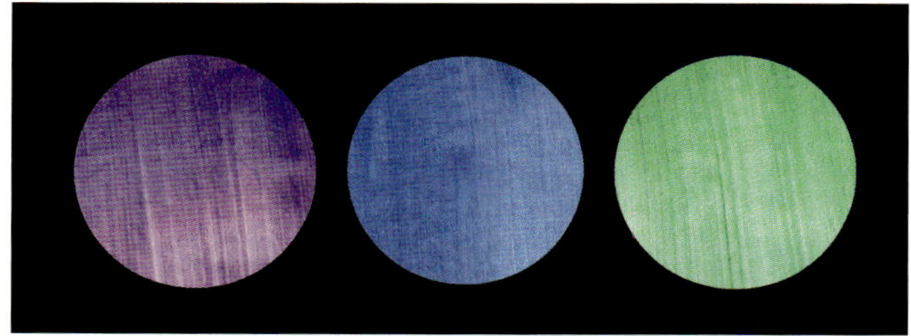

Interference colour range

The Interference colour range is available in both heavy body acrylics and in Fluid colours.

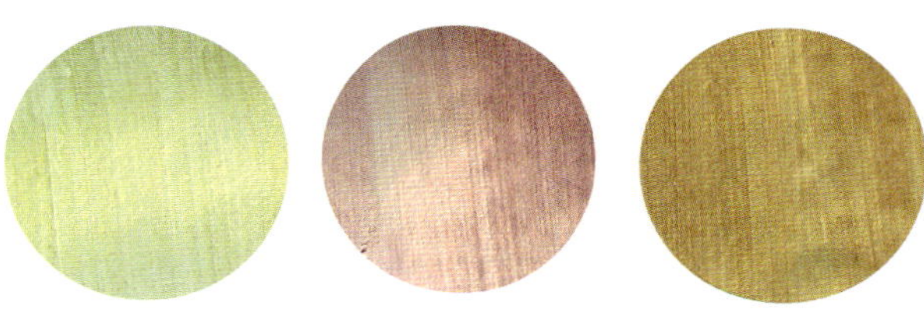

Iridescent colour range

The Iridescent range in Golden colours is very extensive: you can choose from Bright Gold, Deep Gold, Copper, Bronze and many more.

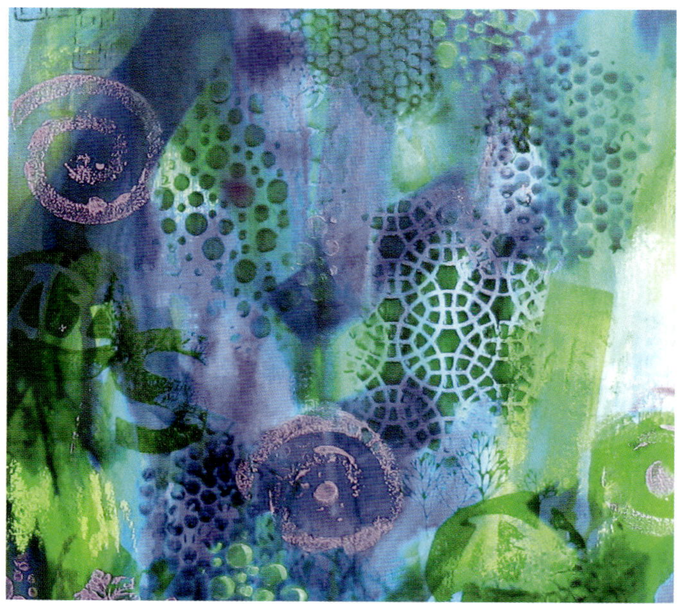

Connective passages with stencils and stamps

Using Interference or metallic Iridescent colours, stamps and stencils are just some of the ways to jazz up the background of semi-abstract floral paintings. These shapes add interest to the connective passages and bring a more exotic element to the image. Home-made stencils are ideal for adding an extra individual touch to your painting, but there are numerous interesting ready-made designs to enjoy. While they are not innovative, I still like the patterns made with sequin relief, bubble wrap, lace and other simple materials.

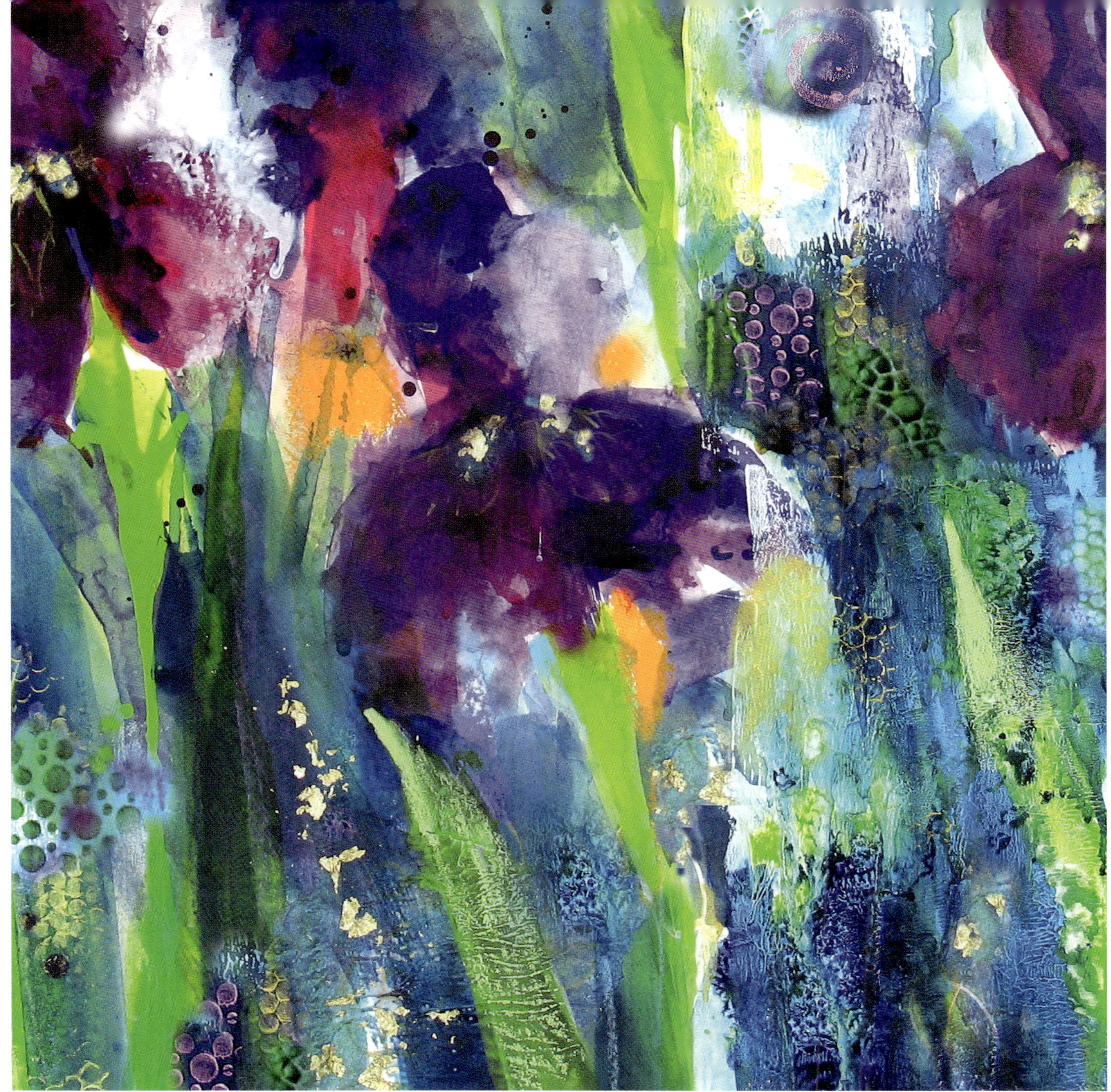

Irises

36 × 36 cm (14 ×14 in)

Acrylic paint and collage on paper

Stamps and stencils can enhance and revitalize a painting that is becoming slightly dull in the background.
Adding some gorgeous patterns with sequin relief and stencils as well as Interference Violet on the irises
and Interference Green over the foliage, plus a few dabs of the exquisite Bright Gold Iridescent heavy body
paint, enlivened this image of irises.

EXPLORE FURTHER

Flowers provide an unlimited source of inspiration, and given the many ways they can be depicted using the creative possibilities of mixed media you should never run out of fresh ideas to explore. The life force of flowers and plants animates the subject and brings colour and vitality to any painting they are included in. In this chapter we shall be exploring flowers within a landscape, woodland, seascape and meadow, as well as a couple of flower markets in an urban setting to expand your horizons further.

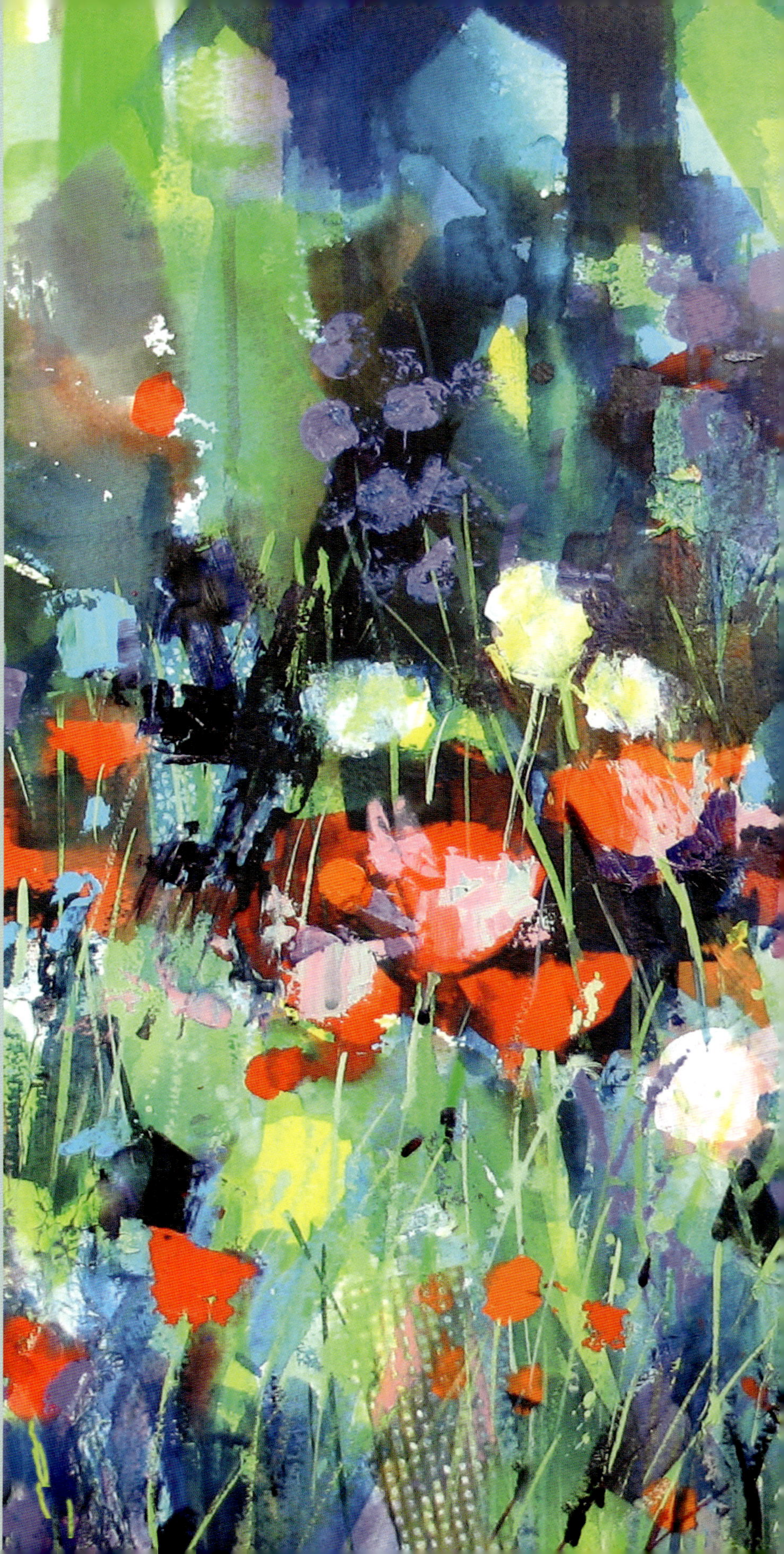

Urban Summer Hedgerow
73 × 48 cm (29 × 19 in)
Mixed media on watercolour paper

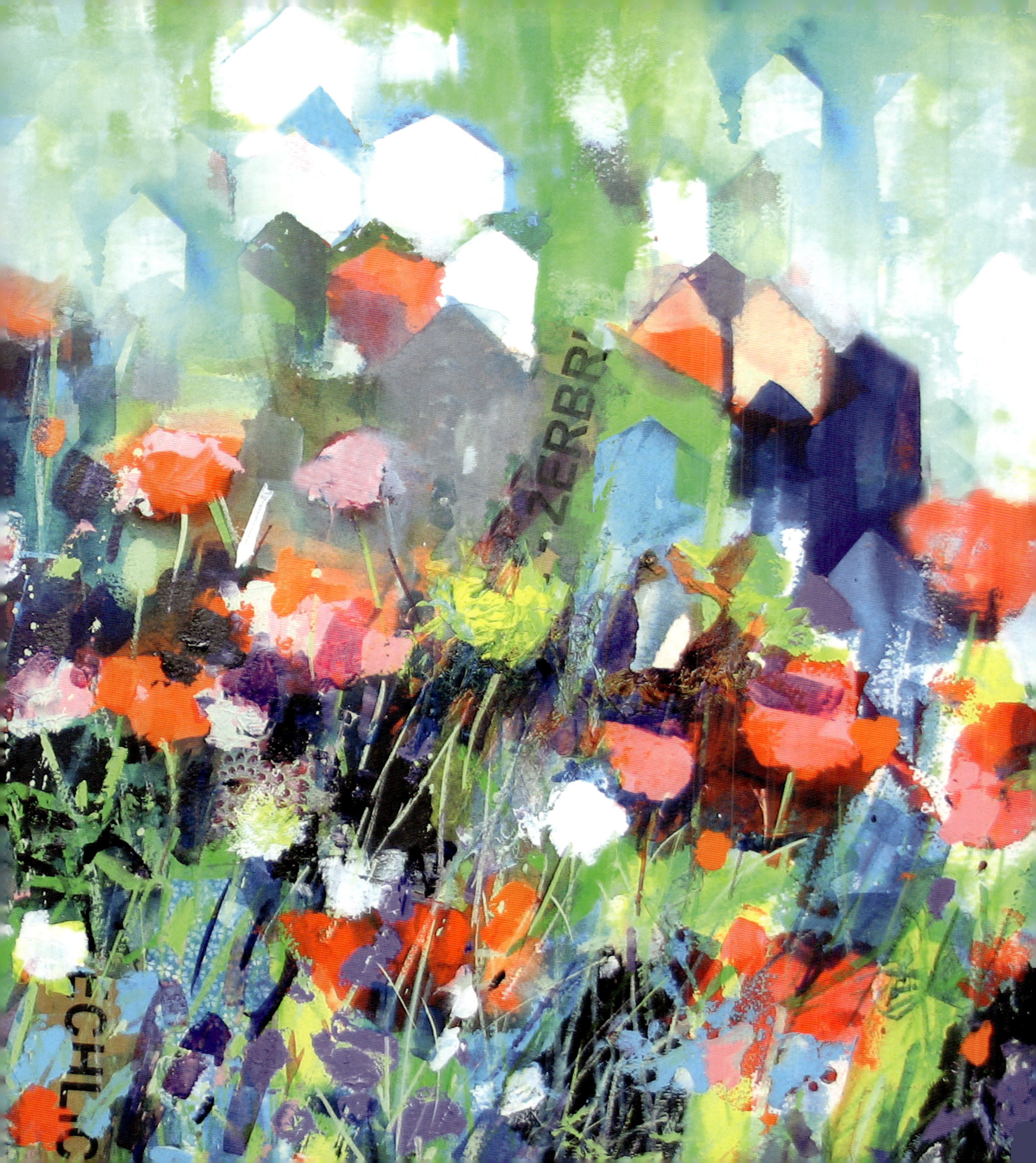

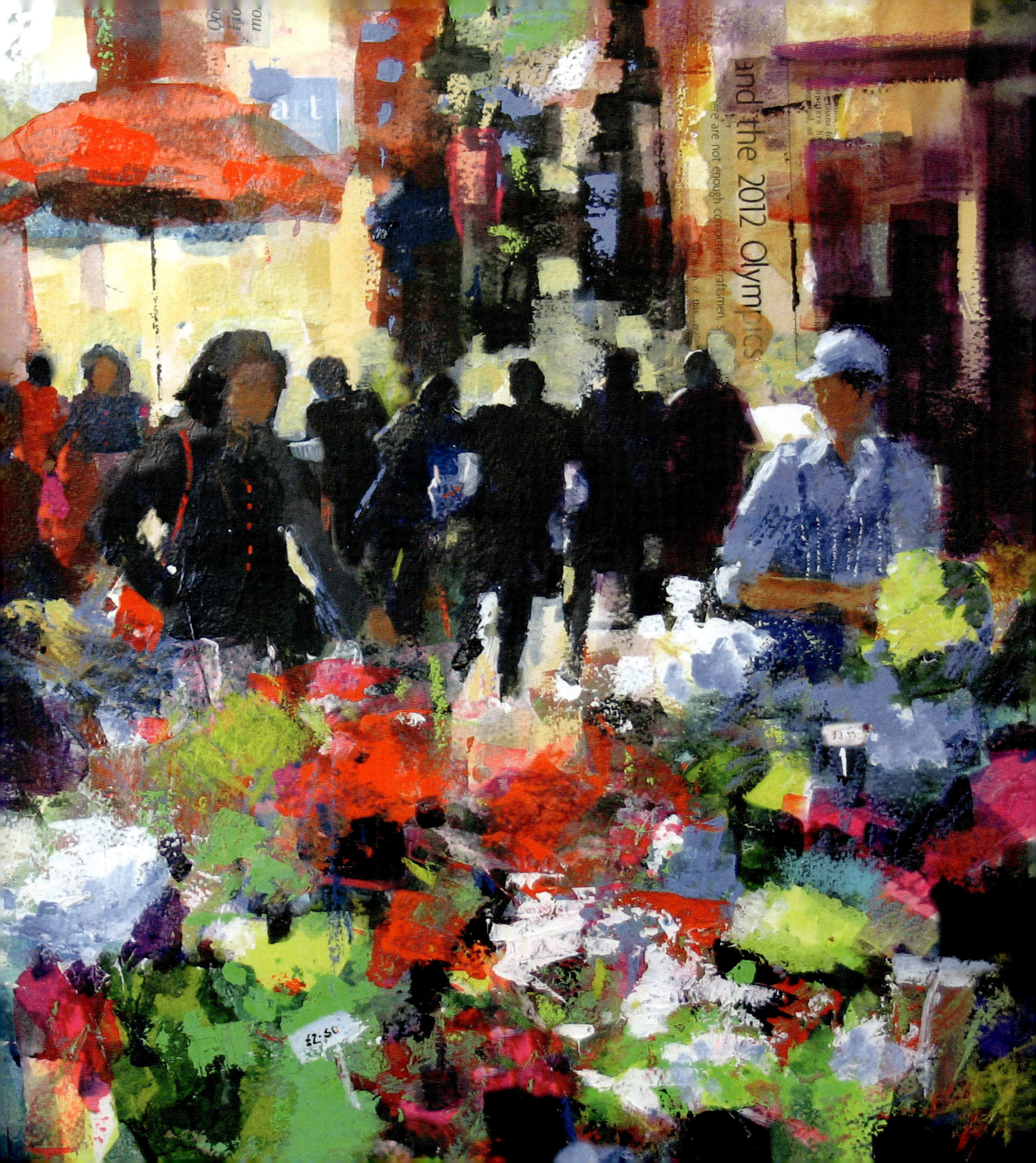
at
and the 2012 Olympics
£2.50

Busy Flower Stall
46 × 16 cm (18 × 6½ in)
Mixed media on mount board
This is an example of cropping a bigger
painting that became rather boring and
had areas that were not contributing
anything significant. I like this little corner
and the narrative of the conversation
between the punters and the flower seller.
The abstracted flowers in the foreground
are an uplifting addition.

(Opposite page) **City Centre Flower Market**
46 × 37 cm (18 × 14½ in)
Mixed media on watercolour paper
Urban landscapes are among my favourite
subjects and flower markets within the urban
scene bring the extra touch of colour that enriches
the subject further. In this painting, I used a fair
amount of collage to begin with, especially over
the abstracted mass of flowers which represents
the chaos of the flower stall without much detail.
Up close, the tactile surface of the painting also
helps its liveliness.

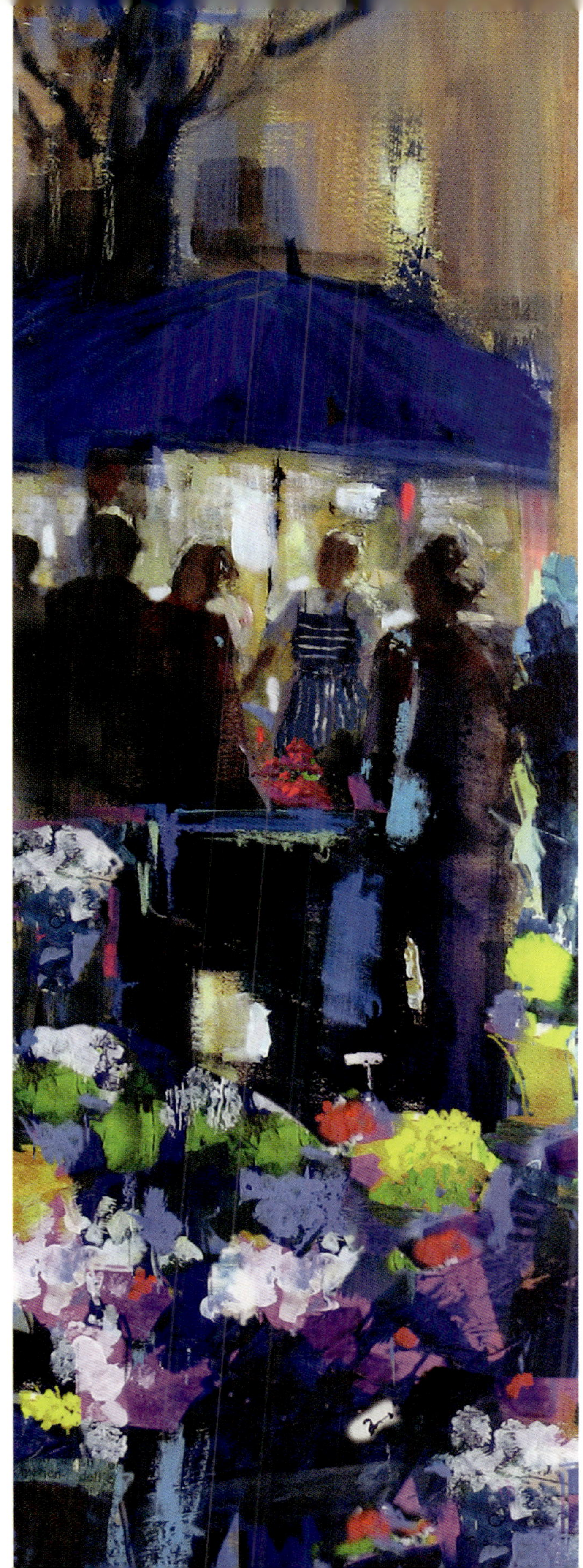

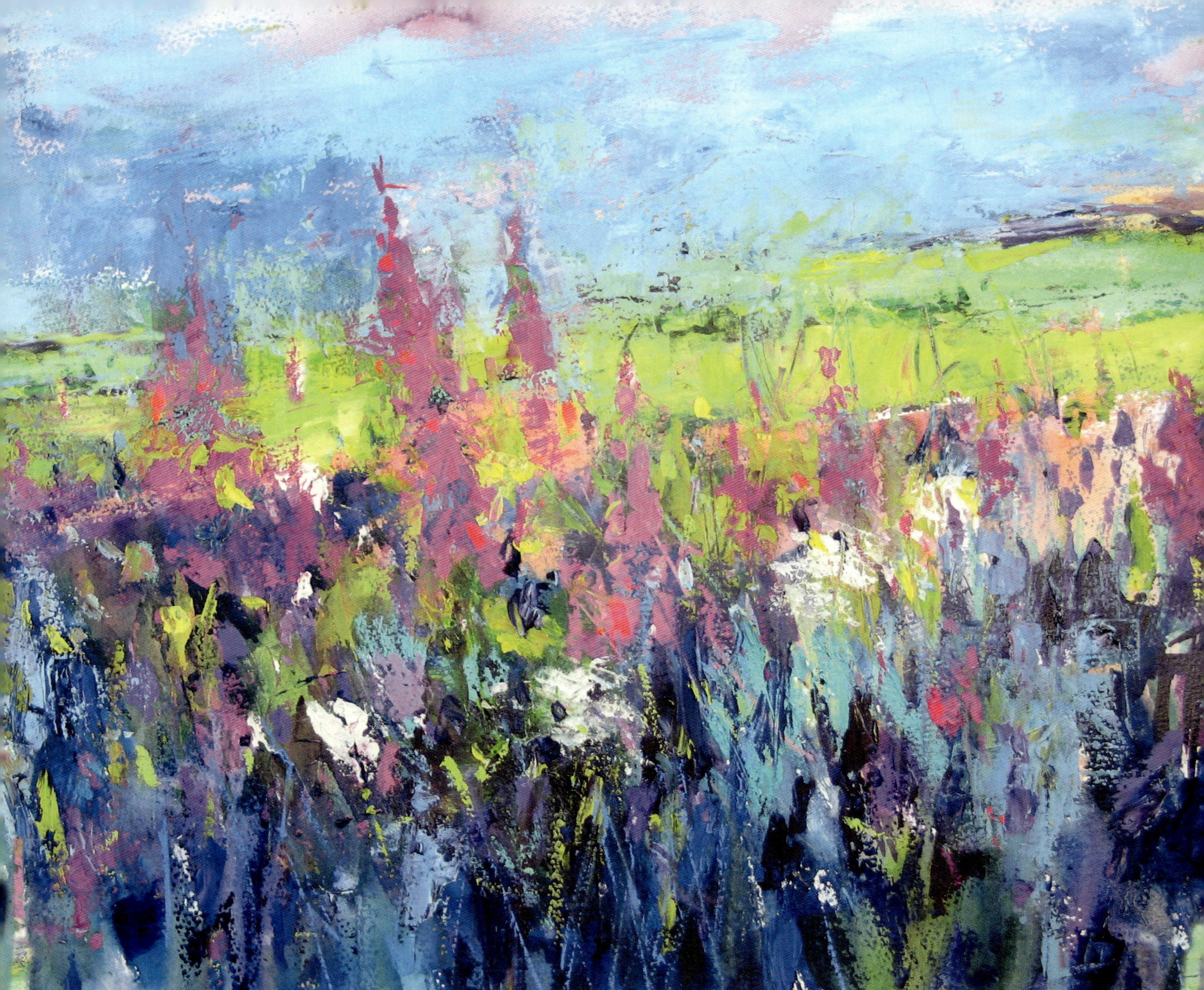

Willowherb Time

50 × 44 cm (19¾ × 17½ in)

Oil and cold wax on oil-painting paper

The breathtaking tapestry of the British countryside is a rich store of inspiration
in every season. Prolific and invasive wild flowers such as willowherb and
hogweed that are not suitable for the garden bring the spring and summer
hedgerows alive with their striking shapes and colours.

Hogweed Patterns

36 × 25 cm (14 × 10 in)

The lacy white flower heads of hogweed create an irresistible display for the flower painter during spring and summer. I have painted so many versions of them. In this one I used the red flowers in the distance to offset the white flower heads, and the unusual stems create pleasing patterns.

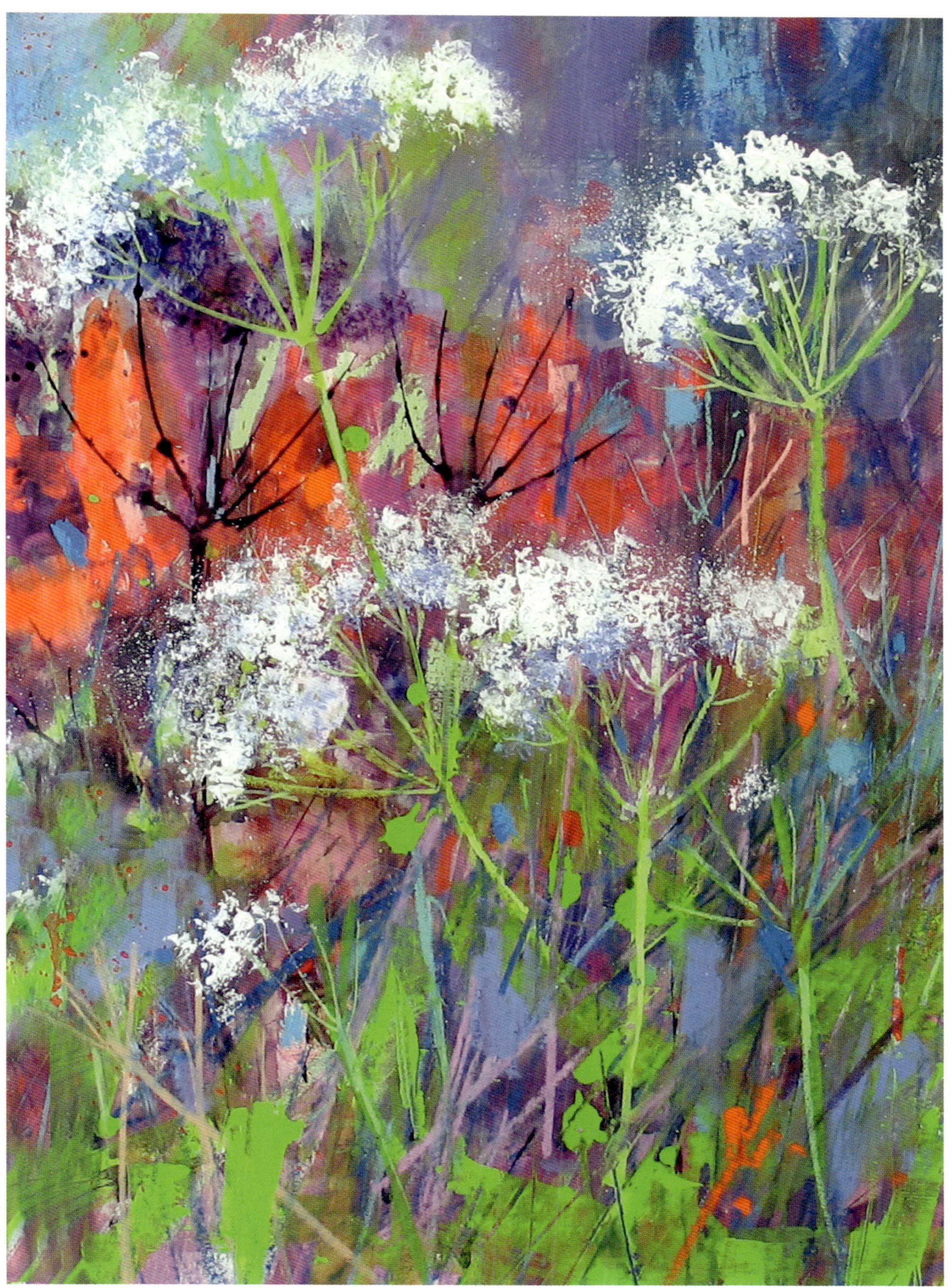

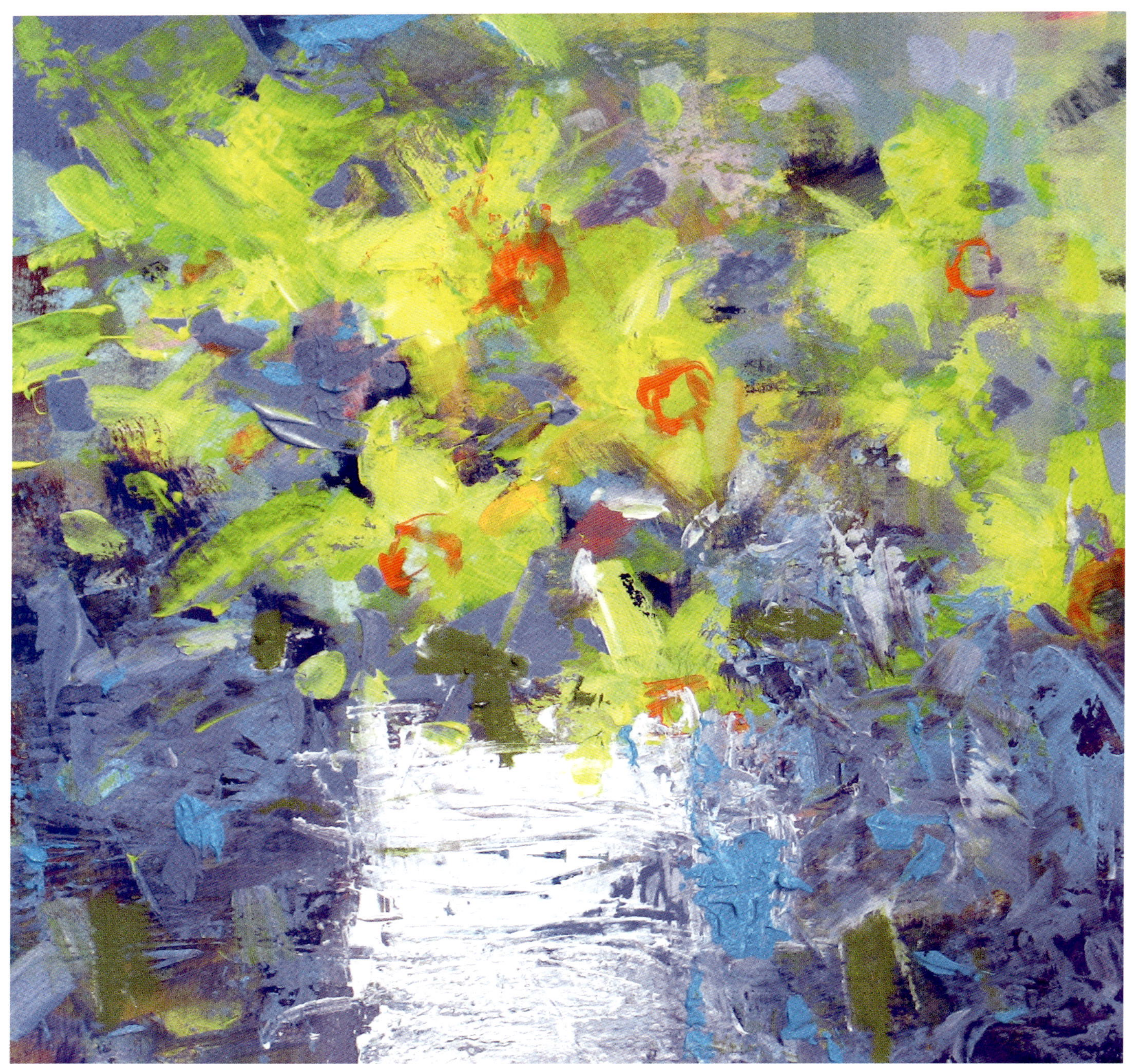

Daffodils in White Porcelain Jug

18 × 18 cm (7 × 7 in)

Mixed media on watercolour paper

Despite its impasto appearance, I used very little paint to do this small still life. I mixed heavy
gel with a small amount of paint and used a palette knife to give the painting an expressive
quality. I applied a few dabs of yellow pastels on the petals at the end to enhance the colour.

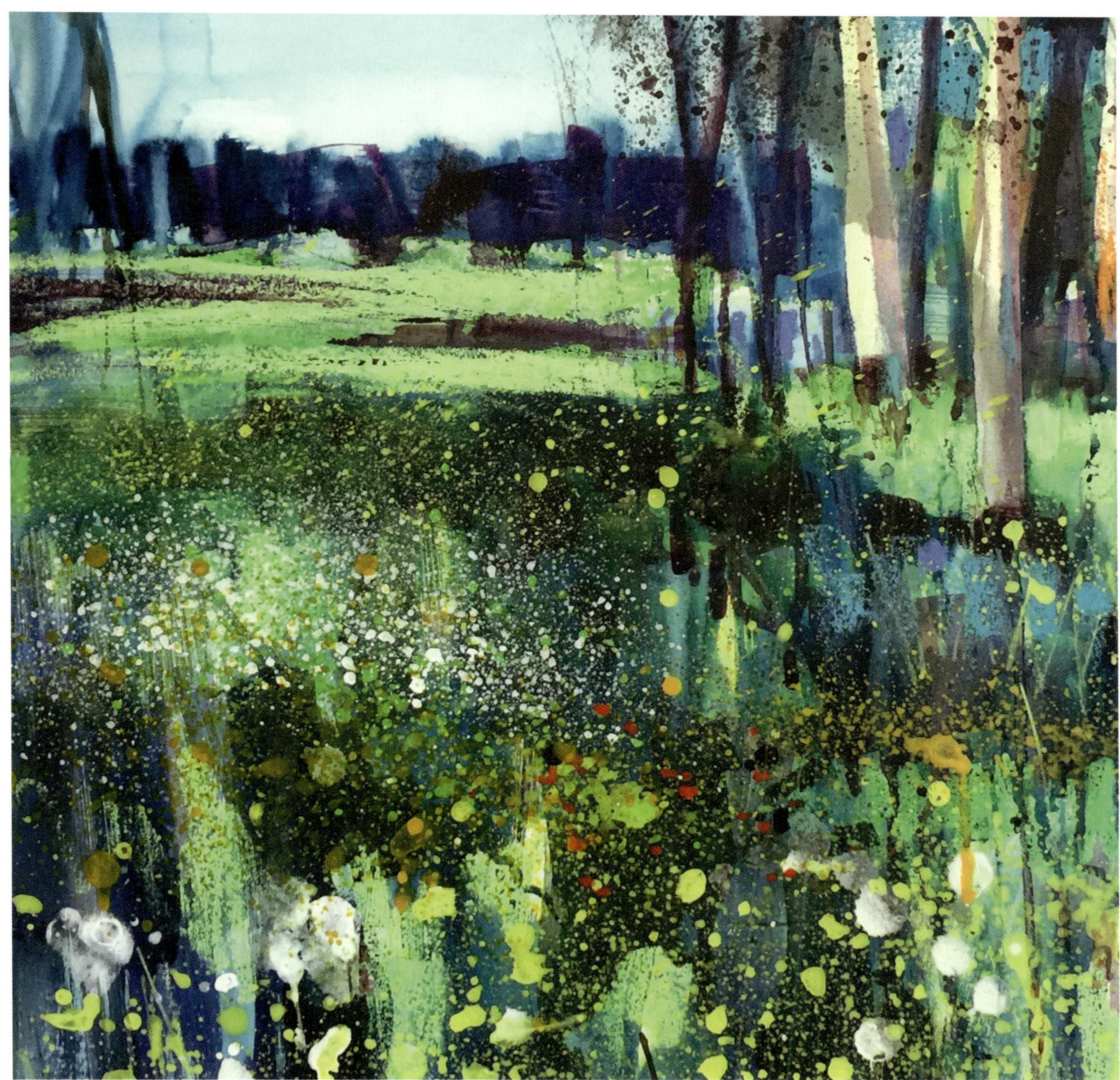

Spring Woodland

41 × 41 cm (16 × 16 in)

Mixed media on watercolour paper

The passage of the seasons brings the refreshing and inevitable change of the artist's colour palette. The season of renewal of nature calls for fresher and softer colours to paint with.

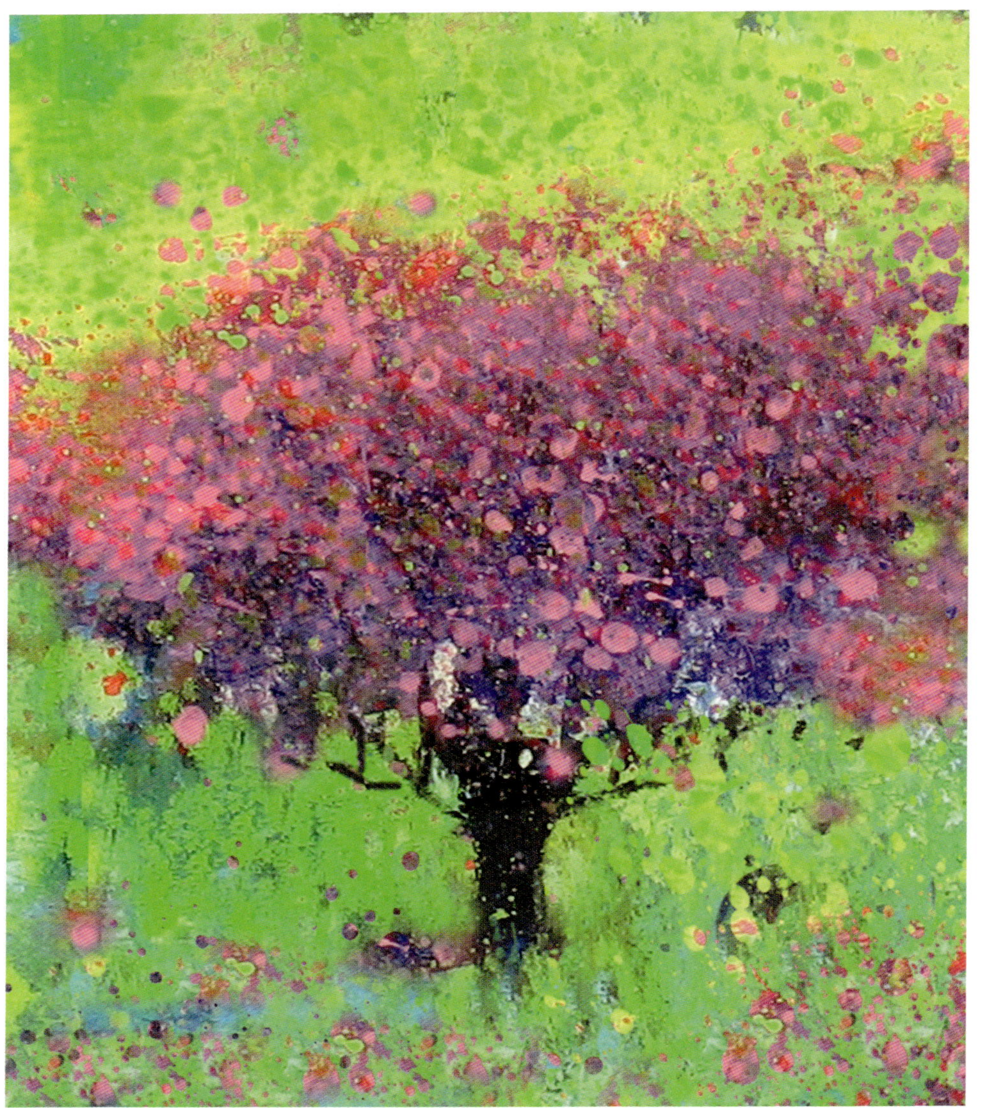

Solo Cherry Blossom

30 × 25 cm (12 × 10 in)

Mixed media on watercolour paper

I find the best way to tackle a subject like this blossom tree is by dabbing the paint with a sponge or splattering. The more you can make the marks look incidental the better the result will be. It is best to layer the colours and make a dark base colour for the lighter ones to show up on top. Without this base the lighter colours will not be able to have the impact they should and the painting will lack a cohesive quality.

(Opposite page) **Cherry Blossom Time**

36 × 26 cm (14 × 10¼ in)

Mixed media on watercolour paper

Blossom trees have a magical quality and turn the garden and the countryside into a fairyland. I love painting them, as they are such joyful subjects.

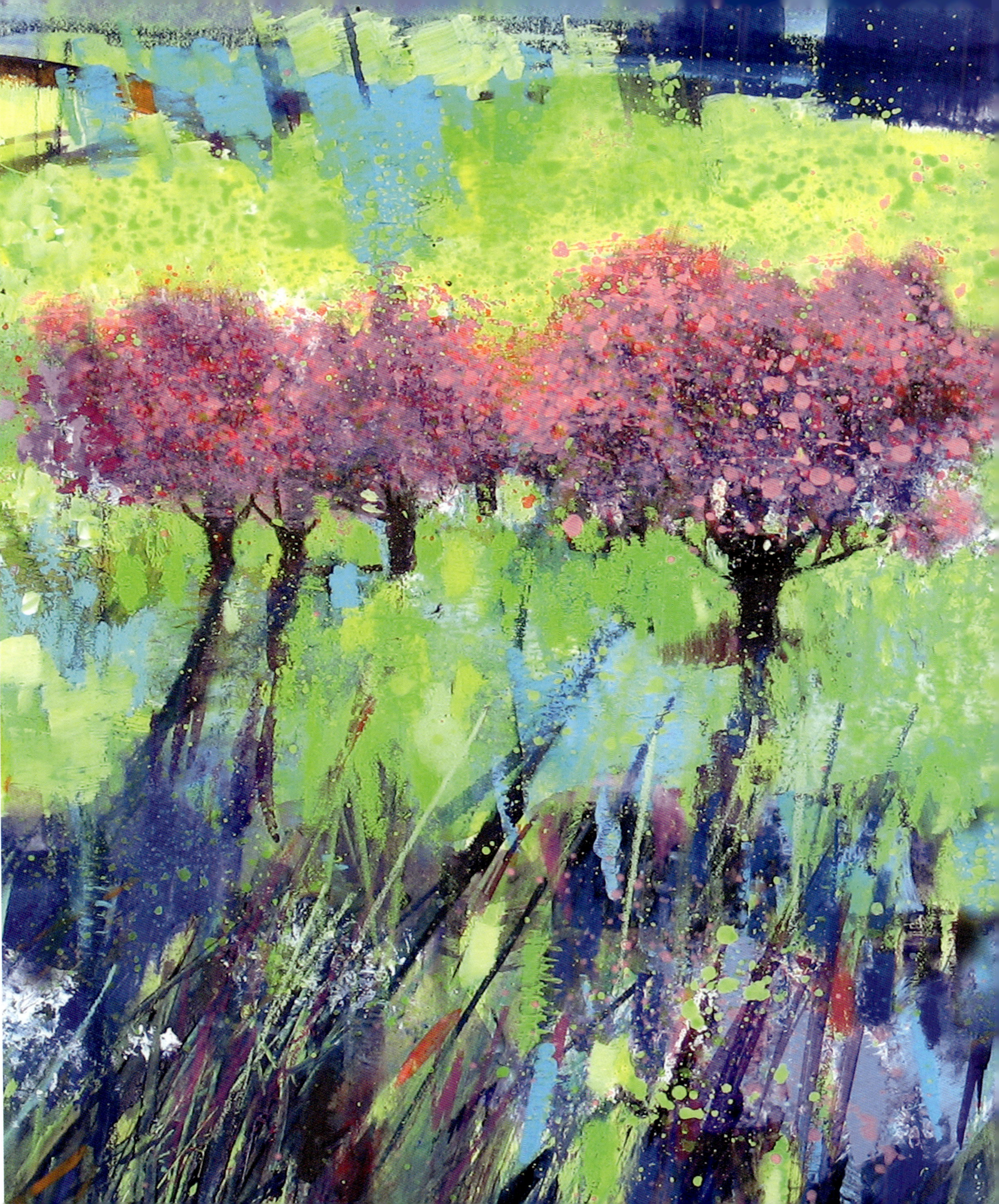

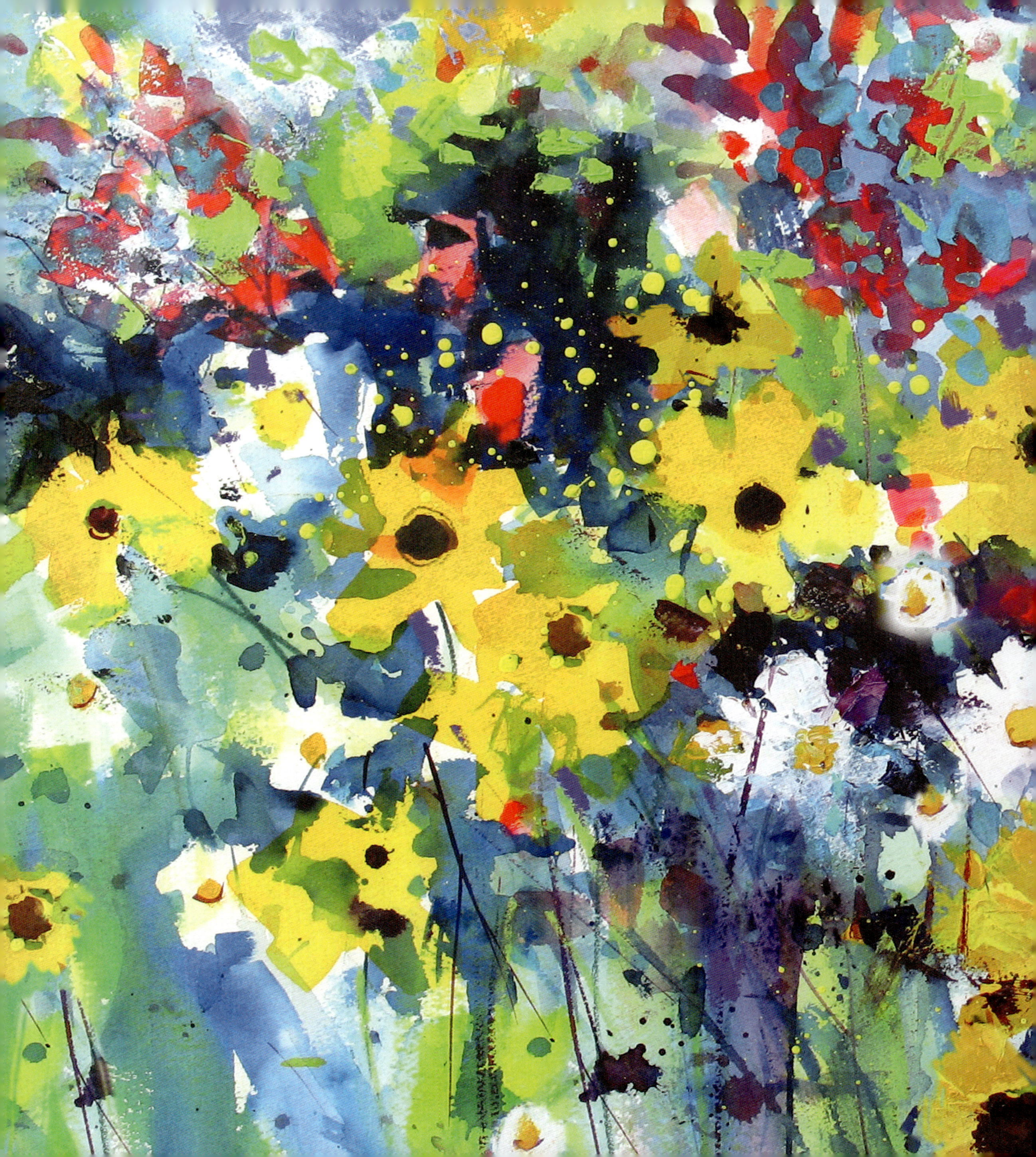

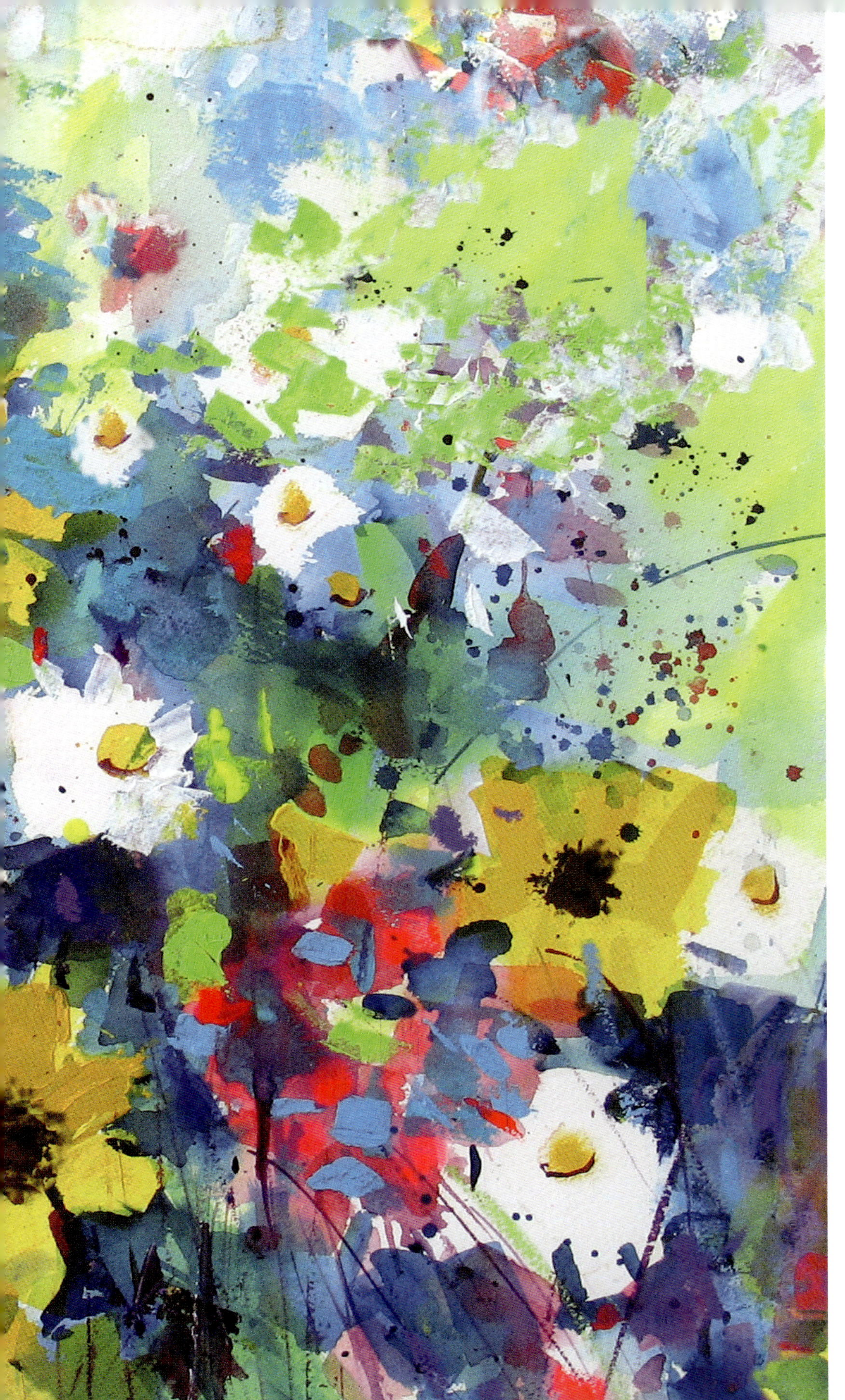

Autumn Flower Border

71 x 51 cm (28 x 20 in)

Mixed media on watercolour paper

The more hardy plants that continue
to flower until the first frosts, plus the
berries and the fabulous colours of
autumn leaves, make for some stunningly
colourful borders, compensating for the
arrival of cooler weather and shorter days.

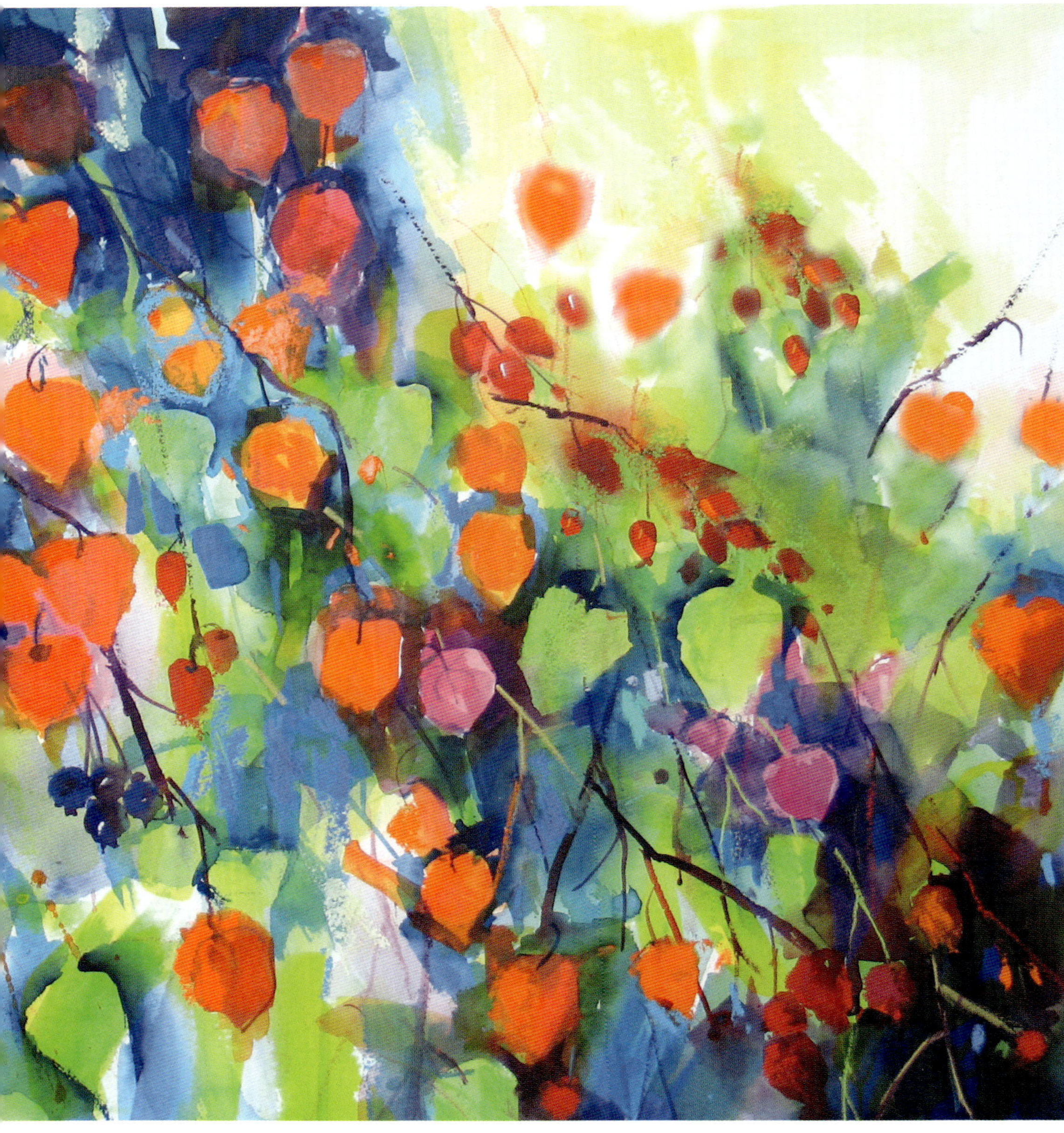

Fruits of Autumn

50 × 50 cm (19¾ × 19¾ in)

Mixed media on watercolour paper

By September the entwined mass of plants such as Chinese lanterns, rosehips and
berries in rich shades of red adorn the flower borders and the countryside and make
for truly enchanting subjects. I like to create the atmosphere by either spraying the
background or using wet-into-wet washes of inks or watercolours, then I build up the
rich colours using oils, acrylics or gouache. Accents of a few brighter tones added
with oil and soft pastels or wax crayons can further enhance the colour scheme.

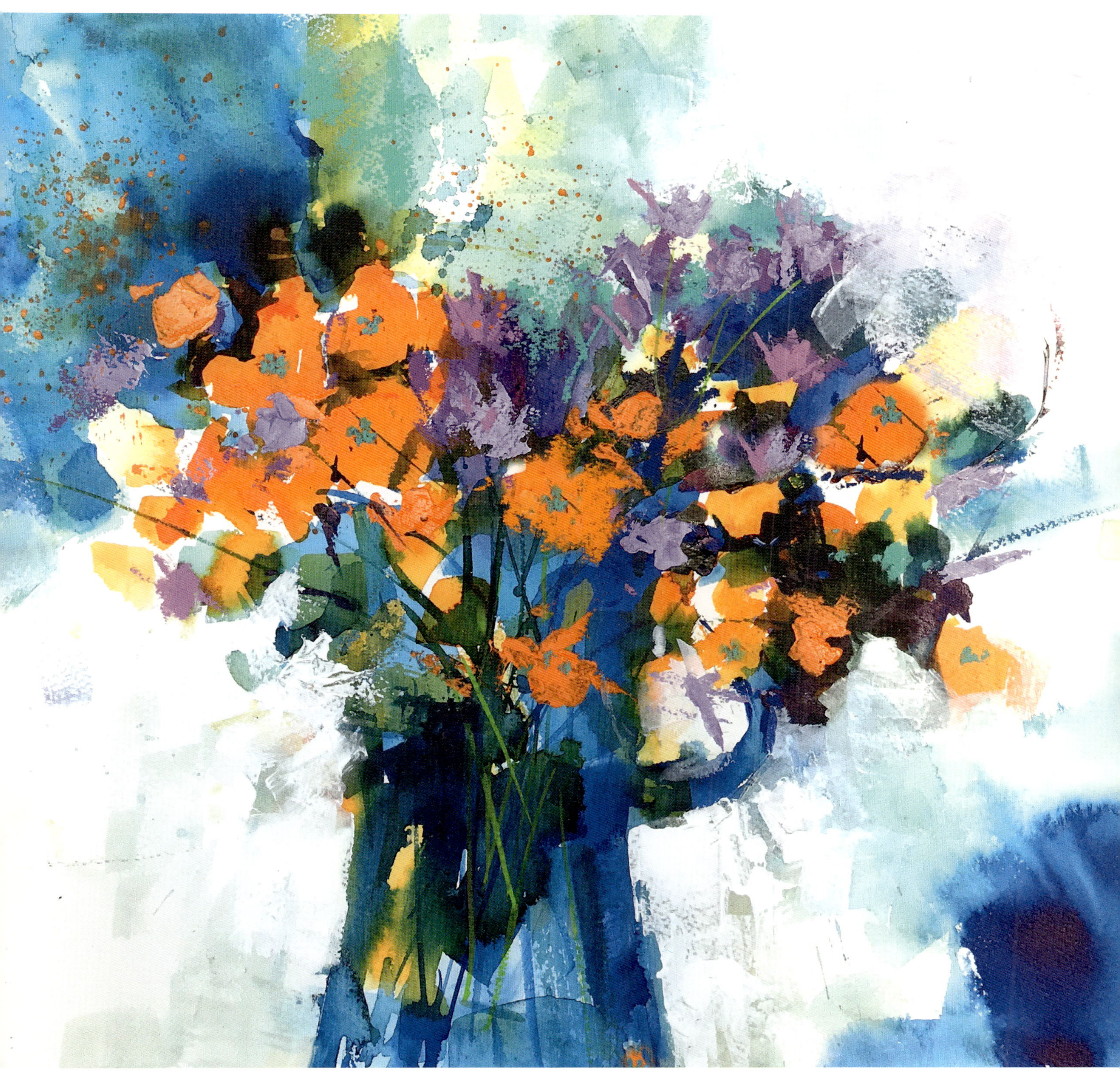

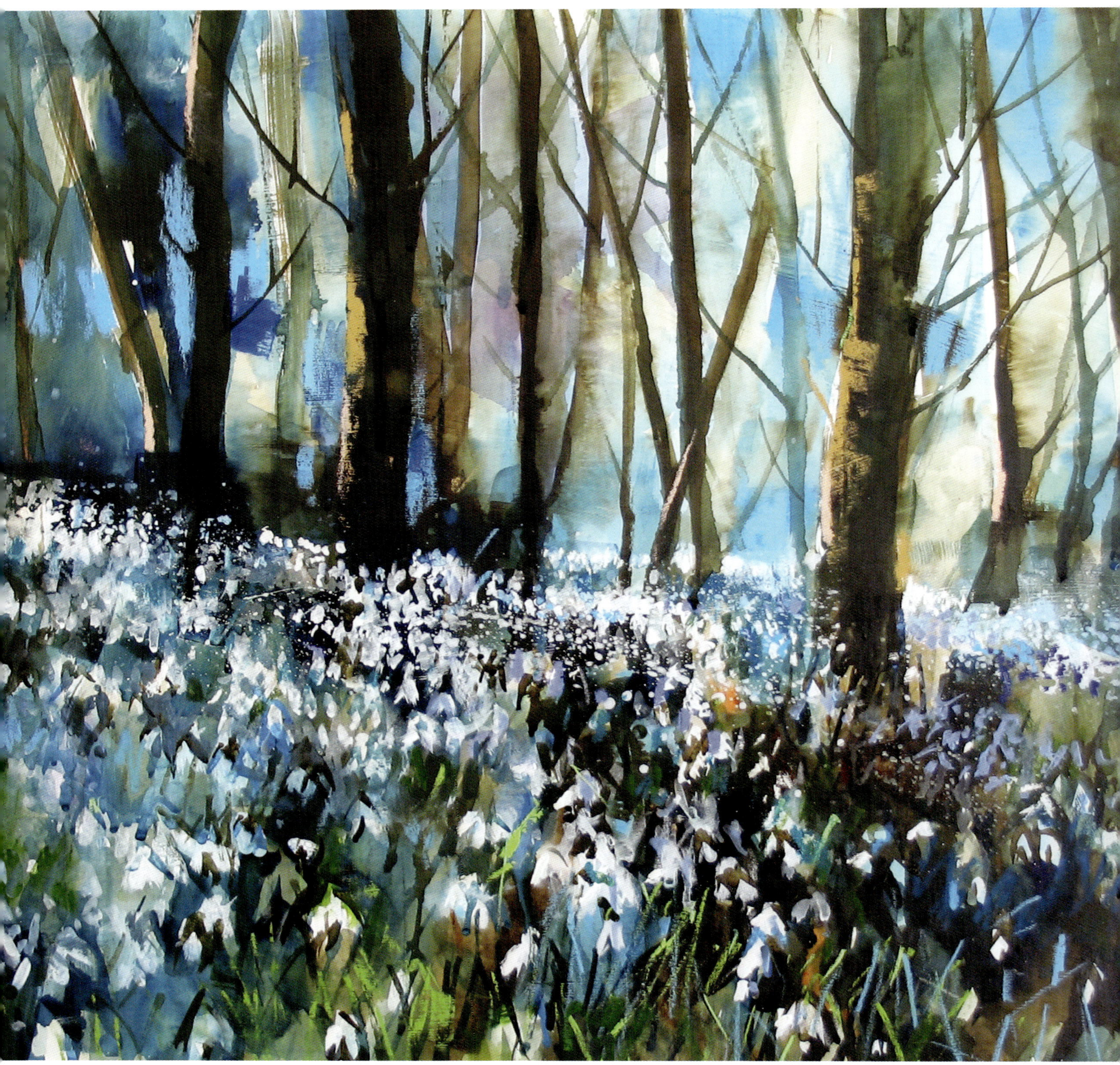

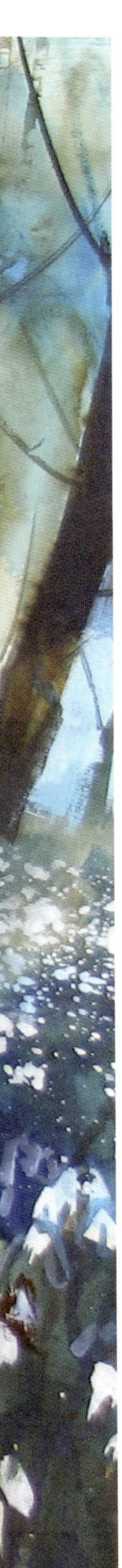

Carpet of Snowdrops

48 × 41 cm (19 × 16 in)

Mixed media on watercolour paper

Snowdrop-covered woodlands are
truly a sight for sore eyes and make
woodland winter walks into
a magical experience.

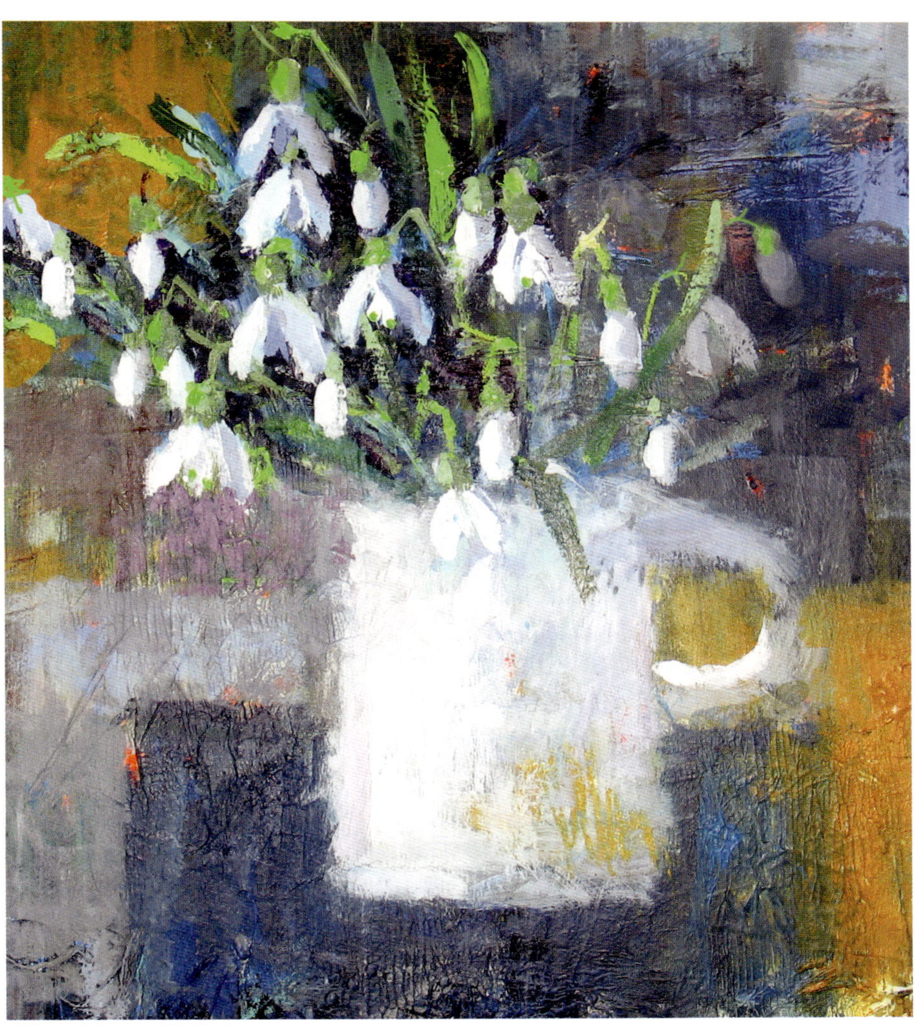

Snowdrops in White Jug

25 × 21 cm (10 × 8¼ in)

Mixed media on artist's wooden panel

This small still life of snowdrops was done over a textured surface created with crumpled tissue paper and
soft gel then painted with heavy body acrylic colours. The grey shadow colour is a mix of all the colours
in the painting plus white. The lighter parts of the snowdrops were painted with Titanium White in the
foreground and cooler Zinc White in the background to create recession.

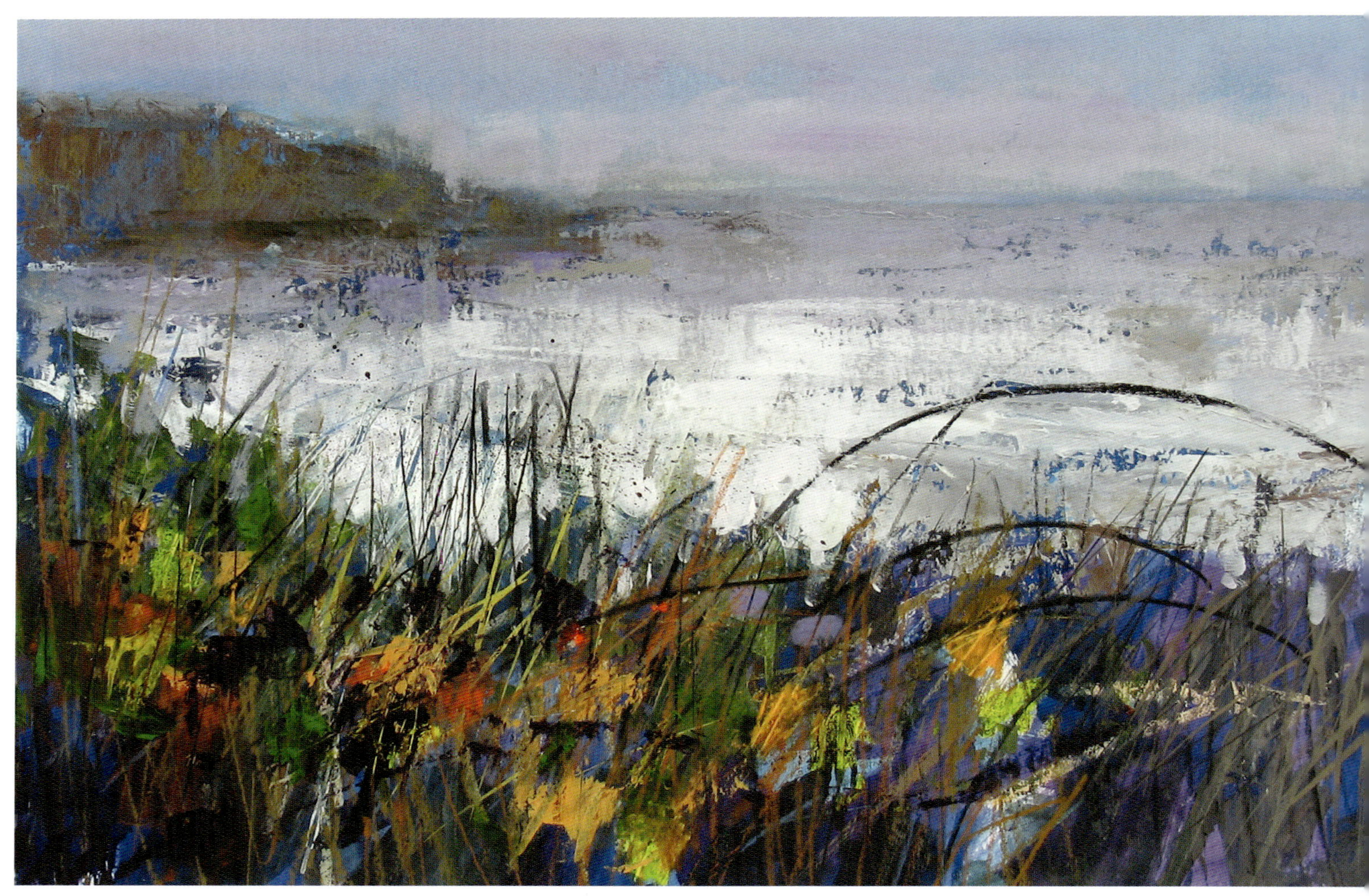

St Ives in December

23 × 31 cm (9 × 12¼ in)

Mixed media on watercolour paper

This was a breathtaking view of St Ives in late December, showing that the
winter landscape can still be surprisingly colourful even though it mostly calls
for a more sophisticated palette of various greys. Here the chromatic greys of
the seascape are punctuated with the remains of autumn colours.

ACKNOWLEDGEMENTS

My sincere thanks and gratitude to the following as without their help and support
this book would not exist.

Tina Persaud for commissioning the book, Diana Vowles for the thorough and
sympathetic editing, Sarah Crookes and Kei Ishimaru for the superb design, and
Nicola Newman for being the most patient and wonderful editor; it is great working
with you again.

To Golden Artist Colors, Jason and Sandy Mackie at Global Art Supplies for their help
and support throughout the year and providing me with the best quality art materials
to work with.

Catherine Frood of St Cuthbert's Mill for the annual supply of the most amazing
watercolour paper.

And finally to all my students and supporters for appreciating my multi-coloured
vision of our beautiful planet.

INDEX